MANCHESTER UNITED

BUSBY'S LEGACY

teammates were then quick to tell of the on-field battles they had to endure thereafter, as Al quotes, "That was the longest hour of my life, and I was hurt. If someone punched me from the front, it didn't hurt, but it shattered when they were about. They were continually putting the bottom in your skin, they pretended to shake hands – or pinching your ribs as they helped you up."

Willie Morgan was so shaken that he had qualified for the Mexico Olympics, as I was doing 90-yard hurdles on the wings. What the hell was that all about? I felt like laughing... for about five minutes. Then I saw the studs coming at my chest and I realised this wasn't much of a joke.

"I didn't even go for 50/50 balls, never mind 60/40 against Nobby Stiles. And I don't think I was being a coward. You couldn't react in there. I'd like to hear one of them ever talk. They must spend hours... thinking up different ways to injure you."

In reality, it was simply 'half-time', with United aware to face a further 90 minutes at Old Trafford. Withdrawing from the competition and simply giving the world crown to Estudiantes, in an attempt to avoid any further confrontation, was certainly an option, but it was one that Sir Matt Busby was not going to consider. Busby confirmed,

> We shall continue to play in this competition because we want to be the best in the world. You cannot stop playing these games because of certain incidents. What better exponents of football have there been in the last ten years than the Brazilians – and they are from South America. I was of course upset at some of the things that happened, but there is no question of us calling off the return match at Old Trafford. We can take tough play, but we are not used to what went on in Buenos Aires. I think my players were wonderful under the conditions. I am confident that the second leg will be more of a football match. We have certainly got to play football to win it.

Many felt that United did have what it took to become world champions, including Jackie Charlton. But, having watched his teammates play under such threatening conditions in Argentina, and although he being hoisted to win, he thought that the worst was yet to come... and that there was every possibility that the game would perhaps not even finish.

"The events of Buenos Aires... could well have produced a prolonged domino effect, with certain players requiring a sustained period of convalescence in order to get back into some form of normality. Thankfully, United's scheduled fixture against Nottingham Forest at the City Ground, originally scheduled for 28 August, had been postponed by the Football League until 4 October, as the United party were not due back in Britain

MANCHESTER UNITED

BUSBY'S LEGACY

IAIN McCARTNEY

AMBERLEY

First published 2014

Amberley Publishing
The Hill, Stroud
Gloucestershire, GL5 4EP

www.amberley-books.com

British Library Cataloguing in Publication Data.
A catalogue record for this book is available from the British Library.

ISBN 978 1 4456 3895 9 (print)
ISBN 978 1 4456 3907 9 (ebook)

Typesetting and Origination by Amberley Publishing.
Printed in the UK.

CONTENTS

Acknowledgements   7

Introduction   8

1   The End of an Era   10

2   Testing Times   79

3   The Revolving Door Is in Motion   110

4   New Man at the Helm   146

5   A Season of Disarray   173

6   A Change of Position   212

ACKNOWLEDGEMENTS

Mark Wylie (Manchester United Museum), Martin Buchan, Mike Berry, Stephen Sullivan, Jim Platt, Frank O'Farrell, Malcolm Macdonald, Alan Gowling, Nick Hoult, Kim Book, Jimmy Ryan, Ivan Pointing, Wilf McGuinness, Paul Anthony, Kevin Donald, Ray Adler and Alan Tyler.

The following newspapers were used in the course of writing this book:

Manchester Evening News, Daily and Sunday Express, The Sun, The Daily Mail, The Guardian, The Observer, The Daily and Sunday Telegraph, The Times, The Sunday Times, People, News of the World, The Sunday Post.

INTRODUCTION

Winning the European Cup in 1968 was the pinnacle of success for Matt Busby and the thousands who followed the club. It was akin to climbing Mount Everest. You knew the route, you could see the top, but the climb was a steep one, with numerous hazards on the way.

In *Rising from the Wreckage: Manchester United 1958–1968* that story was told. It told of how Manchester United, under the guidance of Jimmy Murphy, rose from the ashes of Munich and, with Matt Busby back at the helm, went on to become a force in both the English and European game, shrugging off the heartbreak and other setbacks.

But, having conquered Europe, the chances of continuing success in foreign fields, and also on the domestic front, were far from guaranteed. Those who saw ultimate success at Wembley on that balmy May evening in 1968 were growing old. Times were changing, and the search for the Holy Grail had blinkered the need to look to the future.

It was to be a future far removed from the 'swinging sixties', the carefree days that seemingly passed without a care when everything was considered perfect.

Yes, Busby guided his team to the verge of a second consecutive European Cup final appearance, but it simply papered over the cracks that had begun to appear. Busby, like his players, was growing old. He had been through so much and was now at the point where he felt he could do no more.

Here, within the pages of *Manchester United, Busby's Legacy*, we pick up the story immediately after that European Cup success, and follow the descent from the lofty heights. It was a journey downwards that gathered momentum with each passing month, and one that saw many fall by the wayside.

It was a harrowing time. A period when, at times, Manchester United were unrecognisable from the team they were during those halcyon days of the fifties and sixties. For those who were there, they may be haunted by the past.

For those who were not, it is a horror story of how United could fall so quickly from greatness.

Iain McCartney

1
THE END OF AN ERA

There were tears.

Amid the euphoria that submerged Wembley, engulfed Manchester and produced mass celebration, not just throughout Britain, but across Europe and beyond, there were tears, of joy, relief and sadness.

United had, at last, completed a long and arduous journey, one that had begun in Belgium way back in September 1956 and now, a little less than twelve years later, in North London, had seen Matt Busby capture his Holy Grail, the prize he had sought above all others – the European Cup.

Thousands of miles had been travelled, bringing relative success, despair, disappointment and disaster. Having succumbed to Real Madrid in that initial campaign of 1956/57, experience was gained and lessons learned, and it was thought that should the two sides meet in the competition the following season, then United might well have the edge over the Spanish giants. The disaster seen on that slush covered German runway waylaid those ambitions, pushing thoughts of any European triumphs to the back of everyone's minds. Securing the future of the club and rebuilding the shattered team was the number one priority. It took time after the initial wave of emotion subdued a little, and the realisation of the enormity of what lay ahead finally sunk in.

Thanks to Jimmy Murphy's patience and guidance, the early days following the crash confirmed that the club would survive and continue. Somehow, the runners-up spot in the First Division was secured in that initial post-Munich season, but it was soon to become something of a stuttering existence, as the Welshman, and the still recuperating Matt Busby, attempted to elevate United back to the heights secured by that memorable squad of footballers who attracted praise and admirers wherever they played.

Relegation threatened as the personnel changed. There was the brilliance of Scottish internationalist Denis Law, a player that Busby had admired since first setting eyes on him as a teenager, and his fellow Scot, Pat Crerand, whose domination in midfield did more than most to guide

United to FA Cup success in 1963. It was a triumph that was to be the springboard to greater things and thrust the name of Manchester United back to the forefront of the English game.

Slowly, a foothold was regained on European fields. But when it was thought that a place in the European Cup Final was within their grasp, those dreams were once again shattered, but ten years after Munich, United once again came face-to-face with Real Madrid. It was, however, a much changed Madrid side from the swashbuckling days of DiStefano and Puskas, but the Spaniards were still a team to be reckoned with. If United did want to succeed in Europe then, as before, it was Madrid who stood in their way.

Once again, with United only managing a delicate 1-0 victory in the first leg of that 1968 semi-final at Old Trafford, it looked as though the white-clad Spaniards would be akin to some ghostly spectre and achieve a result that would haunt United for yet another season, as they strode majestically into a 3-1 lead with a mere 15 minutes remaining. It looked as though, like many a horse in the Grand National, United were to find that the semi-final stage of the European Cup was to be their Becher's Brook, a hurdle that they simply could not overcome.

But Busby's team found some inner strength, their own ghosts from the past combining with the red-shirted heroes of the present to carry them forward when all looked lost, with goals from David Sadler and Bill Foulkes, the latter having been a member of the side that had taken those tentative first steps in Europe against the Belgians of Anderlecht, taking United into the final.

That it was to be played at Wembley was an added bonus and, having at last reached that elevated plateau, there was no way that Benfica, who had been trounced 5-1 on their own ground two years previously, were going to gatecrash the party. And a party there was following United's 4-1 triumph.

An additional half an hour was required to achieve this ultimate success, but no one cared, as a Brian Kidd birthday strike, and yet another of those archived goals of notable individuality from George Best, confirmed Manchester United as champions of Europe. Tears of joy were shed on those terraces and stands below those famous old twin towers, while deep within the bowls of the North London stadium, there were tears in the United dressing room. Both of relief and in remembrance: relief that at last Busby's vision had become a reality and all those disappointments were now forgotten, and remembrance of those colleagues who had been there as those first steps were taken, but had lost their lives at Munich.

Undoubtedly, United would have won the European Cup long before that humid and emotional May evening in 1968, but some of those who had perished could well have been involved in that triumph, adding yet another medal to a hoard of others. Duncan Edwards would have been only thirty-one, as would his sidekick in midfield, Eddie Colman. Kenny Morgans, whose career had just been in its infancy back in February 1958, would have been twenty-nine, while Albert Scanlon and David Pegg would have been thirty-two, just a year older than Bobby Charlton. Bill Foulkes, the elder statesman of that European Cup winning side, was thirty-six, the same age as Tommy Taylor would have been, while the defensive duo of Jackie Blanchflower and Mark Jones would have been a year younger. Irishman Liam Whelan, at thirty-three, might well have still been able to run the midfield for Busby's team.

Some of the pre-Munich side, like captain Roger Byrne, who would have been thirty-nine, and Johnny Berry, forty-one, would not have been around, but Shay Brennan and Tony Dunne were thirty-one and twenty-six respectively, while Brian Kidd, (nineteen), John Aston (twenty), along with David Sadler and George Best, who were both twenty-two, ensured that the team maintained a youthful look. This, coupled with the maturity of Stiles (twenty-six), Stepney (twenty-five) and Crerand (twenty-nine), those players would most certainly form the cornerstone of the side for a number of years to come.

Despite the quality in Busby's side, there was always room for improvement, and it was with an eye to the future that the United manager had, on a couple of occasions during that European Cup winning season, run his fingers over the chequebook tucked away in the back of his desk drawer.

There was little urgency to increase the Old Trafford payroll, but, with the continuing fitness of Denis Law, who had missed the Wembley final due to an operation on a knee that had troubled him over the course of the previous two years, and at one point looked like it would bring premature end to the twenty-eight-year-old's career, Busby had toyed with the idea of signing a replacement forward.

Approaches had been made during the previous nine months, with six attempted signings all being rebuffed by opposition clubs. West Ham and England frontman, Geoff Hurst, was well to the fore in Busby's list of possible recruits, with a fee of around £200,000 being quoted, as was Leicester City's England Under-23 centre-forward Alan Clarke, but even the reported figure of £150,000 failed to tempt either the Upton Park or Filbert Street sides into selling their prize assets.

It wasn't as if there had been a lack of goals, as even without Law, at times, United still managed to find the back of the net eighty-nine times during the 1967/68 campaign, three more than champions Manchester City.

Law, recovered from his operation, however, was fighting fight and looking forward to getting back to goalscoring in the coming season, as he relaxed in the Majorcan summer sunshine. 'I can't wait to get back into training again, now that my knee is better. Despite the rumours that went round, I've never considered for one minute giving up soccer', he said, while adding:

> I'm just longing to get stuck into that training. It's going to be tough, but I'm going to enjoy it. I shall start training earlier than the rest of the team. I've only done simple leg exercises so far, but there's no pain at all now. When I came round from the anaesthetic and saw this inch-long piece of cartilage in a bottle of spirit I was amazed at its size. No wonder I had been in pain.

As the Scot worked on his tan, his manager was working on his plans for the months ahead, but under something of a new guise, as he was now Sir Matt Busby, a knighthood coming his way ten days after the European Cup triumph. It was certainly a well-deserved honour, coming ten years after he had lain in severe pain on that snow-covered Munich runway with many of his prodigious team lying close by, but in certain quarters north of the border and also among certain Labour MPs, who while having rejoiced in United's victory and in Busby's personal honour, it was felt that similar recognition should have been bestowed on Jock Stein, whose Celtic side had become the first British side to be crowned European champions, having beaten Inter Milan 2-1 in Lisbon the previous May. This was even more so as all but one member of Stein's green-and-white hooped squad had all been born within a 10 mile radius of Celtic's Parkhead ground.

For the newly crowned kings of Europe, there was no far-flung continental pre-season tour to try and boost the club's coffers, and the already more than favourable following, by displaying the large silver trophy in numerous destinations to a host of recently materialised supporters. Instead, it was the old tried and trusted 90 minutes against the German side Hamburg, and an even shorter trip across the Irish Sea for a more relaxing 90 minutes against Drumcondra, a testimonial match for John Whelan, brother of former United inside-forward and Munich victim, Liam.

In Germany, the spotlight was on Denis Law as he returned to the fray, but it was not in the role of captain as he had relinquished the position, with Bobby Charlton continuing in the role he fulfilled at Wembley in May. 'I mentioned the captaincy to him', said Busby, 'and he felt that handing it over was something he had to do because he is more concerned about getting fit and in form.'

There was no real pressure on the Scot in the role of captain, but he was more than happy to pass the baton to Charlton and concentrate on his fitness, as there certainly was pressure on him to regain as much of his previous form as possible. Prior to the friendly in Germany, Busby said of his forward,

> He is short of confidence and still afraid of the knee, but that is only natural. We shall have a look at him under actual match conditions and go from there. He still has something to find. His little flashes have been missing in practice matches.

Law's fitness was indeed a worry, as Busby could not even consider the consequences of losing his talisman, as his forward department was already a man short with the transfer of David Herd to Stoke City. Herd had been a major force in Busby's rebuilding in the years following Munich, but the broken leg against Leicester City in March 1967 had severe implications on his overall performances at top level, with only half a dozen in that European Cup winning campaign. So much so, he was offered the option of a free transfer or another season with United.

The former Scottish international had numerous options if he decided upon a move, with the likes of Walsall, Stockport County, Huddersfield Town, Oldham Athletic and Bolton Wanderers all showing an interest in signing him, but he felt that he still had something to offer at First Division level and opted to join Stoke City. The Potteries were a short drive from his south Manchester home.

Law's return to action in Germany saw him manage to complete the 90 minutes and, although not scoring in the 2-0 victory over Hamburg, he was back to his swaggering best, looking sharp and eager, going on to score both goals in a 2-1 win in Ireland over a Drumcondra Select. This allowed Busby, in the meantime at least, to push the idea of scouring the marketplace for a new striker to the back of his mind. Indeed, Law was the only change to Busby's European Cup final starting X1 for the opening fixture of the 1968/69 season, with him taking over the No. 10 shirt from the unfortunate David Sadler for Everton's visit to Old Trafford.

A sun-kissed afternoon, with the pitch looking akin to a snooker table, brought the curtain up on the new season; only a fanfare of trumpets and velvet drapes across the mouth of the tunnel were missing, as first the gleaming European Cup was paraded, and then the presentation of the Manager of the Year award to Sir Matt Busby. It was the visitors who made all the early running, brushing the European champions aside with ease. Royle volleyed over the crossbar and Ball, twisting and turning past four rather half-hearted tackles, could then only aim a somewhat feeble shot in Stepney's direction. Harvey hooked the ball wide after Ball once again tormented the lacklustre United defence, and then Husband forced Stepney into making a superb two-handed save.

They were opportunities that the Goodison Park side were to rue, as United, in a rare attack in which Law was totally ineffective, meant they took the lead. Stiles robbed Ball, then found Charlton, whose finely measured pass picked out the on-running Best. Feigning to shoot, West, in the Everton goal, committed himself, and cheekily the Irishman prodded the ball into the opposite corner. Ball scrambled home an equaliser, but, within 2 minutes, United were back in front from Charlton driving home a George Best pass into the bottom corner from the edge of the penalty area.

Everton continued to dominate the game, with Harvey and Kendall prominent in midfield, but it was their forwards' inability to beat Stepney, through their poor finishing and also the 'keeper's outstanding form, that prevented them from taking not one, but both points from the game. Best actually had the ball in the net right at the death, but was denied a goal by the referee's whistle for full-time. Despite the victory, it was something of an early warning to Busby's team – despite their title of European Champions, the opposition were certainly not going to consider them unbeatable.

Foulkes, starting his seventeenth season with the club, was caught out on several occasions by the more mobile Royle. Law, despite having the niggling, ongoing pain removed from his knee, was missing his instant touch and quicksilver movement. Stiles was, at times, uncertain, while his midfield partner, Crerand, was also far from his normal, assured self. 'We were fortunate to win', said Busby in reflection. 'We will have to do better than that … a lot better. It just wasn't good enough. Everton were much sharper than we were. We weren't really in the game at any time. They were making openings and we weren't.'

Ronald Crowther certainly did not beat about the bush in his *Daily Mail* match report writing, 'Somewhere between their conquest of Europe and their creaking and cumbersome return to League football, Manchester United have gone off-tune.' While it would be so easy to allow the glowing memory of two exciting goals to obscure the many flaws in United's patchy performance, Sir Matt Busby struck a sternly realistic note when he admitted 'We were fortunate not to be three goals down before Best put us in the lead.' Crowther continued,

> While Everton can accept that tribute [of being much sharper than United], the champions of Europe must settle for the fact that the party's over. The glories of last season will soon fade if they allow opponents as many chances per game, as Everton's tremendous team effort created on this occasion.

The Stretford Enders had been warned. Not just of the pending threat to their favourite's lofty position of European Champions and First Division runners-up, but of the petulant behaviour that was causing the men in the boardroom much embarrassment. So much so, that Busby had spoken out prior to kick-off on the opening day fixture about the behaviour of the wayward element of the club's support. 'Give us the support you did last season, please, and for the small minority who misbehave, do try and correct yourselves on behalf of the great name of this club.' Many felt that the opening day performance was due to nothing more than a lack of match action, and that once the cobwebs were blown away and the summer inactivity was worked out of the legs, the show would be back on the road and it would be the United of old: swashbuckling, devil-may-care football, steamrolling opponents to one side in the quest for further honours.

Was this an opinion shared by players though? Jimmy Ryan, who had made only seven appearances during the previous season, was asked if he detected a different atmosphere around Old Trafford in those post-European Cup winning days, and replied:

> I certainly didn't detect a 'different' atmosphere and if anything, pre-season seemed to be very upbeat which I suppose was to be expected. My 'personal atmosphere', however, was different in that I realised that it was about time for me to leave and in view of what had happened the previous year and the great affection [if not love] that I had for the club, I knew this was going to be a wrench. Everybody else seemed to be in fine fettle. I was expecting Denis Law to return to full fitness and this would have made the team that much stronger so I expected them to have another great season, even if I didn't expect to be part of it.

Four days later and, not having learned the obvious lessons from the Everton encounter, United travelled to the Hawthorns and were duly thumped 3-1. Never mind United being natural slow starters to their league campaign, their two opening fixtures proved them to be slow starters full stop. Fortunate not to be three behind against Everton early on, they were to find themselves 3-0 down in the opening 18 minutes against West Bromwich Albion, the team who had more or less ended their hopes of retaining the league championship last term with that notable 6-3 defeat.

Albion, the FA Cup holders, had been humiliated 6-1 by champions Manchester City in the FA Charity Shield, but the defeat was simply brushed aside as they dismantled the visiting defence with ease. 'United's defence was an utter shambles', uttered one report, conceding the first goal as early as the 4th minute, when Astle, totally unmarked, headed past Stepney from Hope's teasing cross.

Another Hope cross found the head of Brown, who, having eluded Crerand, made it 2-0 in the 9th minute and, a further 9 minutes later, yet another cross, this time from full-back Williams, saw Astle sneak between the statuesque figures of Dunne and Foulkes to send another header past Stepney.

United pulled a goal back 3 minutes prior to the interval scored by Charlton, but despite being slightly more threatening in the second 45 minutes, or at least George Best was, the Irishman hit the woodwork on three separate occasions. It was mainly thanks to Alex Stepney that Albion did not increase their goals tally.

The performance of the home side failed to impress not simply the United support, but also one of the Albion players, as Jeff Astle, who had now found the net five times in the last two meetings, was critical of the red-shirted defenders. 'I would like to play against them every week', the previous season's top scorer declared in the wake of his two goals in Albion's 3-1 win. 'They lack height and are suckers for the cross ball. I've always wondered why Sir Matt Busby never bought Mike England when Blackburn Rovers put him on the transfer list.' Harsh words, but enough to sow seeds of doubt in many minds.

It was certainly not the start that Busby wanted from his team, with certain individual performances raising cause for concern, particularly that of Denis Law. At the Hawthorns, Law had clearly struggled, with his manager confirming that, 'The knee is still worrying us and Denis is still very sore. He feels the effects when he gets his leg into certain positions.' Although only two games into the season, there were alarm bells ringing. Certainly, as European Champions, United had no God-given right to continuous success, nor even to play every game in their familiar swashbuckling fashion, but, during the 180 minutes played, there was an obvious difference in their play from a few months previously. Certainly then, they had been challenging on two fronts, but the recent performances were a far cry from the 1967/68 season.

But why were they struggling?

'I couldn't really say why the team struggled at the start of the season', commented Jimmy Ryan,

but there are a couple of things that I think may have affected their results. First they were now 'European Champions' and this was probably motivation for the teams who played against them. A situation that has survived until the present day. Certainly I think that teams would have been pumped up playing against the first English team to win the European Cup! The second factor that may have affected their early season form was that very few people really understood the emotional effect of the European triumph. It is better documented nowadays that emotional highs and lows can affect physical performance and thus results. This was not an ordinary win but the climax to a ten-year story that involved more than just football.

That stuttering start against Everton and West Bromwich Albion was about to be tested even further, with the first 'derby' match of the season, a visit to Maine Road, thrown into the mix on the second Saturday of the new campaign. European champions vs. League champions, a heady concoction and a meeting between the two rivals that had been simmering away like few previous encounters, since before the fixture list had even been compiled. City's 3-1 hammering of United at Old Trafford the previous March was still fresh in the memories of those of the red persuasion, but there was also the underlying concern that the fixture, always a high profile one no matter how either team was performing, would be overshadowed by the more mischievous followers of both clubs.

The dark shadow of hooliganism had overshadowed the game since the mid-1960s, not just in Manchester, but the length and breadth of the country. England's World Cup triumph had brought a wave of new interest to the game, as had United's European Cup success. But United had always been the lamp that attracted most moths. Munich brought national sympathy, and there were countless numbers who followed the club's fortunes following that grim Thursday afternoon in 1958. Some were enthralled by Busby's entertaining, attacking policy, augmented by the tantalising trio of Law, Best and Charlton and their supporting cast. Best, of course, was an attraction on his own, his mere presence adding hundreds, thousands perhaps, to any attendance figures. But there were also others who latched onto the United bandwagon, an undesirable feature, who, although wanting to see a successful Manchester United, were seeking a bigger fix than the 90 minutes of football could provide, happily causing all sorts of mayhem on the terraces and streets of Manchester, or wherever Mat Busby's team played.

The friction between the United and City support had reared its ugly head before the season had even started, even away from the packed, swaying terraces: not too far away though – a mere few hundred yards from the towering Old Trafford floodlights, down at the opposite end of Warwick Road, at the home of the Lancashire County Cricket Club.

Arranged as part of Lancashire fast bowler Ken Higg's testimonial fund, United faced City at cricket, in what was intended to be a light-hearted, although still competitive, Sunday afternoon's entertainment. The visitors, if City could be considered as such, had the likes of Mike Summerbee,

Colin Bell, Tony Book, Neil Young and Harry Dowd in their team, while United called upon the services of Messrs Herd, Sadler, Charlton, Stiles, Stepney, Crerand, Brennan and Best. Sufficient enough names to persuade anyone to forget about the Sunday roast and head towards Trafford Park. Some with little interest in cricket, or the individuals who were participating, never mind their Sunday lunch, decided that a confrontation with their local rivals was too good to miss, and headed off among the estimated 15,000 who decided to attend.

As the City players dismissed their United counterparts for 79 runs before going on to amass 171 from their own innings, the hooligan element, adjudged to be mainly teenagers, threw bottles and even staged a pitch invasion, as the organisers debated whether or not to call a premature halt to the proceedings. It was later reported that five youngsters, aged between thirteen and sixteen, had been arrested for carrying offensive weapons, breaching the peace and assaulting a policeman. The problems that materialised that afternoon were still fresh in the mind of the local police, as some 250 officers reported for duty on the morning of 17 August, with a further fifteen mounted policemen and dog-handlers also heading for the Main Road cauldron of hate. Shopkeepers closed early, preferring loss of income to hefty repair bills and increased insurance premiums. Around sixty-five supporters were treated for cut heads or similar injuries, either at Manchester Royal Infirmary or in the city gymnasium before and during the match, as trouble continuously broke out and bottles flew in the Kippax Street end. Fifty were ejected from the ground.

As the officers of the law contemplated their confrontation with the unruly mob that would make their way to Moss Side, Matt Busby had his own moments of concern as he considered his options for the 90 minutes ahead. Should he wield the axe or keep faith with his tried and trusted? 'Injuries' were mentioned as giving the manager cause for concern, but Law was the only real casualty as he was still, in effect, recuperating from his recent operation and had not looked himself in the opening fixtures. Pat Crerand had also failed to impress, as had Shay Brennan, but Busby was giving nothing away, naming a squad of sixteen to make the short journey across town. By the time he had arrived at Maine Road, he had decided that there would indeed be changes. Out went the previously mentioned trio, along with Bill Foulkes, and in came Frank Kopel, John Fitzpatrick, Alan Gowling and David Sadler, to give the side something of a younger look.

Much was expected from the match itself, as the two 'champions' went head-to-head and, despite the injuries (or whatever it was), there was still a vast array of talent on show. But those expectations failed to materialise as United approached the 90 minutes with something of a defensive attitude.

Perhaps the *Sunday Post* correspondent hit the nail on the head with the opening paragraphs of his match summary:

> Brawn took the place of brains, physical toughness took over from skill, and bitterness substituted for rivalry as these two giants clashed head on. Fifteen fans were arrested. Two players – England international Mike Summerbee and long-haired Aberdonian John Fitzpatrick – were booked, and several others were lucky not to have met a similar fate as the game erupted into a series of vicious fouls. It was inevitable that somebody was going to get seriously hurt before the end and, unfortunately, that was what happened.

Other headlines and reports were equally scathing. 'Shambles' proclaimed one, 'no classic – just crude and ugly', said another.

Summerbee was booked in the 33rd minute for a raised foot challenge on Dunne, having already been spoken to twice, while Fitzpatrick's followed suit 5 minutes later after tangling with Doyle, but there should have been other entries into the referee's notebook by then, not players names but goals scored, as United spurned a couple of opportunities. Best put the ball wide of the post as early as the fifth minute, after Gowling created the opening, and five minutes before the interval, Aston also shot wide after taking a return pass from Best.

This was to be more or less Aston's last involvement in the proceedings, as, with seconds remaining before the interval, City forced a corner having enjoyed a period of immense pressure, and as the ball was cleared to the edge of the United penalty area, Francis Lee and Aston challenged for the ball. With the whistle having been blown for half-time, the players began to make their way off the pitch, but Aston remained on the ground, obviously in much pain, while surrounded by concerned and angry teammates. Carried off the pitch by trainer Jack Crompton and Wilf McGuinness, it was later confirmed that the winger had broken his tibia and cracked his fibula in his right leg; an injury that was expected to keep him out of action until at least Christmas.

What United lacked up front, they more than made up for in their defensive duties, especially during the second 45 minutes, which City dominated, often throwing caution to the wind as they sought a breakthrough. They did manage to put the ball past Stepney midway through the half, when Young ran onto an Owen header, but was denied by the raised flag of a linesman for offside against Lee. A decision that did not go down very well with the City camp to say the least.

Their onslaught almost cost them dearly, but, as they had in the first half, United again scorned the opportunities that came their way, with

Charlton sending one shot inches over and Best crashing the ball against the crossbar.

It was a point that many perhaps did not expect United to obtain, and the determination shown by the likes of the tiger-like Fitzpatrick, the promising display of Kopel (who had only started one game during the previous season) and Sadler, who had shown considerably more mobility than Bill Foulkes in defence, were all encouraging. It was also a performance that City coach Malcolm Allison likened to a 'relegation battle', saying, 'United came with the wrong attitude to the game. It was as grim as a relegation battle at times with United looking like the side afraid of going down. There could be no joy for the spectators.'

The resolute display of the patched up United side certainly created plus-points for the under pressure United manager, but the loss of John Aston, Man of the Match the in European Cup final, was a severe blow. With Denis Law's fitness still being debated, along with an injury to his replacement, Alan Gowling, Busby now found his attacking options somewhat curtailed. Law could return at anytime, whether or not to the effectiveness of the past no one knew. As for Aston, it was even more long term. 'I am quite sure Denis will be fit eventually', said Busby, 'but he is has got to start again, slowly and methodically, but I don't know how long it is going to be before Aston is fit. Perhaps six or seven weeks.'

With the new season still in its infancy, these were all problems Busby did not need. He now had to seriously consider whether to move into the transfer market to re-enforce his front line, while also bolstering his squad for a renewed championship challenge. Any signing, however, would make little difference to the forthcoming European campaign, as the deadline for making any additions to your personnel had passed on the eve of the Maine Road encounter.

Money was certainly available, as the previous season had seen the club rake in record gate receipts of £530,800, having enjoyed an average league attendance of 57,696, another record in itself. Opposition clubs also benefited, as twelve of them enjoyed their best gates for the visit of United. Such attendances at Old Trafford created a profit of £120,842, enabling Busby to casts his eyes around the country to see who he felt could be beneficial to his rather lacklustre side. Some considered that the club's profit, plus more, would be splashed in the search for recruits, with the first £200,000 transfer hovering on the not too distant horizon.

Aston's loss was a major one, but there were already suggestions that the United manager was considering signing a replacement, casting his eyes a few miles north of Manchester towards Burnley, with a move imminent for their Scottish winger, Willie Morgan. But even a move for the Turf Moor favourite would not guarantee success in obtaining his signature as other clubs were also showing an interest, with Leeds United reportedly ready to test the water with a £100,000 bid.

A small flicker of light did appear in the Manchester evening gloom as the depleted United secured two very grateful points, courtesy of a solitary goal victory over Coventry City; a somewhat nondescript 90 minutes that almost didn't last its course due to the constant whistling from the crowd. There was a 57th minute announcement that if it did not cease then the referee would abandon the match. From an entertainment point of view, it might not have been a bad thing, but United needed a victory, badly, if only to reinstall some confidence within the ranks.

Despite countless names having been thrown about as possible United targets – everyone from Ron Davies and Jeff Astle to Peter Lorimer and Bobby Lennox – some of them being totally unlikely, it soon became apparent that Willie Morgan was the player at the top of Matt Busby's shopping list.

Morgan, a player who had given United problems in the past, had refused to sign a new contract with Burnley and had been banned from training, and consequently was left out of their opening fixtures, becoming something of a leper. The Turf Moor club did eventually grant his request for a move, while hoping to receive somewhere in the region of £100,000 for their prized asset.

Busby, however, was not the only manager to show an interest in the winger, as Don Revie was keen to take the Scot to Elland Road. He had even gone as far as to tell Morgan not to sign for anyone else, and if the eventual transfer fee could be kept to around £75,000, then he would receive £20,000. Morgan's wife, Pat, however, insisted that her husband was completely in the dark about any proposed move, but claimed 'we don't mind where he goes as long as it is not too far from Bacup', where she had a boutique.

Burnley scout and former player, Jimmy Adamson, along with other members of the back-up team, had been spotted at a couple of recent United reserve team fixtures, adding to the rumour mill that a cash and player exchange deal could be in the offer. United's interest kindled a flame within Morgan, immediately nudging Leeds United into touch, with his heart now set on a move down the road to Old Trafford. All that stood in the way of his dream move was the two clubs agreeing on a fee.

Bob Lord, the Burnley chairman, had ruffled a few feathers in his time, perhaps none more so than those of Manchester United, after commenting that people felt sorry for the club after Munich as they searched for players, and also the Teddy boy accusation directed towards Mark Pearson, following a rather robust 90 minutes around the same time. So, it was perhaps with some trepidation that Busby met the Burnley butcher. There was, however, little for the United manager to be concerned about as talks went amicably, with the national press reporting that United had agreed to pay Burnley's asking price of £90,000, or in some cases £100,000. However, the player himself later said that Sir Matt Busby had told him that the clubs had agreed a fee of £117,000. Had United paid £17,000, or indeed £27,000, more than necessary?

If it was £17,000 more, then perhaps they had also agreed to pay Morgan's share of the fee out of the desperate need and urgency to strengthen the side more than anything else, as he was entitled to 10 per cent as he had not asked for an actual transfer. In any case, Willie Morgan became a Manchester United player, immediately bolstering the flagging spirits of club and supporters alike. So eager was Morgan to sign, he did so without as much as looking at the contract placed in front of him. 'I signed without going into details', he confirmed.

The signing of Morgan was somewhat akin to that of Johnny Berry back in the early fifties, when Busby need a replacement for Jimmy Delaney, moving for the Birmingham City winger, who had often been a thorn in United's side when the two clubs came face-to-face. Upon securing his latest winger, the United manager commented that, 'He's a player I have always admired and been somewhat afraid of when he has played against us.'

Signed on the morning of 24 August, Morgan was unable to take his place in the United line-up for the visit of Chelsea, due to the 48-hour clearance ruling, and had to take a seat in the stand, enduring an agonising afternoon. 'Watching the game was sheer murder', he was to confess. 'I was aching to jump into my kit and go on and help them.' Help they could certainly have done with, as any hopes of a United revival, following that 1-0 victory over Coventry, were completely unfounded as their failings were made only obvious even to the most biased supporter, as Chelsea showed little compassion and scored four with reply. If United's crown had reportedly been slipping against Coventry, then it had certainly done so against the Londoners, obscuring their vision as they failed to spot the dangers as Chelsea dismantled them with ease. It took the visitors a mere 30 seconds to open the scoring, and in a totally mundane 90 minutes, United, and their defence in particular, were exposed at ease, showing uncertainty and little in the way of inspiration.

'Chelsea surely will never gain two points so easily again this season', 'Unless they [United] can find a quick remedy, their supporters, so long drunk on success are in for a long period of sobriety', and 'It was United's heaviest home defeat for six years. Not since Burnley won 5-2 at Old Trafford in September 1962, have the Reds conceded four goals at home' were only three of the comments to be found within the reports in the national and local newspapers following that embarrassing afternoon.

Into the line-up against Coventry City and Chelsea came Jimmy

Ryan, for his first appearances since the end of the previous March, but the opportunity for the Scot to nail down a permanent place was not to materialise. Something that was to leave him disappointed.

> Naturally I was disappointed not to get more games in the team, but by that time, as I mentioned before, I already felt that I needed to move and my mind was more on that than playing in the first team. The signing of Willie Morgan didn't really affect me that much, other than being one more indication that I needed to find a new challenge. It wasn't a particularly nice situation to be in since I was newly married and felt the responsibilities that marriage brings. I have to add that since John Aston and I were great friends, I had no desire to profit from his misfortune and would have preferred to have got into the team on merit.

The arrival of Morgan would certainly add a new dimension to the lacklustre attack, with the team as a whole relying solely on George Best for much more than inspiration. Worryingly, defensive problems were also beginning to surface, and the transfer kitty, for so long neglected, looked as though it would soon be plundered, with long-term target Ian Ure once again being spoken of, along with Blackburn Rovers and England full-back, Keith Newton. The latter was keen to leave the Second Division behind in order to cement his place in the England international side. But Manchester United were master of the unexpected and could go from pathetic to perfection at the drop of a hat. Down and depressed when there were black clouds overhead, but as soon as the sun reappeared, there was a spring in the step and a smile on the face. Denis Law was that sun.

Back in the fold for the visit of Tottenham Hotspur, four days after their London neighbours Chelsea had ventured up the M6, Law was the difference between the two teams. Certainly Willie Morgan savoured his debut in red and white, turning on a display that augured well for the future. Best was simply Best, but it was Law that showed a sharpness and hunger, persistently tormenting the Tottenham defence to give United that little something that had been missing from the earlier fixtures. Although failing to get his name on the scoresheet, Law created the opening for fellow Aberdonian John Fitzpatrick to score United's second, 5 minutes into the second half. An own goal, after they had pulled one back, added to their woes. The 'King' and United were back in the groove. Or were they?

Willie Morgan moved from his seat in the stand to Sheffield Wednesday's Hillsborough dressing rooms for his debut in the red No. 7 shirt. The Yorkshire stadium was certainly not one of United's favourite venues, and the newly promoted 'Owls' had begun their season well, with seven points from their opening half-dozen games – on par with

United. Few of those making their way to the ground on that last day of August could have imagined what they were about to witness, nor could they convince themselves to put the visitors down for an away win on their football coupons.

At times they were to regret not having taken the gamble of betting on a United victory. At the end of what was to be an enthralling 90 minutes, the packed ground rose as one to salute both sides in what was a memorable afternoon's entertainment. Wednesday were a goal up within 3 minutes of the start, as Dunne approached a Ford pass with a distinct lack of concern, and Whitham snatched the opportunity and slid the ball past Stepney. The United full-back paid for his unusual tardiness by picking up an injury in his attempted tackle on Whitham and was replaced by Burns.

On 10 minutes, United were level after Best scored, latching onto a pass from Burns. Two minutes later, they were in front, as Springett failed to hold a shot from Best and Law pounced to score. The United support was still celebrating when Wednesday equalised; Ritchie heading home a Ford centre. Despite this setback, the United machine of old kicked into gear. Law showed his old awareness in front of goal, Best tantalised the Wednesday defence and Charlton pulled the strings in midfield. Awesome to watch.

Half-time was still 20 minutes away when Law, playing his 200th game for the club, scored his second with a shot off the underside of the bar ,before turning away in delight with the arm raised skywards in salute. Then, 8 minutes before the interval, Kidd's centre was met by Charlton, whose powerful drive left Springett little more than a spectator and gave United a 4-2 lead. Whitham pulled one back for Wednesday seconds from the interval, but the half-time conversation still centred on how many United would score in the second half, such was their performance during that opening period.

But, 3 minutes into the second half, Wednesday were on level terms, after Nobby Stiles headed past Stepney while under pressure, then, soon afterwards, the United 'keeper was beaten by Megson, but a linesman's flag denied the goal. Within minutes, United had lost their penetrating edge, their authority diminished as Wednesday sniffed victory. With 13 minutes remaining, Stepney dropped the ball at Whitham's feet, unable to hold Ford's shot, and the Wednesday outside-right stabbed the ball over the line. But back came United. Stiles had a shot cleared off the line, McCalliog robbed Charlton while he was on the verge of shooting, then Law shot narrowly over. But it was all to no avail, as, despite the crowd pleasing 90 minute game, it was yet another pointless Saturday afternoon for Busby's team.

Conceding five goals was certainly a worry, and it was clear that United's fragility was in defence, confirmed seven days later with a giveaway point at Old Trafford against West Ham United. Two further points were lost in a rough-and-tumble affair, as could be expected at Burnley, a side who had been humiliated 7-0 by Tottenham Hotspur the previous weekend. Four defeats in nine outings was not expected from United, and the concern surrounding the indifferent displays was not helped by the impeding start to the defence of the European Cup and World Club Championship encounter with the Argentinian side Estudiantes.

The draw for the first round of the European Cup had paired United with League of Ireland side, Waterford, a tie switched from Dalymount Park Dublin to the headquarters of the Irish Rugby Union at Lansdowne Road, much to the displeasure of Bohemians who lost out on some much needed income from renting out their ground for the tie. But moving the much awaited visit of the European champions to the rugby ground did ensure that more people would have the opportunity to be present.

Vinny Maguire, player manager of the Irish part-timers considered that the tie was not simply about Waterford against Manchester United, but 'this is Ireland playing England'. Well aware of the gulf between the two sides, along with the possibility that his players could be humiliated over the course of the two legs, he still insisted that he would, 'Let United do all the worrying as I know we can do well in Dublin.'

Waterford's main hope in causing an upset was Alfie Hale, a former Aston Villa player, but he was realistic as regards the magnitude of the task in hand. 'Of course we don't expect to win the tie' he said, 'we're no fools, we know Manchester United are capable of tearing us apart, but right now, we're mainly concerned with putting up a good show in Dublin. By switching the tie from Waterford, we have lost any little advantage there would have been in having the game on our own ground. But the Irish are very patriotic, and most of that Dublin crowd will be behind us.' Against a lesser side, Waterford may well have achieved a favourable result in that first leg, but, having finally brushed away the cobwebs and nudging his career back on track with three goals in the previous three games, Denis Law was virtually unplayable.

Two reverse passes from Crerand and Best allowed Law to open the scoring in the 8th minute, adding a second 4 minutes before the interval, with a header from a Kidd cross. Nine minutes into the second half, which was delayed in order to allow George Best to sign autographs for two female admirers, Law claimed his hat-trick, stroking the ball past a bemused Thomas after Best had left half the Waterford side in his wake. In between those three goals, Law should have had another two, hitting the post in the 29th minute, doing likewise with a penalty kick almost on the hour mark. Best saw a superb effort disallowed due to Law, poaching again, in an offside position, following a breathtaking move between Charlton and Sadler.

Waterford had their moment of glory in the 65th minute when Matthews shot past substitute Rimmer. Although nothing more than a consolation, it did cause United considerable concern due to the resulting pitch invasion by hundreds of youngsters, forcing the referee to announce that any further encroachments would lead to the game being abandoned. Thankfully, the match proceeded without further incident and United returned to Manchester to concentrate on their forthcoming league fixture against Newcastle United at Old Trafford and their impending trip to South America. If Busby and his players, not to mention the supporters, needed a lift prior to the World Club Championship first leg, then the 3-1 victory over the Magpies was perhaps as good as it could get, although it was all down to one certain individual.

As on numerous previous occasions, George Best secured a United victory, scoring two goals. According to Peter Slingsby of the *News of the World*, 'Best's wizardry gave United the goals that mattered in two shattering minutes – goals with a magical quality because in a football sense neither was *on* and certainly could not have been scored by a mere mortal.' The first saw the Irishman make the ball curl in a 5-yard arc, leaving his boot and arching past a helpless McFaul. 'Frankly I have never seen a goal to equal it', commented Slingsby. The second, after winding his way through a mesmerised Newcastle defence, once again leaving the goalkeeper little more than a spectator, was pale by comparison. As was Denis Law's 30-yard drive in the 27th minute for United's third. The show was slowly getting back on the road, but for now the domestic front could be forgotten momentarily as the bags were packed for the long-haul trip to Argentina, a journey many had advised the club against taking, as Sir Matt Busby looked to add the World Club Championship to the Manchester United honours board.

It was a fixture that many felt should never have been a feature of United's season, as, twelve months previously, when Celtic contested the trophy against Racing Club, they were faced with trouble almost from the offset of the second leg in South America, when their goalkeeper, Ronnie Simpson, was hit on the head with a bottle during the pre-match warm up and was unable to take part in the game itself. Losing that second leg 2-1, but having won in Glasgow 1-0, Celtic were forced into a play-off to decide the eventual outcome of the trophy, but, had they known what they were about to encounter, already having had to endure irate Argentinian fans invading their dressing room, they would have simply presented Racing with the trophy and returned to Scotland.

As a sporting fixture, the play-off fell well short and evolved into a seemingly continuous running battle between the two sets of players, with the referee at one point losing complete control. Two Racing Club players were sent off along with four from Celtic, with one of that quartet, Bobby Lennox, being ordered to the dressing room at least three times and another, Bertie Auld, remaining on the pitch for the whole 90 minutes. There was also problems on the pitch – the 1966 England/Argentina World Cup tie at Wembley to throw into the mix, creating an almost certain volatile situation.

'I believe one will only break these continental barriers by playing more, not less. Football is a world game and I do not think that a problem can be solved by running away from it.' Busby was quick to tell those who thought he, and Manchester United, were making a grave mistake in following the Parkhead sides' footsteps to South America. United's opponents, Estudiantes de La Plata, although formed in 1905, had only broken the dominance of River Plate, Boca Juniors, Racing Club and Independiente the previous season, winning the newly formed Metropolitan championship, while also achieving the runners-up spot in the National Championship, which lead to a place in the South American Cup. Competing in the latter, and due to their success in winning the trophy, they had to play sixteen games over a three-week period, which was over and above their regular league fixtures; although in the latter stages of the tournament they did play somewhat weakened sides on the domestic front.

Played in a group format in the opening two rounds, they progressed with ease into the semi-finals, where it took a play-off to overcome Racing Club on goal difference. In the final, where they faced the Brazilian side Palmeiras, they were once again involved in three games. Having won the home leg 2-1, they lost the second 3-1 and, with the aggregate score not being taken into consideration for some unknown reason, it was down to a play-off in Montivideo to decide the winners, where Estudiantes ran out 2-0 victors. Formed by students of the University of La Plata; numerous lessons had been learned over the years – they were now a formidable side. Although their fixture against United would be switched from their modest 25,000 stadium to the 80,000 capacity Buenos Aires home of Boca Juniors, they would still have a formidable support, with the atmosphere bordering on the hostile.

Given United's current fragility and the tempestuous nature of the likes of Law, Stiles and Crerand, the South American sojourn had the possibility of being a step too far. Simply getting to Argentina was fraught with problems, as United had to dash from Old Trafford under police escort, almost as soon as the final whistle blew on their match against Newcastle

United, in order to catch their flight from Manchester to London before heading into the unknown territory of South America and Buenos Aires, via Paris, Madrid and Rio de Janeiro. Prior to leaving, Matt Busby cast the threats of a troubled visit to one side, stating there was a prospect of misbehaving players being thrown into jail. He said,

I have had a personal assurance from Estudiantes that they wish to play this game without any fury. They did the kindness to write and say how honoured they were to receive such a great team and expressed the hope that this contest would be a credit to international football. My players have been around the world sufficiently to know that they are only inviting trouble if they step out of line. We have had a series of talks and the players have agreed that they must be prepared for anything. The only menace can come from the crowd. I know that Estudiantes are not one of the Argentinian millionaire teams who can be pretty ruthless in these prestige games. Their captain is a dentist, two are fully qualified doctors, and there are lawyers and law students among the team. We expect a hard game. It should be a great test of courage and skill. I have repeatedly told my players that the only provocation can come from the fans who can get a bit het up. Luckily, we are accustomed to this terrace menace. But just to make sure that we do not let British football down. I have given a stern warning to every player that if they step out of line they will face a sentence from me they will never forget.

The United party were met in Buenos Aires with the words of warning from EUFA officials ringing in their ears, mirrored by pacifying comments from one of the Estudiantes directors. The former stating that should there be any misbehaviour from players of either side then they would face up to three years' suspension. Newly drawn up regulations also stated that fines and suspensions of clubs, with the possibility of ground closures for EUFA or South American Football Confederation controlled games also in place, with a EUFA spokesman adding that, 'if the worst came to the worst, we would invoke the whole lot. Something had to be done after last season. We could not allow such play to carry on, and though rules can never completely cut out misconduct, we hope the new ones will act as a brake.'

Having arrived at their destination following the 24-hour flight, the United party were greeted with surprising friendliness, with an Estudiantes director proclaiming

We don't want a war as there was last year in Argentina; we want to play football. We are a different team from other clubs in the country. We will not go out to win at all costs. I cannot predict what the nature or style of the game will be against Manchester United, but my attitude is that this is a football match – not a national war. There will not be any heroes. Like Sir Matt Busby, I too have impressed upon my team the need to play this match in a sporting manner, repeat sporting, worthy manner. But as Sir Matt must have also told his team, my team, I have told my team to go out and win ... repeat, win.

A pre-match cocktail party was also organised for the officials and players of both teams, with numerous interpreters recruited to ensure that conversations were allowed to take place between all in attendance. It was all, however, nothing more than a smokescreen, as no Estudiantes officials or players showed up and, following a quarter of an hour wait, the United party returned to their hotel. *Señor* Mariano Mangano, the Estudiantes president, said, 'The time of our last training session had to be switched and it was impossible for our players to come.' It did little to pacify the annoyed visitors, and neither did the comments of coach Zubeldia. 'Football is a game for men. I see no point in teams kissing each other. If they want to do that they may as well stay at home.' A clear hint that no one from Estudiantes ever had any intentions of turning up and it was yet another form of gamesmanship.

With efforts to keep some peace and goodwill surrounding the fixture disintegrating, such an idea had never been an item on the agenda of the local police department or the press. Gen. Mario Fonseca, the local chief of police, had decided that should any player get sent off, then he would be subject to thirty days behind bars, without any mere formalities such as a trial or an appeal. When word of this reached Sir Matt's ears, he immediately set off for the British Embassy to ensure that none of his players would find themselves in such a situation.

In the press, Nobby Stiles was the United player singled out for attention. 'Assassin' screamed the headlines, with the bespectacled half-back portrayed as a kicking, spitting demon; the reporters only stopping themselves from going as far as to add that he also ate children! Even the official match programme went as far as to call him a brutal player and a bad sportsman.

The match venue was the totally inappropriately named Candy Bowl Stadium where the bumpy and rutted pitch was far from ideal. 'My back garden where all the local kids play is in better condition than that', said Pat Crerand, when they surveyed the arena which was also surrounded by a 12-foot deep moat – ready for emergency flooding. Alongside would be 2,000 uniformed and plain-clothed police and firemen with high-powered hoses and strategically placed tear gas bombs. Remember, this was only a football match.

As the minutes ticked away to kick-off, Sir Matt Busby professed his confidence:

> If we play as well as I know we can over the two matches then I am quite
> confident we will become world champions. I was satisfied before we
> played Benfica in the European Cup final that the lads would have the
> skill to do their job. Out here they will need so much more than skill.
> But they are a mature lot now. They have had plenty of experience at
> the highest levels and I think they are in the right frame of mind. But
> now the gloves are off, and soon we will have the answers to a lot of
> questions. Let us hope we are prepared for all eventualities.

In the build up to the game, Busby only had two injury concerns: Tony
Dunne, who had a cut head, and Pat Crerand, who had only returned to
the fold against Waterford, nursing an ankle knock. Both, however, were
to be pronounced fit, allowing the United manager to select the starting
line-up of his choice.

Back in Britain, the United support had two options: go to bed in the
hope that when they awoke in the morning the news would be favourable,
or stay up into the early hours and tune into Radio 2, who were
broadcasting a commentary of the match from 2.05 a.m.

As Estudiantes took to the field, fireworks filled the air, adding an
additional backdrop to the already menacing arena, with a band in its
eighteenth-century costume of top hats, blue coats and white knee
breeches, giving the scene something of a surreal appearance. The opening
stages were always going to be a clear indication as to how the game
would unfold, with United fouled eight times in the first 10 minutes. It
came as no surprise that the Argentinians, although more than capable
of demonstrating a wide array of skill, adopted a cynical, underhand and
sometimes evil approach.

From the offset, the Estudiantes players made their intentions
more than obvious. An early disgraceful foul on George Best clearly
achieved its intention, virtually killing off the undoubted threat from
the Irishman, as, from that moment on, he seemed to lose all appetite
for the game. In the 14th minute, Nobby Stiles was headbutted by the
consistently transgressive Bilardo, resulting in a deep cut over his eye,
while Bobby Charlton, closely marked by Togneri, was brutally hacked
down by Pachame, and later required two stitches in a leg wound.
Stiles suffered blurred vision following a second assault, this time by
Togneri. United's trainer, Jack Crompton, was on the field so often that
many an observer could have been forgiven for thinking that he was
actually playing.

With the United players warned to steer well clear of any confrontations, their play and overall confidence was somewhat diminished, fearful that any tackle, slightly mistimed or otherwise, might light the blue touchpaper with disastrous consequences. Law was constantly shadowed by two defenders, with Willie Morgan, perhaps something of an unknown to the Argentinians but arguably United's best player, showing a brave edge to his game as he took on defenders, while well aware that if he did not meet a raised foot or an obstructive challenge from the first defender, there was more than a possibility he would from the second.

Estudiantes came close to scoring in the opening minutes when a free kick, awarded for obstruction on Ribaudo, was headed just wide by Bilardo. But it took them until the 29th minute before they eventually managed to prise open the United defence. Stepney failed to hold a shot from Pachame and, as it bounced towards goal, it was cleared off the line by Charlton. Then, as Ribaudo's corner swung into the United penalty area, the defence stood as though hypnotised, allowing Conigliaro both space and time to head home. United, although momentarily deflated, were soon back in the game, never for one minute allowing their opponents to believe that they had the upper hand, either from their subversive tactics or their one goal lead, and within 10 minutes, had the ball in the net.

Morgan, in yet another attempt to make progress down the wing, was fouled, and from Charlton's low, hard free-kick, Sadler flicked the ball past Poletti. The joy, however, was short-lived, as no sooner had referee Miranda signalled the goal and began walking back towards the centre, his attention was attracted by linesman Marino, who ironically was the referee in the previous season's encounter between Celtic and Racing, and who attempted to run this one from the touchline with a number of clearly controversial decisions.

Following a brief discussion between the two officials, the referee changed his mind and awarded a free kick to Estudiantes for offside against a United player. One photograph shows Bill Foulkes hovering in mid-picture as the ball flashes past the 'keeper, with one defender looking to be playing the United centre-half on-side. While another, taken from the opposite side a fraction earlier, shows Foulkes nearer to the goal line with no Estudiantes players in sight. David Sadler was later to insist that 'there were three Estudiantes defenders on the goal line', while George Best added, 'the only reason it was offside was because the ball went in the net.'

Dejected, United plodded on, now seemingly with even the match officials doing their utmost to prevent them from taking something from the game. Estudiantes, in their underhand methods and determination to demoralise United, lost much of their effectiveness, while demeaning the fixture as a footballing contest. To United's credit, they plodded away manfully in what was described by one observer as being similar to 'an end of season Fourth Division affair, rather than one for the regal title of world champions', with Stepney keeping their hopes of salvaging something from the tie alive with an excellent block from a Madero shot, then performing further heroics as he leaped and squirmed to prevent Veron and Ribaudo from latching onto the loose ball. But those slim expectations of escaping the cauldron of hostility with a goal, as well as credit for their performance against adversity, were dealt a blow 10 minutes from time, when Nobby Stiles was sent off.

A pass down the wing saw Stiles run onto the ball, but a raised linesman's flag for offside halted the attack. The Argentinian public enemy number one threw his arm into the air in frustration, nothing more, but was immediately dispatched to the dressing room by the referee. He was offside, but his reaction, considering what had gone on during the previous 80 minutes, deserved to be ignored, or received a mild finger-wagging at the very most. The United No. 6 was now banned from the return leg in Manchester. The game petered out, but the furore that followed maintained considerable momentum over the course of the next few days.

In the cold light of day, United and Busby's decision to take part in the fixture was furiously debated, while the United players, now in more peaceful surroundings, spoke of their experiences in a game that did nothing to benefit or do anything for international relations.

United did know what they were getting themselves into when they agreed to enter the competition, perhaps naively thinking that a leopard could change its spots. Sir Stanley Rous, the President of FIFA, commented after the 90 minutes, which at times ignored the Geneva Convention, stating, 'To me, the most outstanding feature of the match was the quite remarkable tolerance of Manchester United.'

Speaking about the sending off, Nobby Stiles said:

I knew before I came that something like this could happen, yet I wanted to play. I had such a grip on myself I thought they could not get me. I was handing the ball to opponents and walking away from fouls like a proper little saint. But I couldn't win – I should have known that. When the linesman called the referee and an interpreter to me in the second half, do you know what they told me? I was playing too near the No. 8 Bilardo. I ask you! But he was marking me. The lads kept telling me to get away from him and I started making runs up on the wing to keep out of his way. I would have had to take my shirt off to get clear. He grabbed me the moment I started to move. But what chance have you got? These bastards were after me before I even got on the plane. I am scared to talk about this. Scared about talk that I may be suspended for three years – what have I done to deserve this?

Teammates were also quick to tell of the on-field battles they had to endure throughout the 90 minutes. 'That was the longest hour of my life', said Denis Law. 'Pachame punched me from the kick-off, it didn't hurt, but it showed what they were about. They kept coming and pulling the hairs on your arms as they pretended to shake hands – or pinching your ribs as they helped you up.'

Willie Morgan was confident that he had qualified for the Mexico Olympics, as 'I was doing 80-yard hurdles up the wings. What the hell was that all about? I felt like laughing ... for about five minutes. Then I saw six studs coming at my chest and I realised this wasn't much of a joke.'

'I didn't even go for 70:30 balls, never mind 50:50', confessed George Best. 'And I don't think I was being a coward. You couldn't live out there. I'd like to hear one of their team talks. They must spend hours thinking up different places to pinch you.'

In reality, it was simply 'half-time', with United having to face a further 90 minutes at Old Trafford. Withdrawing from the competition and simply giving the world crown to Estudiantes, in an attempt to avoid any further confrontation, was certainly an option, but it was one that Sir Matt Busby was not going to consider. Busby confirmed,

> We shall continue to play in this competition because we want to be the best in the world. You cannot stop playing these games because of certain incidents. What better exponents of football have there been in the last ten years than the Brazilians – and they are from South America. I was of course upset at some of the things that happened, but there is no question of us calling off the return match at Old Trafford. We can take tough play, but we are not used to what went on in Buenos Aires. I think my players were wonderful under the conditions. I am hoping that the second leg will be more of a football match. We have certainly got to play football to win it.

Many felt that United did have what it took to become world champions, including Jackie Charlton. But, having watched his brother play under such threatening conditions in Argentina, and although backing United to win, he thought that 'the worst was yet to come', and that there was every possibility that the game would perhaps not even finish.

The events of Buenos Aires could well have produced a prolonged domino effect, with certain players requiring a sustained period of convalescence in order to get back to some form of normality. Thankfully, United's scheduled fixture against Nottingham Forest at the City Ground, originally scheduled for 28 August, had been postponed by the Football League until 1 October, as the United party were not due back in Britain until the Friday morning. So it was some seven days before the players saw action again with Waterford visiting Manchester for the second leg of the European Cup First Round tie.

As expected, the Irish part-timers once again put up a spirited fight, but there was no Argentinian hangover, and United put seven past an exasperated Thomas in the Waterford goal, with Denis Law claiming four as United eased their way into the Second Round. Back on League business, with some ground to be made up if a championship challenge was to be maintained, Arsenal arrived at Old Trafford, setting their stall out with the perception of denying United few, if any, scoring opportunities. A cause helped by the inadequacy shown by Law in front of goal, who wasted and spurned numerous chances. The drab, error strewn, goalless encounter almost never lasted the 90 minutes. Many would have been grateful had it indeed been cut short, but the thought of calling a halt to the proceedings certainly passed through the mind of referee Ken Burns midway through the second half. 'I was showered with hundreds of pennies, aspirin bottles, conkers, apple cores and everything else these fans could get their hands on' admitted Arsenal goalkeeper Bob Wilson. 'Coins could blind you if they caught you in the eye. It was frightening. And this was only an ordinary League match.'

Arsenal captain Frank McLintock added:

At the station, about fifty youngsters – aged thirteen or fourteen, I'd guess – surrounded our coach, swearing, waving their fists and spitting. I don't know what's happening to the game. If this goes on, someone is going to get killed by these mobs. If they are like that when the Argentines play up there, I hate to think what will happen.

Hooliganism had been bubbling away for a number of years, not just at Old Trafford but around the country. However, due to the number of people attracted to United games, such disturbances always looked greater. This latest outbreak of trouble caused the club much concern, particularly with the forthcoming meeting with Estudiantes on the horizon. It was even suggested that United switch the game to Wembley in an effort for sanity to prevail and the safety of the visitors preserved.

Worried about the on-going threat of trouble on the Old Trafford terraces, United had gone as far as making an unprecedented move in trying to create a less hostile environment prior to the recent meeting with West Ham, by asking the London side if they would be first out onto the pitch prior to the kick-off, and if they would warm up at the scoreboard end. Minor details perhaps, but anything was worth a try in the on-going war against the hooligans.

'Between now and the world championship, we have got to get it over to the fans that they could destroy us and the club if they do anything foolish', said a concerned Sir Matt Busby. 'We want them to shout, cheer and encourage us. But they stepped over the mark on Saturday [against Arsenal].' United chairman Louis Edwards added

> The fans know the score, they know what trouble from them could do to the club. We have to take all the precautions we can, and then rely on their good sense. They have never let us down. This is United's match and it should be played at United. Wembley is terrible – they treat us badly over tickets for our fans, they treat us badly over everything. I would never play there again if I had my way.

The local police force also showed obvious concern, with a spokesman saying, 'We have a meeting with United to discuss arrangements. Obviously we are a bit apprehensive. An early goal for United will help us – for it's anybody's guess what will happen if United look like losing.'

A creditable 2-2 draw against Tottenham Hotspur in London, 90 minutes which portrayed the mirror opposite of United previous encounter against a North London side, was followed by a 2-0 defeat at Anfield. Little, however, could be read into the latter, as United were beset by injury problems against Liverpool; ten players were under treatment prior to the journey along the East Lancs Road.

Only four recognised first-team players – Alex Stepney, Nobby Stiles, Pat Crerand and Bobby Charlton – made the starting eleven on Merseyside, where they were joined by six players under the age of twenty-two, with Busby more than happy to produce medical certificates for those taking up the space on the Old Trafford treatment tables. Francis Burns was a long-term casualty in need of a cartilage operation, Law had fluid on the knee, Morgan, an injured thigh, Fitzpatrick, a twisted ankle, Best and Dunne also had ankle injuries, Foulkes was suffering from a cold, while Kidd had a groin strain. Added to these were the other long-term injuries – a chipped ankle bone for Sadler and Aston a broken leg.

The defeat against Liverpool, although unwanted, was of little concern to the United manager, nor was the possible fine from the authorities for fielding an under-strength team; his immediate worry was the quality of the side he would be able to field against Estudiantes. By strict contrast, the South Americans enjoyed something of a ten-day break between their last game and travelling to Manchester. Even then, with the blessing of their League authorities, they were allowed to field a complete reserve side in the 3-0 defeat against Colon.

In the run-up to the Estudiantes encounter, the European Football Union warned both sides of the consequences should they step out of line, while United sought out the media in order to make their feelings as clear as possible. Having previously appealed for calm in the club's match-day programme, they now attempted to send the message out to a much wider audience. Sir Matt Busby wrote,

> There is a great danger that the supports at large may become incensed at the play of our opponents and be tempted to take matters into their own hands. This, of course, is the last thing we all want; not only will it destroy the spectacle of this great occasion, but obviously could ruin the chance of us becoming world champions. As you are aware, the ground can be closed for three years and we can be banished from UEFA competitions for up to three years. Also, we can be adjudged to have lost the match 3-0 if there is any misconduct. This is important, but the all-important thing is that we should have a match which should not bring disgrace upon our club and supporters and country.

The message, however, did fall upon deaf ears, as one youngster during a Granada interview insisted, 'If Estudiantes are in front ten minutes from the end, there will be trouble.'

Estudiantes arrived in Manchester on a win bonus of £1,700 a man, some £300 less than the United players could look to pick up if they achieved success, and their captain, Oscar Malbernat, was quick to divert matters away from the controversial first leg saying, 'We feel that the stories about the first match have been grossly exaggerated. We are not a dirty side and are hoping for a fine game of football. We know United have some great players, but believe we can hold on to our lead.' His manager, Zubelda, added,

> If there is any trouble or if any of my players are attacked, we will not continue with the game. We have come here to play a game of football. This is not intended to be a battle – just a game between two sides of eleven players. We want the players and the crowd to behave and we see no reason why there cannot be a really good match.

With all the talking done, it was down to the twenty-two players on the pitch to decide the outcome of the match, which even the neutrals eagerly awaited and viewed with bated breath.

United's medical team worked as hard pre-match as the players they had patched up, and prepared for the following 90 minutes, but their efforts were soon looked upon as futile as the visitors increased their advantage after only 5 minutes. Dunne robbed Veron, but gave away a throw-in and, as the ball came back into play, Bill Foulkes was judged to have raised his foot too high as he challenged Coniglari and was penalised. From the resulting free-kick, Madero curled it over the heads of the United defence and in crept Veron to head home, with Stepney static on his line and two defenders failing to pick up the player dubbed as 'the Witch'.

Two goals behind on aggregate, United had a mountain to climb, not simply to win the tie on the night, but in order to force a play-off in Amsterdam. The visitors had reduced their repertoire of underhand tactics, but the little niggles and off-the-ball incidents were still obvious to the eye. There were hard, no-holds-barred challenges, but, as in the first leg, United had to ignore them and get on with the job at hand – one that was now considerably more difficult.

From the offset, United had attacked – they had little option – although they had to do so with caution, and twice in the opening minutes they came close to reducing arrears. Crerand shot for goal from 25 yards, only to see Poletti grasp the ball at the foot of the post; then both Law and Best were denied by the luck of the bounce. Best beat Malbernat, but Poletti saved at the second attempt, while Sadler's threw himself at a Morgan cross, but looked on in anguish as the ball curled past the post. Then, Charlton, like Best, was denied by Poletti, who dealt comfortably with his 30-yard drive. It wasn't until midway through the half that the hostility of the first leg resurfaced with a 5 minute spell of pushing, obstruction and sly digs. Veron was booked for a ridiculously late challenge on Crerand, but thankfully, such injury-threatening incidents were few and far between.

Continuing their forages towards the Estudiantes goal, and urged on by a voracious crowd, Kidd pushed forward and his cross was met by Law in mid-air, but Poletti was equal to his effort, as he was just before the interval when United's best opportunity of the opening forty-five again fell to the usually decisive Law. It was Crerand on this occasion who found the blonde-headed Scot, but uncharacteristically, he delayed his shot, allowing the goalkeeper time to pounce on the ball. Not only did Poletti rob Law of a goalscoring opportunity, it also deprived him of the chance to make amends later in the game, as the 'keeper's challenge produced a cut down the back of his leg. Carried off, with four stitches given, it was considered unwise for him to return to the action and the Scot was replaced by Sartori.

Estudiantes went about the job at hand with prolific professionalism, but there were occasions that looked like they were cracking under pressure. Brian Kidd took up the mantle left by Law and led the United front line forward in search of a goal that would at least get them back into the game. A Charlton flick sent him through on goal, but once again

Poletti saved, Sartori created the opening, but the final shot flew across the face of the goal. As the minutes ticked away, the tension mounted and tempers began to fray. Following one challenge on Best, both Togneri and Malbernat ended up sprawled on the sodden ground, with the Irishman lucky to escape a booking. Then, with only 2 minutes remaining, and many supporters having decided heading for the exits, Best and Medina were sent off.

Having endured one over-robust challenge too many, Best threw a punch at the already booked Medina. Both this and the retaliation went unnoticed by the referee, but were clearly observed by a linesman, and upon his verdict, both players were dismissed. From the resulting free kick – taken quickly – Morgan raced forward and, catching the Estudiantes defence unaware, slotted home the equaliser.

Many piled back onto the earlier vacated terracing in the hope that some form of miracle might be achieved in a final last surge towards the Estudiantes goal, and they were rewarded with the sight of Morgan wriggling down the wing before crossing into the crowded goalmouth, where Kidd prodded the ball over the line. Old Trafford erupted, United had secured a draw, and the chance of a third meeting in Holland. But had they? It was the Estudiantes players who were celebrating, not those of United, as it turned out that the referee had blown for full-time seconds before the ball had crossed the line.

United had failed in their challenge and were perhaps let down by Best's inability to remain calm in the face of provocation and Stepney's action at full-time when, as Pachame stood sportingly at the side of the pitch applauding the United players and shaking their hands, he was rewarded for his civility with a slap across the face from the United 'keeper.

Had United not conceded that early goal, then things could have been different, something admitted by Bobby Charlton, the United captain, who added 'It was our own fault that we didn't win. We didn't play well enough I knew that we hadn't equalised with the last kick because I heard the whistle go before Brian Kidd put the ball into the net.' The United support, upon whose shoulders much had rested, remained calm throughout, but had the Estudiantes players decided upon a lap of honour at the end, then events might have taken a nasty turn. In reality, it was the players who had let the club down.

In the aftermath of the Estudiantes confrontation, United struggled pitifully against Southampton, a team that had not won on the road during the opening weeks of the season, but needed little in the way of luck or an upsurge in their normal game plan to leave Manchester with both points, following a 2-1 victory.

Defensively, United were poor. Bill Foulkes was stretched to the limit by Ron Davies, who made the first and scored the second for the visitors, and was withdrawn from the action after an hour. It was at 90 minutes that saw United, already having lost half as many games as they had during the whole of the previous campaign, drop to sixteenth in the table, casting a huge dark shadow over Old Trafford.

The season continued on a stop-start basis, with a 3-2 victory at newly promoted Queens Park Rangers, followed by four successive draws, although sandwiched in between the 1-1 at Sunderland and a goalless stalemate against Ipswich at Old Trafford, Anderlecht were defeated 3-0 in the European Cup Second Round first leg in Manchester, and this was without the suspended George Best, who was to miss both this and the away leg as punishment for his sending off against Estudiantes.

Fingers were also pointed at the players during the club's AGM, not exactly for their performances, but for their on-field behaviour. A Mr Arthur Heatley stood up and said,

There are some players who are not helping the good name of the club. They could be much better mannered on the field. If Nobby Stiles had not been sent off against Estudiantes in Argentina for a silly gesture, we might have won the world championship, plus a lot of money and prestige.

In reply, Sir Matt Busby said,

I am continually reminding our players to keep their heads. But some of the things I saw happening out in Buenos Aires during our first leg match against Estudiantes nearly made me lose my head – and that's saying something. Time and again I stress to the players, 'If you lose your heads you lose the match.' But on certain occasions they have been expected to stand too much. It is silly in some respects I know, but you have to accept that human nature comes into it. Intimidation goes on throughout football. A player may take two kicks, but the third time it is very difficult not to show some form of expression.

A record crowd of 31,138 squeezed into the Loftus Road home of newly promoted Queens Park Rangers and, with a little more luck and composure, could have enjoyed a much more productive 90 minutes against United. Perhaps a little overawed by their majestic visitors, they were a goal behind after 25 minutes, although had Bridges took the opportunities presented to him, missing two in the opening 9 minutes and a further two later on, then United's somewhat dismal defence would have been more exposed for its frailties. On four occasions, the Rangers outside right shunned scoring chances and his team were to pay for his recklessness in front of goal.

Two own goals, despite what the record books say, gave United what should have been a comfortable cushion with only 30 minutes remaining, but panic set in when Leach headed past Stepney 2 minutes after United's second. Although Law was to restore that two-goal advantage 5 minutes from time, the visitor's nerves were to remain on tenterhooks, even more so when Wilks scored a second to make it 3-2 and then, with virtually the last kick of the ball, Allen blasted it over.

If we turn through the pages of history, even just a matter of some two or three years, we have a Manchester United of free-flowing supremacy and the ultimate goal machine, but suddenly those goals were at a premium, with a mere one, and an own goal at that, over the course of the following four league fixtures.

Against Leeds United, goals have never been in abundance, so a 0-0 'Battle of the Roses' at Old Trafford could have been expected. A creditable performance, accompanied by a goal 2 minutes from time at Sunderland, earned a valuable point, although United could still be found in the bottom half of the table, but against Ipswich Town and Stoke City, it was a tale of 'inadequate finishing' and a 'wretchedly uneventful' game, when 'there was not even a goal to relieve the tedium'. Yes, this was Manchester United they were talking about.

Three days prior to the Ipswich fixture, Busby's team had returned to Europe, with the Belgians of Anderlecht, United's first ever opponents in the European Cup back in September 1956, flying into Manchester then returning home, wondering how they might attempt to reverse a 3-0 defeat in a fortnight's time. But had the East Anglican side found themselves involved in a two-legged affair with United, a second 90 minutes would have been anticipated with relish. The 0-0 scoreline looked upon as a victory of sorts, despite the actual blandish afternoon.

Spectators and journalists alike were rooting among their memories to recall a worse match at Old Trafford. 'They failed', wrote Paul Fitzpatrick of the *Guardian*, while two of his press box colleagues, Henry Weston and Michael Parkinson, were equally scathing. The former penned, 'Sir Matt Busby faces one of the great challenges of his managerial career. This is not said lightly. It comes after watching an unbelievable inept performance from the champions of Europe', while the latter wrote,

> United moved sideways and backwards but rarely forward, and while they played about in midfield Ipswich chased back in defence, so that when United finally arrived in the penalty area the sentries had

been posted, the gates locked and what is more United had forgotten the password.

England 'keeper Gordon Banks, as much as a dysfunctional United forward line, kept Best and the others at bay at the Victoria Ground, and it was of little surprise that the short trip across the English Channel for the return match against Anderlecht should see a further struggle.

Leading 3-0 from the Old Trafford first leg, seven less than the previous occasion, when the two sides met in Manchester at City's Maine Road ground, United stunned the cautious Belgians with an 8th minute Sartori goal. Certainly an excellent start and something of a safety cushion, but it was also a start that invigorated the home side and pushed United onto the defensive for lengthy spells. Equalising in the 20th minute, it was not until 13 minutes into the second half that Anderlecht managed a second, the experience of Bill Foulkes doing much to keep the visitors in the game, that the Belgians finally emerged from their shell and attacked with a hint of desperation and abandon.

A third goal in the 70th minute brought further inspiration, as Anderlecht realised that there was more than a possibility that they could prevent the champions from making further progress in the competition. As the minutes ticked away, goalkeeper Trappeniers cut a lonely figure in the Anderlecht half of the field as the Belgians set up camp around the United 18-yard box. But United weathered the storm, edging through 4-3 on aggregate and Busby was grateful to be making progress, despite his opposite number bemoaning an injury to Peteers in the Old Trafford first leg; something be believed cost his team dearly.

Back to the grunt and grind of the First Division. A 2-1 defeat at Leicester City kept United stranded in fifteenth place, nine points off the bottom and sixteen off the top. That the home side had lost 7-1 against Everton at Goodison Park the previous Saturday stood for nothing, that United had opened the scoring and that it was Leicester's first win in ten, mattered little either, as it was simply just another mediocre performance from a team that much more was expected from. It was a worrying time, as there just did not seem any light at the end of the tunnel, with no miraculous cure to this stuttering and indecisive form, although the visit of Liverpool to Old Trafford was more than enough to push current league form to the back of the mind, if only for 90 minutes.

There was certainly not the intensity or all out hatred that this particular fixture in future season's would create, although the local constabulary kept themselves warm and occupied with regular ventures onto the Stretford End terraces to extract nefarious juveniles. The overpowering necessity to put one over their Lancashire neighbours was most certainly there, although, as league leaders, everyone wanted to try and knock you off your perch, but, on current form, the odds on United doing just that were as big as the points margin between the two.

For two players, the battle between the two clubs from opposite ends of the East Lancs Road produced completely different emotions. For Willie Morgan, it was a feeling of despair, as only three months since moving to Old Trafford, he found himself dropped for the first time despite having, by some accounts, a favourable outing against Leicester City the previous week. Obviously Matt Busby thought differently.

But for nineteen-year-old Steve James, 3 p.m. on that particular Saturday afternoon just could not come quick enough, as the youngster, who had previously only been used as something of a stopgap on three occasions, found himself thrown into the fray, but this time on merit. The young Midlander had ironically made his debut against Liverpool at Anfield back in October, replacing the injured Bill Foulkes, but he was now given the opportunity to step out of the Central League shadows and make the No. 5 jersey his own, as United sought a replacement for the aging Foulkes.

On a partly frozen, bone-hard pitch, covered in the frost of the previous evening, amid a backdrop of mist and freezing cold air, both sets of players looked ill at ease as they slipped and slithered, even although some had tried and tested at least three pairs of footwear prior to kick-off. Having to overcome the conditions, which added to the excitement of the afternoon, as well as the opponents, it was United who adapted the best, testing Lawrence on several occasions. It wasn't until 8 minutes after the interval, when footwear was again changed, that he was finally beaten. A lob from Best on the edge of the area flashed past Lawler and, as the ball bounced, Law bent forward to nod the ball past the Liverpool 'keeper. Soon afterwards, Lawrence was again the hero of the day, saving attacks from Best and Sartori, while at the opposite end Stepney made a double save from St John, amid claims that the ball had actually crossed the line, with several other efforts flying wide and over his goal.

Despite this minor scare, United held on to their solitary goal lead, with Tommy Lawrence in the Liverpool goal remaining the difference between that and a heavier defeat. As for young Steve James, he came through the 90 minutes with much credit, doing enough to ensure that further appearances were on the cards.

In defeating the league leaders, there should have been a surge of confidence ebbing through the club, with the victory used as a springboard to better things, despite the current crop of injuries and loss of form having severe consequences on the season to date. Some twenty-one players had already been used, as Sir Matt Busby tried to guide his team towards a position more in keeping with its recent history. 'We are improving', he insisted prior to the trip to Southampton. 'We could start coming to the boil in time for the FA Cup competition, which is really important to us this season and could be our passport to Europe next season.'

He obviously considered the fourteen point gap between United and Liverpool, despite having two games in hand, as being a mountain that could not be climbed, something that the most biased Stretford Ender would have reluctantly agreed with. But what of Europe, where his team were in the last eight and not due to play Rapid Vienna until the end of February, when the tide could certainly have been turned? Did the United manager consider that this was also beyond the capabilities of his players, or had he simply mellowed with age or taken his eye off the ball so to speak, following that ultimate success against Benfica at Wembley? 'Let us hope that this is not the end, just the beginning', Busby was to say following that European Cup triumph, a message from the heart, but in his head there would certainly have been thoughts of retirement, having achieved his ultimate goal with age, as well as those demons of yesteryear weighing heavily. His every move was being carefully studied, with each result scrutinised and bisected with a fine toothcomb. The clock was slowly ticking down.

If there was an improvement to the recent form, then it was certainly not obvious on the south coast, where there was little in the way of pre-Christmas goodwill, with frustration creeping into the mix as Southampton hit United with two goals in the space of 2 minutes, leaving any thoughts of an instant revival blowing in the cold winter air. It was difficult to imagine that United were indeed the current European Cup holders, their position enhanced by the announcement that George Best and Bobby Charlton had been named first and second in the European Footballer of the Year competition, although it was the performances of the United duo in the Real Madrid semi-final and the final against Benfica that earned them the plaudits and the Irishman's claim to the Golden Ball. Perhaps a golden lamp, producing a genie when rubbed, would have been a more acceptable award, as United not only lost their second consecutive fixture, but failed to score, conceding three against Arsenal at Highbury on Boxing Day – the first time that they had failed to score on the north London ground since October 1950. It was also a game seen by some, as the beginning of the end.

While a number of observers considered United to be playing better than their league position suggested, others, such as Brian James, a journalist with the *Daily Mail*, thought otherwise, as he began his report on the Highbury defeat with 'Manchester United's last great talent as a team – the power to scare other sides into submission by calibre of their component stars – was shattered by Arsenal yesterday.' So, difficult times at Old Trafford as 1968 merged into 1969, with the possibility that the new year could have a far from happy start, as the FA Cup third round draw had presented the type of tie that no one at the club would have wished for, with an away draw against lower league opposition and the distinct threat of a giant killing.

Fourth Division Exeter City, the ninety-first club in the Football League and United's first opponents in the Football League Cup (a game in which they had struggled), rubbed their hands at the prospect of the European champions visiting their homely St James Park ground, but, having reached the third round of the cup only once since the war, their hopes of progressing were always going to be slender to say the very least. They certainly had the experience, if not to cause a major upset, then to make things somewhat difficult for United, with two of their defenders being able to boast of First Division experience. One of those players, Newman, in fact played in the 1956 FA Cup final with Birmingham City, while another two had mustered twelve years' experience between them at St James Park.

Perhaps United's current league form painted a picture of a team in decline, but they were still a far cry from the talented performer doing the rounds on nothing more than his back catalogue. They still had the name, the players and, at times, the panache, to lure the intrigued, as well as the interested away from the comfort of their own homes. The comfort of their own homes was indeed something that residents in the five terraced houses on St James Road, adjacent to Exeter's ground, cherished. But with the visit of a marauding red army from the north, they were living in fear. Of the 18,500 tickets available, almost 5,000 had gone to the away support and, in the eyes of the locals, it was 4,999 too many. Chimney sweep Terry Plumer, who lived in No. 11 St James Road, admitted that he was scared of what would happen on the day.

> It was bad enough when they had a gate of 16,000 for the League Cup clash with Sheffield Wednesday last September. Wednesday supporters trampled all over my garden and five crowded into my hall and watched the game from the porch steps. I'm asking for police protection this time. Since the draw was made, my phone and doorbell haven't stopped ringing. Complete strangers have been trying to watch the match from my upstairs windows. I have been offered as much as £10 a seat. I could make more than £100 for the afternoon, but it's not worth the risk of having your home smashed up. I know a sixty-seven-year-old pensioner who couldn't get a ticket although he has supported Exeter all his life, so I have invited him.

Two doors along, at No. 9, widowed Mrs Grace Elliott admitted that she would be keeping her door locked and only close friends would be allowed in. A similar situation to Mrs Grace Alford at No. 12, who threatened to set her dog on any hooligans who strayed too near to her front door.

If a dreaded fear simmered in the minds of the locals, a similar fear of the unexpected preyed on the minds of the United players en route to the West Country, and it exploded into startling reality in the 15th minute when Exeter took the lead. Catching United cold, Exeter surged forward. Pinkney surged down the flank and from his cross, Banks headed towards goal. Stepney, thinking the ball was going wide, barely moved and was stunned to see it bounce over the line. A deafening roar enveloped the ground, and one observer, unable to gain access to the packed ground, almost fell off his advantage point – the roof of a nearby house – in the hysteria that followed. A disallowed Exeter goal in the 27th minute seemed to awaken United from their slumber and slowly they began to take control, finally managing to pull a goal back on the stroke of half-time thorough Fitzpatrick. Two more in the 65th and 66th minutes were enough to turn the tide and ease United into round four. The victory produced a huge sigh of relief around Old Trafford, as, despite the lowly status of the opposition, given United's current form, this tie was a potential banana skin and defeat could well have had a devastating effect on the weeks and months ahead.

When a team isn't playing well, luck seems to be somewhat non-existent, with countless borderline decisions going against them, and the bounce of the ball spiralling in a completely opposite direction than would have been preferred. Such was the 90 minutes across the Pennines at Elland Road. Visiting second in the table, Leeds United was always going to be a difficult encounter, and, although the Lancashire/Yorkshire mutual dislike and loathing that often soured this volatile fixture did not surface, on the field at least, there was still enough in the 90 minutes to make even the placid Bobby Charlton lose his temper.

Against a lacklustre visiting side, it still took Leeds 29 minutes to breach the United defence and, even then, Alex Stepney should have done better with Lorimer's cross, which allowed Jones to head home with ease. But strangely, there was a slightly different mentality about the United side as the second half got underway and, within 8 minutes of changing ends, they had drawn level. Sartori, having made ground down the right, crossed into the centre, and although Charlton missed the ball, Best was on hand to slot home. It was a goal that seemed to give United some encouragement, and from seldom having threatened the home defence, they began to realise that perhaps they could gain something more than a point from their afternoon in Yorkshire.

Nine minutes after the equaliser, United thought they had edged their way in front, gaining an unexpected advantage. Charlton, pushing forward on a more regular basis, was tackled from behind by Bremner on the edge of the Leeds penalty area. Picking himself up, he stood poised over the ball alongside George Best, but it was the latter who took the kick, curling it over the defensive wall and past the outstretched arm of Sprake. The instant jubilation was soon curtailed, as referee Gow immediately indicated that the goal would not stand as it had been an indirect free kick.

There had been no indication from the official that it was an indirect free kick and after the game George Best said, 'We asked if we could score from it and the referee said we could. Otherwise, there would have been no point in me having a pot at goal would there?' Bobby Charlton was furious at the decision, protesting vehemently to the referee, something in itself that surely indicated some injustice had occurred. But the decision stood and, as luck would have it, Leeds snatched a second, 15 minutes from the end to secure both points, with James, Stiles and Burns all dwelling too long to see which of them would make the challenge on O'Grady.

Although it could have been considered something of an unfortunate afternoon, the critics were still out in force, claiming that United were a mere shadow of their former selves, with 'Crerand too slow and his passing becoming imprecise', while Best was seen as 'failing to assert the sum of his marvellous gifts at a time when his club most needed them'. Indeed, as previously mentioned, Manchester United were a far cry from the team of old. It was the swashbuckling side that had destroyed Benfica at Wembley only a matter of months before, and of course, left the Portuguese side totally mesmerised on their own ground as recently as 1966. A side that had overcome the threat of Real Madrid to reach that Wembley final and on the domestic front played to capacity crowds across the length and breadth of the country with their all-star cast lead by three European Footballers of the Year. But now there was a dark shadow hanging over the club, with performances certainly lacking consistency, and that special United buzz more than often missing from those 90 minutes out on the pitch. It was a black shadow that suddenly became much darker on the afternoon of 14 January, growing in size, taking on a much greater magnitude and hovering over Old Trafford like an unidentified visitor from outer space.

It was midday at Old Trafford, a non-match day, with the feverant, red-and-white scarved supporters missing from the backdrop of the vast stadium, but there was still much activity as the north west press corps, accompanied by countless photographers, alighted from the cars and taxi's and scurried into the bowls of the stadium and the sanctified area of the players' lounge. No one knew why a press conference had been suddenly called, although rumours circulated on numerous subjects, but more than a few of those present half expected to discover Leicester City's talented duo of Alan Clarke and David Nish to appear alongside Sir Matt Busby, with the announcement that United had paid out around £250,000 for their signatures. Instead, beneath pennants that recalled memorable encounters from the past, sat a grim faced Louis Edwards, the club chairman, secretary Les Olive, director Denzil Haroun, who toyed nervously with his pipe, and a stone faced Sir Matt Busby. This was serious.

Once the last of the journalists and cameramen had jostled for position in the not too spacious lounge, where it was now standing room only, club secretary, Les Olive, announced that he had a statement to read and to a hushed audience he said,

> Sir Matt has informed the board that he wishes to relinquish the position of team manger at the end of the present season. The chairman and directors have tried to persuade him to carry on, and it was only with great reluctance that his request has been accepted. The board fully appreciate the reasons for his decision and it was unanimously agreed that he be appointed general manager of the club, which Sir Matt is very happy to accept. The position of manager will be advertised at a later date.

The only sound was the scrape of pens and the rustle of paper, as the pages of notepads were quickly turned in order to capture every word of this momentous announcement. Even more so, when the secretary finished his task and glanced along the row to where the manager sat after clearing his throat, Sir Matt Busby said in rather subdued tones,

> It will have come as a great surprise to a great many people that I have relinquished, or at least that I am about to relinquish, control of Manchester United. But it will come probably as a greater shock, and I'm not sure that I have fully accepted my own reasons, to everybody to know why I have done it. And I don't mind admitting here and now that the reason is – I am losing my grip. It's not by a long way a decision that I have reached overnight, but it is the honest reason of months of heart searching. I have not had enough time with the players. Too many things away from the playing side have happened, and yet in soccer, players are the all-essential being. Therefore a manager must be with them and must live with them and know them. As things happened over the last few months, this has not been possible. Therefore, it is time for me to go. And eventually the decision, which is my decision only, was inevitable. Manchester United needs new blood, a new supply of ideas

from which they will progress and do better if it is possible. There has got to be a new young lease of life, and if I have to step into the sidelines on to the touchline, aye if necessary into my bath-chair to keep the club great, then I'll do it. From the end of the season I will become general manager and in a lot of ways my work may be harder, but I have turned down the opportunity of directorship so that I can stay within the game. I knew that the minute I offered my resignation from team managerial duties that I would be offered either a place on the board or that a post of general manager would be created. But I did not want to become a director because, after twenty-three years of waking up and living the life of Manchester United, a directorship seemed to me to be a sort of vacuum. And that I didn't want. Eventually, if it is still the wish of the then present board, then I shall join the board because Manchester United is my life. The board work hard now and without them, and their predecessors, I don't think I would be in a position to be writing this now. But my time to join the board has not arrived yet. We can worry about that in the eventuality. The big thing now is for Manchester United, which I believe to be the greatest club, not in England, or in Britain, or even Europe, but in the world, to appoint my successor. And there is no point in beating about the bush or being falsely modest. I shall have some say in whom my successor shall be and I have ides on that subject. One: He must be young, in his early thirties up to the absolute age of forty-five. Two: He must have experience, because Manchester United are not in a position to experiment. Three: He must be a manager who has proved himself to be a leader, who commands respect, and can only command respect by having been proved honest and straightforward. And the players must know what he is talking about. Four: He must have the human touch and the advice he gives will have to be the best for the players but, more importantly, the best for the club. Five: He must never ever make a promise without ever being able to fulfil his words. I know a lot of people will think we at Manchester United are now looking for a man who does not exist. I know that it is going to be a difficult task and that the man who takes over is going to have a difficult time to say the least. For there is a sixth quality, which Manchester United now expect – the man who takes over is going to have to be right in his decisions. And though he will be given time to prove that he is right, this is the final condition – until he is dreadfully wrong. And I hope I am not sounding too big-headed if I say that the lad who takes on Manchester United has a difficult job. He must, and I repeat must with all possible emphasis, have success in the terms of championships or cups, or otherwise he is going to be deemed a failure. And quite frankly it's not the sort of job that I might have taken on thirty years ago. For the last twenty-three years or so, footballers in general, and the lads of United in particular, have kept me young. I have lived through a personal crisis or two and a disaster that was worse for others than it was for me, but I have, in all those years, lived with the lads. They have kept me laughing, and if you can't laugh or smile, then it's a poor outlook. But recently, I have not lived with the players and they are paramount to any soccer team's success, as much as I feel I ought to have done. So, we need a new face, we need new life in the club, we need new blood, and though in my opinion I'm not too old, we need this complete transfusion to take the club even further. My successor will have heartbreak, heartache, headache, success and happiness in some order or other. But I promise him this – he will never, ever, have any interference from me. Because as this season ends, and in whatever position we finish, Matt Busby, who was knighted on behalf of some great boys, past and present, is bowing out of football team management. From there on I shall be on the administration side and, who knows, maybe I will start being able to enjoy a game of soccer again.

Chairman Louis Edwards added

When Matt told us of his decision, we were of course, very down hearted at first. He has been with us for twenty-three years. He is under contract, a hell of a long contract, and we will go on drawing one up for as long as we can. We are going to make sure that he stays in Manchester.

So there it was, the manager's chair at Manchester United was about to become vacant and, as the conference came to a close, some made a mad dash for telephones, while others, with no immediate deadline to make, sat around debating and speculating on who that next manager of Manchester United might be. There was one lingering question though, had Busby considered retirement before, perhaps immediately following the victory over Benfica last May, when the long arduous task had finally been completed? 'No, no definitely not', said his son Sandy. 'It wasn't something he had thought about back then. But now, it was slightly different. He was fifty-nine years old and he felt that it was time for a younger man to take over.'

But what of the players? Was there any indication that their manager was going to announce his retirement? Jimmy Ryan certainly didn't see the announcement coming. 'No, it came as a complete surprise to me. It may not have surprised some of the senior players such as Bobby or Nobby, but I had no idea that he would leave.' The two World Cup winners, however, were just as equally surprised. Charlton was to say

I was stunned when Sir Matt told me the news of his resignation. It was a real blow, although it had often been suggested that he would 'move upstairs' after our European Cup victory in May. Sir Matt deserves a rest. It is obviously a great blow to players like myself, Billy Foulkes, Shay Brennan and Nobby Stiles, who have been with him all our playing life.

Nobby Stiles added, 'I did not think it would ever come to his retirement. He has been like a father to me. But as he is to be general manager we shall not be losing him.'

So, who was going to be the next Manchester United manager? Who would the annual salary of around £9,000 attract? There was no lack of immediate suggestions, although no hats were immediately thrown into the ring, with Eric Todd of the *Guardian* suggesting that the job could well be kept 'in the family'. Would Jimmy Murphy be prepared to take over the reins once again? This time on a more permanent basis compared to his unwanted and forced sojourn at the helm back in 1958? 'A few years ago I think I could have done the job here', replied the fifty-seven year-old genial Welshman when the question was put to him. 'But not now, as we want a younger man', before going on to admit that he had declined a managerial position, at a club he would not name, only the month before.

So Jimmy Murphy was out of the running, but trainer and former goalkeeper, Jack Crompton, his former teammate and now a coach at the club, John Aston, and assistant trainer and England youth team manager, Wilf McGuinness, could all be possible candidates, but the list of names being bandied about in the hours following the monumentous announcement was long and certainly impressive. There was Jock Stein, a friend of Busby's and the manager who had guided Celtic to countless successes, including the European Cup the year before United had their name etched upon the trophy. The Celtic manager was strangely tight-lipped when asked about the possibility of relocating south.

Another early suggestion, Leeds United manager Don Revie was more forthright in his reply, saying

I am not interested in the job. We have built up a family at Leeds. It has taken us a long time to get where we are and we have a lot to do yet. I would also like to emphasise that I am very happy at Elland Road and my big ambition is to finish as team manager of Leeds in the same proud manner Sir Matt has done.

Had Revie thrown his hat into the ring, there would certainly have been a very mixed reception around Old Trafford as the Yorkshire side, along with the near neighbours along the East Lancs Road and of those much nearer to home, were despised, not so much for their emergence as one of the country's leading sides, but for the manner in which they played. A style that was often considered, not just by those who supported United, as little more than downright dirty.

Jimmy Adamson, Dave Sexton, Alan Ashman, Don Howe, Brian Clough, Ian Greaves, Frank O'Farrell and Jimmy Meadows were other early suggestions, along with Noel Cantwell, currently manager of Coventry City, who like the aforementioned Greaves, was a former United player and captain. Noel Cantwell, however, did have the slight advantage of having been somewhat endorsed by Busby and was the early favourite for the vacancy. 'Noel is a wonderful leader of men', Busby once said of his former captain, 'and he will make a fine manager one day'. This was something that filled two of the necessary criteria. Hitting the headlines when it did, Busby's announcement was a bolt out of the blue and perhaps could not have come at a worse time, although one suspects that it was made much sooner than intended as the club did not want any of the whispered rumours that had begun to spring up suddenly explode onto the front and back pages, creating much embarrassment for the club and forcing them into some hastily compiled announcement.

Challenging for the First Division title was out of the question, even to the most blinkered supporter, as United were closer to the foot of the table than the top, floundering in sixteenth place, their twenty-two points some nineteen fewer than leaders Liverpool, although they did have two games in hand. But they did retain an active interest in two cup competitions – the FA Cup and the European Cup – both trophies well within United's capabilities of winning. But, with Busby's end of season departure now blasted out into the open, there was added pressure on the sometimes underachieving players whose performances had been at times erratic (and that is perhaps being polite), as the team clearly struggled.

It is perhaps the performance of the team in the first half of the season that prompted Busby into making the decision to 'relinquish his position', not, please note, retire. 'Losing my grip' were the words he used. Had the emotions of winning the European Cup last May finally caught up with him? Did he now wish that he stepped into the background after that European Cup success? He would never lose his grip, neither would he loose the adoration nor the respect of his players. His authority would never be questioned. But perhaps it was the players who inadvertently forced his hand.

Having watched them struggle at times, Busby perhaps realised that his team needed some major surgery in order to keep them challenging for silverware at home and abroad on a regular basis. He was well aware that those individuals who had taken the club back to its former glory in the aftermath of Munich, and given so much to the United cause, were growing old and would, in the very near future, need replacing. Did he not want the responsibility of having to cast those players who had become personal friends aside, telling them that they were no longer guaranteed a first-team place? Did he want someone else to do it instead?

For the remainder of the season, Sir Matt Busby was still manager of Manchester United and life had to go on. There were three competitions to be contested. Who knew what the immediate future held? Denis Law, considered 'useful' rather than 'inspirational', was to confound his recent critics against Sunderland, scoring three in the 4-0 win that left Sir Matt Busby enthusing 'This was more like it. We really got moving today and I am very pleased.' It was certainly a relief for the United manager, with two testing cup ties on the immediate horizon against Rapid Vienna and Watford in the European and FA Cups respectively.

First up at Old Trafford was the domestic competition, and if there had been some trepidation surrounding the trip to Exeter in the previous round, then the visit of Third Division leaders Watford, to the banks of the Ship Canal, was certainly taken more seriously. Watford was no longer thought of as simply the last stop on the railway line before London; they were an up-and-coming team under manager Ken Furphy, so much so that Jimmy Murphy had watched them the previous week, bringing back a report that they were 'a very good side. Very disciplined and a team that would not be easy to beat.'

A week on the Channel Island of Jersey was Watford's pre-cup tie preparations, where, along with training on the beach, the players would watch films of recent United games over and over again, while being given the low-down on every United player from detailed dossiers. 'They are a great side with tremendous talent and players able to win a match with one touch of genius' admitted the Watford manager. 'I seems to me though, that they are leaving a lot to Charlton and Best and if these two can be held we must have a chance.'

A chance they most certainly had, as they certainly approached the game in a confident mood. Looking back through the history books they could take encouragement from the likes of Norwich City and Bristol Rovers, who both recorded victories at Old Trafford and even from Walthamstow Avenue, a non-League side, who held United to a fourth round 1-1 draw back in 1952/53.

Furphy had certainly done his homework, while United had heeded no pre-match warnings of a possible giant killing, as Watford stormed into a 3rd minute lead, Scullion intercepting a cross-field pass by Law, before exchanging a quick one-two with Hale and firing past Rimmer from 25 yards, the United 'keeper helping the ball into the net. For almost an hour, Watford held on bravely and, on more than one occasion, it was goalkeeper Walker who stood between United and an equaliser. Best and Sartori both scorned good opportunities after the interval, but the visitors were finally to relent to the almost constant pressure, when Law snatched a 61st minute equaliser, pouncing on a loose ball and nudging it home from 6 yards.

There was sufficient time for United to step up a gear and go on to secure a place in the next round of the competition, but this was not the red-shirted team of old and they were very much relieved, as were the majority of the 60,000 strong crowd, to hear the final whistle, even although they now had to journey to Vicarage Road for a replay.

Prior to the replay, United had a league fixture at Portman Road, turning in yet another undistinguished display in a scrappy 90 minutes that was sadly becoming something of the norm for the European champions who had only won two games away from home all season, against Fourth Division Exeter and Queens Park Rangers, who were propping up the First Division. A solitary Ipswich goal was enough to earn both points, sending an ominous warning to all at Old Trafford that there could be something of a cup upset at Vicarage Road. United's visit certainly did not cause Watford manager Ken Furphy any sleepless nights. 'We must be favourites now', he exclaimed, before going on to say, 'The only thing I was afraid of at Old Trafford was their crowd. But with all our fans shouting us on at Vicarage Road, we will have the atmosphere we need for victory.'

Watford supporters began queuing for tickets as soon as they had arrived back from Manchester, and a record crowd for the Hertfordshire ground lay in wait for United. But their retreat from the forefront of both European and domestic football was certainly not furthered by defeat at the hands of the plucky Third Division leaders, who were disappointed in their attempt to make further progress in the competition.

It was still a much below par United performance on a rock-hard pitch, in a game more on the level of the home side's normal League fixtures, although Law became the first visiting player to score there since 4 November, with the only major incident of the first half coming when a number of supporters spilled onto the running track behind one of the goals, and the first-aid personnel kept busy for a considerable time. Such was the tedious display being played out on the pitch, Peter Lorenzo of the *Sun*, was to write: 'The first aid men were still busy when the second half started. The game, unfortunately, never improved, and I am convinced there were as many people watching the rescue teams as there were watching the football.'

As hard as they tried, Watford could not find that equaliser, or indeed a winner in a tedious match, although they did come close with both Dunne and James having to make last gasp clearances. But it was left to Law to seal the game, adding a second 4 minutes from time, to send United into the fifth round, where yet another difficult tie against Birmingham City awaited.

United Chairman Louis Edwards, admitted that 'had Watford got the goal when the ball hit the bar, we would have been in trouble, real trouble'. But he attempted to disguise his team's inadequacies by adding: 'United are still a top attraction. We had a sell-out at Ipswich last Saturday, a sell-out tonight and we face another sell-out crowd at Birmingham this weekend.' Still a top attraction through the likes of Best, Law and Charlton in the ranks, but they were no longer one of the top clubs in the First Division. What would Edwards prefer? The cash from the supporters clicking through the turnstiles, or the silverware from players on the pitch? For many, the surge of spectators from the terracing at the Vicarage Road end onto the perimeter running track was little more than a regular occurrence at numerous grounds around the country, something that came part and parcel with following football or, perhaps more to the point, a club with as big a support as United. Others felt it was little more than boyish enthusiasm or mischief.

But it was soon to come to light that it was much more than either of the above, as such was the pressure from a section of the home crowd as United attacked, a railing broke, two crush barriers buckled and supporters pitched forward on top of one another. It was later discovered that some twenty-four people had been hurt, and that amid the frightening scenes, sporadic fighting had also broken out. One had a dislocated elbow, another, a broken foot.

Ron Rollitt, the Watford secretary, was more than a little relieved that a major incident had been avoided. 'It wouldn't have taken much for it to have been much worse. A small child at the front could have been trampled to death or suffocated in those circumstances,' but he was quick to insist that the incident was not much else in regards to crowd safety on the night that could, or would have been done differently. 'In hindsight, perhaps the crush barriers higher up could be better positioned to prevent as many people being channelled down to one spot. That will be done when the damaged barriers are repaired.'

When it was suggested that perhaps too many people were in the ground, this was something that he strenuously denied. 'People are bound to say that, but the answer is no', he replied.

> This was a record crowd, but at 34,099 it was still less than 1,000 more than the previous record, and we had no trouble then. Remember, we didn't just fix this limit out of our heads. The ground was looked at carefully with police help. This figure was that we agreed was the top safe limit. When we built the terrace at the other end of the ground, the Bolton disaster [when thirty-three people were killed and countless more injured during an FA Cup sixth round tie between Bolton Wanderers and Stoke City on 9 March 1946 at Burnden Park], was very much in everyone's mind. We were made to build shallower steps and put in very many barriers. We will look at this terrace again after this. We were also well aware of the safety factor for the cup tie. We usually reckon one policeman for 1,000 fans. For this game nearly 100 policemen were in and around the ground, helping to control the crowds. My conclusion is that Watford did as much as any other club would do in similar circumstances. But that is nowhere near enough. The inquiry into the Bolton disaster of 1946 pointed out that the narrow margin tolerated in soccer each week between safety and tragedy could be breached by one unexpected factor. And 23 years after Bolton, the recommendations of that commission have still to be made.

There was a disaster waiting to happen!

But there was little time to catch breath, as no sooner had United progressed through the fourth round of the FA Cup, than they were pitched into the fifth, a matter of five days later, where once again they were pitted against another lower league side who also felt more than a little confident of ending United's interest in the competition.

Stan Cullis, manager of Second Division Birmingham City, was well aware of the task ahead of him, having 'to cope with individual genius, players like Denis Law, George Best and Bobby Charlton, who can turn a match with one flash of genius, in one split second.' But he went on to say:

> Nevertheless, I am confident we can win. Statistics prove we raise our game against tougher opposition. I don't think players do this consciously, I think it's something to do with their own ego. I went to Watford on Monday to look at the home team. We all know what United can do on their day.

Birmingham's leading scorer and former England striker, Fred Pickering, echoed his manager's views. 'We know that United can still produce flashes of greatness but they are not the side they were a season ago. They like to be given plenty of room and time to play their football and that's just what they will not get against us.'

With odds of 9-1 against winning the FA Cup, Sir Matt Busby showed little concern and thought his team had 'a wonderful chance of winning the cup this year'. Many felt that Birmingham City had only the one opportunity to snatch a memorable victory, as two seasons ago they had held Tottenham Hotspur to a 0-0 draw in the sixth round, only to lose the replay 6-0, but, as the match at St Andrew's against United got underway, it began to look as though United would progress into the next round of the competition without too much difficulty.

Heavy snow had covered the Midlands pitch 24 hours previously, but a squad of workmen made the conditions playable, and it was a surface to which United adapted well, creating four first-half opportunities that should have given them an unassailable advantage. Herriot in the home goal, however, foiled Law on two occasions with notable reflex saves, Morgan hit the bar, while Charlton and Law failed to connect with the ball as George Best's cross flashed across the face of the Birmingham goal and trickled past the post. Goalless at the interval and as the second half got underway, United once again scorned opportunities. This time it was Charlton and Kidd who failed to beat Herriot. But, just after the hour mark, the deadlock was finally broken. Kidd centred and Law leaped high above the Birmingham defence to head home. It was a lead that was held for barely four minutes.

Replacing Thwaites with Beard, the substitute took a mere 30 seconds to make a difference. With his first touch, he started a move involving Wylie and Pickering, with the latter beating Stepney to the cross, allowing Beard to tap the ball into the empty net. The groan that emerged from the throats of the visiting support did little to inspire the United players to regain their advantage, and it became increasingly like yet another 90 minutes being added to the already overflowing fixture list. But, with 9 minutes remaining, Charlton centred from the left. Best evaded two tackles before hitting the ball into the top corner of the net. Those groans were now cheers. Surely United could hold onto their lead? But the FA Cup always produces numerous twists and turns and, 3 minutes later, with Best back helping out his defenders, the ball bounced up off the hard ground and struck the Irishman on the hand. The referee, standing only 6 yards away, immediately pointed to the spot, much to the visitors annoyance, as Robinson stepped up and placed the ball past Stepney for the equaliser. United rallied again, but, as the seconds ticked away, Herriot, once more pulled off notable saves, twice denying Kidd, who had already hit the angle of the cross bar and upright when through on goal, securing his place in the following morning's newspaper headlines.

Life was a far cry from normality at Old Trafford and Busby, despite his decision to step down at the end of the season, had much to contend with, attempting to muster his squad and maintain some sort of stability within the ranks. He had dropped Alex Stepney for the first time since the 'keeper's arrival from Chelsea, with David Sadler another who found himself on the sidelines more than he cared for, with the utility player actually contemplating his future at the club. 'I must consider my future very seriously. From my point of view I cannot really afford to be in the reserves at this period of my career.' Ousted from the No. 5 shirt by Steve James, at least he had the flexibility of being able to step into another position if called upon, something that another contestant for that same shirt could no longer do. Bill Foulkes had the experience of playing at full-back, but that was a number of years previously. Now, the rugged defender was no longer a first-team regular, and his omission from the team had not gone unnoticed by Grimsby Town, who had ironically taken another United central defender, Allenby Chilton, to Blundell Park in 1955 as player/manager, looking at the St Helen's man to fill a similar position.

Struggling in the Fourth Division, Grimsby were serious in their attempt to lure the one-time miner away from Manchester, going as far as meeting Sir Matt Busby. The outcome, however, was not in their favour, as Foulkes, although interested in a managerial role, felt that he still had another year as a player.

Before the Birmingham City replay, a point was grabbed in a 2-2 draw with Wolves, in a spirited performance on an unplayable Molineux pitch, but the visit of Birmingham City for that replay was a fixture that United certainly did not want, as, two days later, they were playing hosts to Rapid Vienna in the European Cup quarter final first leg. Indeed, they had to play four cup ties within the space of ten days and, although attempting to retain a grip on the trophy they had won the previous season, which certainly held a higher level of concern and interest than an FA Cup tie, Sir Matt Busby sent his strongest side out to face the Midlanders, hoping that they could remain injury free, while at the same time make progress into the quarter finals.

A somewhat cautious approach could well have been expected against Birmingham City, but, perhaps surprisingly, United threw the shackles aside and caution to the wind, destroying the visitors with a six-goal blast. Birmingham City took a surprise lead as early as the 4th minute, with Jimmy Greenhoff heading home before a United player had even touched the ball. But, within 10 minutes, the game was turned on its head as United took a 3-1 lead. Law equalised from the spot after Crerand was brought down, then Best took centre stage. Beating four men in a mazy run, which saw him actually lose the ball twice before regaining it, he evaded a fifth challenge before hitting the post. A minute later, the already bemused Birmingham defence could only stand and watch as Morgan's cross-cum-shot beat Herriot at the back post.

Best picked out Law, who made it 3-1, with the Scot (celebrating his twenty-ninth birthday) having another goal disallowed prior to half-time. After the break, Law did notch his hat-trick with United's fourth, then, in the final 15 minutes, Kidd made it 5-1, Birmingham grabbed a second and Morgan, with a 70-yard run attempting to emulate Best, scored United's sixth. This was the Manchester United of old.

Rapid Vienna, waiting in the wings, would be an entirely different opponent to that of Birmingham City, perhaps more so due to the fact that the Austrians had overcome a certain Real Madrid, going through on away goals in the previous round. Club representatives, however, had watched United's demolition of Birmingham City, and they knew that they were in for a far from easy ride.

An easy ride it certainly wasn't, as the Viennese visitors came up against the Manchester United of old. The Manchester United that took the European stage by force, the re-emergence of the team that captivated everyone, so much so that it had you sitting on the edge of your seat, marvelling at the wide array of talent in front of you turning in a virtuoso performance. Yes, they had hit Birmingham City for six, but the performances of late had been something of a mixed bag and, with a wider audience watching, United were determined to show that they were more than capable of retaining the title of champions of Europe.

The six-goal beating of Birmingham City should have been repeated under the Old Trafford floodlights against a Rapid Vienna side, who, to be fair, did demonstrate poise and resilience in a defensive display, but one where scoring opportunities were shunned. Content to play with only two front men, the international Rapid side kept United at bay, but were fortunate not to concede two penalty kicks within the space of 10 minutes. Charlton was fouled inside the area, but, to everyone's amazement, he signalled for a corner rather than a penalty. Seven minutes later, Best escaped his marker, only to be blatantly brought down by Flögel just inside the area. Again, the referee ignored United's pleas. He was far from biased however, allowing fouls by Crerand and Stiles to go unpunished.

The deciding factor in this first leg tie came in the 44th minute when a Kidd, Law and Best move saw full-back Gebhardt, in an attempt to clear, kick the ball against the foot of the post. Morgan was on the rebound in a flash, pulling the ball back for Best to shoot home through a crowded goalmouth.

The referee's performance became as much of a focal point of the fixture as United's display, something signified no more so than in the 56th minute, when Fak and Best exchanged punches in the penalty area, the Irishman slumping to the ground holding his face. The official looked the opposite way unconcerned. For most of the second half, the action was concentrated around the Rapid penalty area, and it was of no surprise that United increased their lead with two goals in 4 minutes, Morgan taking up Kidd's flick-on to make it 2-0 and Stiles chipping the ball over the rapid defence for Best to delay his shot, before turning across the face of the goal and shooting high into the roof of the net to give United an advantage that would be difficult to overcome.

The games continued to come thick and fast and, no sooner was the European Cup out of the way for the time being, than it was back to the FA Cup and a quarter final, First Division head-to-head against Everton at Old Trafford. Expensive times for the home support, with three consecutive cup ties thrown into the mix of the normal domestic league fixtures. Having struggled against the lower opposition of the previous rounds, there was no room for error against the Goodison Park side, but the expectations were high following the midweek victory over the Austrians; this, however, produced little more than something of a false dawn.

Everton were to prove themselves a far superior team to Rapid Vienna, and even more so compared to Birmingham City. Even without their star player in Howard Kendal, they were more composed and tactically superior to their hosts. For most of the game, both forward lines were thwarted by equally strong defences. Inspiration for the home side was virtually non-existent compared with that of recent games, and it was looking as though yet another replay was on the cards.

Best and Morgan both had opportunities to swing the game United's way, with Labone alone often standing between United and a goal. But red could not overcome blue, even when the visitors lost another influential player in Harvey on the hour through injury, and the game continued to remain goalless. This deadline was broken, however, with 12 minutes remaining. Everton, on one of their quick counter-attacking raids towards the United goal, saw Fitzpatrick beat Morrissey to the ball, but at the expense of a corner. Morrissey swung the ball into the United goalmouth, where it was back-headed by Husband towards Royle, who forced it beyond Stepney with his knee. Steve James, who had closely marshalled the Everton forward all afternoon, paid dearly for a moment's hesitation.

It was an often physical encounter and, in the time that remained following Everton's goal, United were perhaps fortunate to end the game with eleven men. Stiles had his name taken for a bad foul on Royle, with Best following his teammate into the referee's book after speaking out of turn. The Irishman was later to turn on Morrissey following a tackle and, despite lashing out at the Everton winger, he managed to avoid any further punishment, much to everyone's amazement.

The FA Cup defeat was yet another blow to United's slowly diminishing confidence and with the return leg of their European Cup encounter with Rapid Vienna next on the agenda, it was perhaps just as well that they held a 3-0 advantage. Although not the United of old, they could still be considered a major attraction. Prior to the match, an Austrian official said that he expected only around 35,000 would assemble at the Prater Stadium, leaving it half-full, with many prepared to give the tie and the cold Austrian evening a miss and watch the game unfold from the comfort of their own homes. As it was, some 52,000 turned up, perhaps oblivious to the visitor's recent downturn in fortune, eager to see the likes of Bobby Charlton and George Best in the flesh. The third of the illustrious trio, Denis Law, was still having problems with his knee and was missing. Charlton was almost another name omitted from the United team sheet having spent a day in bed, but his high temperature and touch of flu could possibly be used as an excuse for shunning several scoring opportunities during a game that saw United do little more than simply play out a cautious 90 minutes, while never being in any danger of relinquishing the tie.

United grew in confidence the longer the game went on, with Fuchsbichler in the Rapid goal doing as much to keep the scoreline blank as Charlton missed chances. Kidd had what looked like a perfectly good goal disallowed for pushing, but, according to Sir Matt Busby, the game went as planned, 'In these competitions, when you have a three goal lead you go out determined to keep that advantage.'

In the semi-finals for the fifth time, United joined Ajax, AC Milan and Spartak Trnava, with the draw giving Sir Matt Busby the one that he did not want – the 1963 winners, AC Milan.

> If I could have had my pick, I would have plumped for Ajax. I fancied us to beat them. Then I thought we could see off Milan in a one-match final. But two games against AC will be a far tougher proposition, particularly when you think of their fanatical following. It's a pity we didn't come out of the hat first. We would have preferred the first match at Old Trafford because previous experience has shown us that this is quite an advantage. Still, you can't pick and choose in a Cup draw. We'll just have to make the best of it.

If things were not going as planned on the field, United enjoyed something of a financial windfall off it, with their three recent home cup ties bringing in around £70,000, leaving the club, after expenses and the

Football Association's cut, with almost £40,000. A nice sum, but one they would have certainly have delved into if they had been able to purchase league points, as the dismal run continued, with a home defeat against neighbours, City, in a game full of mistakes and missed opportunities. So many in fact, that had they all been seized upon the records books would have been rewritten.

One would have expected the local derby to have been an aggressive affair, but it was timid in comparison to the 90 minutes at Goodison Park where United sought revenge for their FA Cup dismissal a couple of weeks previously. Slowly clapped off the pitch at half-time, they certainly had the better of their opponents when it came down to fouls committed, but the referee was surprisingly lenient throughout, and his lack of authority was equally matched by the lack of goals. But at least the 0-0 score line brought United a point in their quest for a more favourable position in the first Division table.

Only two goals in the last four league fixtures was a worry, as was the one victory in the last eight, but two goals against Chelsea at Stamford Bridge looked to be enough to snatch another crucial point, only for their careless incompetence to gift Bobby Tambling what was to prove a decisive strike.

There is always someone worse off than yourself, and where United were concerned, it came in the form Queens Park Rangers, the First Division's bottom club. It had been obvious for some time that they lacked the character and class to remain in the top flight and were a sure-fire bet to be relegated well before the end of the season, while having nothing in their make up to attract the Manchester footballing public to Old Trafford, with the ground hosting its smallest crowd of the season, a mere 37,053, some 10,000 less than the previous lowest. For those who stayed away, they were to miss a strange mishap 90 minutes in: United's first 'double' of the season and their first league victory since January. Despite the 8-1 score line, there were spells in the first half when the visitors were certainly the better team.

Within the first half hour, blunders from Stepney, dropping an easy catch and James with a woeful back-pass, almost gifted Rangers two goals, but, when you are down at the wrong end of the table, luck just never seems to go your way. On the half hour, United made their guests pay for their inadequacies and took the lead through Morgan, stabbing home Aston's back-header from a Best corner. The Irishman made it 2-0 3 minutes into the second half, only for Marsh to pull QPR back into the game in the 62nd minute.

If the crowd had been stifling the yawns during the opening 45 minutes, they felt that they dare not blink during the second in case they missed something. At 2-1, and United capable of doing anything, the game could have swung either way, but the two-goal advantage was soon restored when Best went round three opponents as only he could, before driving the ball home to make it 3-1. Morgan's second of the night, in the 74th minute, appeared to be something of a deciding blow, and this was followed by four goals in the final 5 minutes from Nobby Stiles, Willie Morgan, who completed his hat-trick, Brian Kidd and John Aston.

The victory instilled some confidence into Busby's often lacklustre team. A solitary George Best goal was enough to beat Sheffield Wednesday at Old Trafford, while they should have snatched both points against Stoke City, again at home, but former United favourite David Herd laid on the visitors' equaliser after John Aston had given United the lead. Another point, this time in a 0-0 draw at West Ham, followed victories over Nottingham Forest (1-0 at the City ground), West Bromwich Albion (2-1 at Old Trafford) and 3-1 in the return match against Forest at home, left United unbeaten in seven games; their best run since the tail end of 1967.

The results in those seven fixtures had been painstakingly etched out, but there was another victory during those weeks in March, one that had taken eleven long years to achieve over a decade of nerve-wrenching, health-threatening worry and turmoil.

The end result brought no reward other than simply offering relief. A weight off one's shoulders, but with no guarantee of making a night's sleep that little bit easier. The enquiry into the Munich disaster was a prolonged one, often needlessly drawn out in the search for someone or something to blame.

Since that February afternoon in Germany, much of that blame had been pushed in the direction of the pilot, forty-seven-year-old Captain James Thain, a man who had protested his innocence since that fateful day in 1958. He had spent thousands of pounds of his own money, plus some £12,000 in legal fees, determined that at some point, justice might just prevail.

The original enquiries by both British and German commissions had been of the opinion that 'ice on the wings' of the plane was the cause of the accident, with the pilot 'negligent' in his duties to check for such irregularities prior to take-off. Captain Thain always maintained that 'slush on the runway' was the true cause of the accident.

Having been ultimately sacked by BEA, Thain moved to Berkshire, taking over a farm in order to eke out a living, while at the same time, never giving up in his fight to clear his name. A fight that went way beyond replays, extra-time and penalties.

The inquiry was reopened under Mr Edgar Fay QC, with the pilot of the Elizabethan aircraft having had the continued support of the British Air Line Pilots' Association, MPs and fellow pilots across the globe with the findings, announced in the House of Commons on 18 March by the Minister of State, Mr William Rogers.

Later published in a 191-page document, it was section 189 – the conclusion – which contained the inquiry's verdict. It read as follows:

1. The cause of the accident was slush on the runway.
2. It is possible, but unlikely, that wing icing was a contributory cause.
3. Captain Thain was not at fault as regard to runway slush.
4. Captain Thain was at fault with regard to wing icing, but because wing icing is unlikely to have been a contributory cause of the accident, blame for the accident cannot in this report be imputed to him.
5. Captain Thain was at fault in permitting Captain Rayment to occupy the captain's seat, but this played no part in causing the accident.

The following section, 190 read: In accordance with our term of reference we therefore report that in our opinion, blame for the accident is not to be imputed to Captain Thain.

James Thain returned to his farm to continue his life, but even if the sun was high in the mid-March sky, there was always that black cloud hovering nearby. Although released from blame, the events of that fateful afternoon would never go away.

There were also black clouds on the Italian skyline, despite that favourable spell that had taken United up to a much more respectable First Division mid-table placing, with the uncanny skills of George Best guiding his teammates out of what had been a torturous and embarrassing period. Like the impish Irishman's performances, timing is often everything. With the European Cup semi-final ties against AC Milan beginning to rouse the interest and take on some importance, those results could not have come at a better time, even casting up the possibility of an Inter Cities Fairs Cup place if a second successive triumph in the European Cup failed to materialise.

On the downside, Sir Matt Busby did have his problems. Tony Dunne broke his jaw in the goalless encounter against West Ham, Bobby Charlton was a long-term casualty with a knee injury, while George Best picked up knocks on what was a match-by-match basis.

Dunne's injury was to cause something of a major problem, as the United manager had allowed young reserve full-back Frank Kopel, leave for Blackburn Rovers. Bobby Noble, who had failed to make a recovery following his car crash in April 1967, also announced that he was being forced to retire.

Twenty-four-year-old Noble's plight was indeed a sorry one, with his injury forcing him into claiming a basic £10 6s unemployment benefit plus a supplement, a far cry from his £50-a-week with United.

He said,

> Football was my life and it's not easy to adjust, but United have been good and the boys are helping me find a job, but at the moment, there is not enough money coming in at the end of the week. I always believed I could make a comeback, but in the end I realised I hadn't made it. I still get a feeling of sadness and envy when I watch the lads I played alongside.

Dunne's injury ruled him out for the remainder of the season. The 2-1 defeat at relegation threatened Coventry City and left Busby with yet another sleepless night, due to Alex Stepney's double slip-up, which cost United both points and their unbeaten run.

After only 3 minutes, the United 'keeper failed to deal with a simple header from Curtis, allowing it to slip over his shoulder after juggling with it like a hot potato. Two minutes into the second half, he failed to grasp a Baker corner and the loose ball was snatched upon by Martin for Coventry's first. Could Busby rely on his 'keeper for the important final fixtures of the season?

Stepney's performance at Highfield Road soon fell under the microscope, with suggestions being made by two evening papers at a later date that the 'keeper had actually thrown the game, such was his overall performance. This was vehemently refuted by the player, with Sir Matt Busby quickly stepping into the fray. Stepney said,

> I've never thrown a game in my life. And if there is a chance, I'll take legal action against the people behind this campaign. It was just another match. It was around that time that I hit a bad patch. That's all there was to it. I am happy to have this brought into the open so I can deny it publicly. It's the vilest thing that has ever happened to me – I'm flabbergasted. If anyone had to say it to my face I would have no hesitation in taking legal action.

An annoyed Busby added:

> This is the most ridiculous accusation – just unbelievable.
> I left Stepney out of the team after that match because he was going through a dreadful spell of bad form. There was no other reason. He certainly didn't throw the ball into the net that night.

The matter escaped closer scrutiny due to an announcement on 9 April that Wilf McGuinness was to take on the role of club coach in the summer, an appointment that he would take on for an 'unspecified probationary period'.

The club statement read:

> The board has given further consideration to the changes which will occur at the end of the season and decided to appoint a chief coach who will be responsible for team selection, coaching, training and tactics. Mr Wilf McGuinness has been selected for this position and will take up his duties as from the first of June, and in these circumstances it is not necessary to advertise for applications as was first intended. Sir Matt will be responsible for all other matters affecting the club and players, and will continue as club spokesman.

Strangely, the appointment had been confirmed at the director's meeting of 27 March, but had taken almost a fortnight to be officially announced.

Despite United not advertising the vacant position of manager, around thirty applications found their way through the Old Trafford letterbox, with one or two being considered by the club as 'quite serious'. Obviously 'Fred from Wythenshawe' and 'Billy from Stretford' were immediately ruled out for lack of experience or some other unfortunate blot on their CV. McGuinness, apparently, was not one of those who had applied.

Personally created for McGuinness, the job description for the role of 'club coach' gave him only certain responsibilities. It remained to be seen if the likes of player recruitment and sales would be added to his list of duties following his probationary period.

Following Busby's decision to stand down, Wilf McGuinness immediately thought that his days as a Manchester United employee could be numbered, with the new manager bringing in his own people and he would simply become surplus to requirements. But those initial fears were soon to ease, as he began to get hints from other staff members that 'he was in with a shout' of getting the manager's job. He was said to exclaim after the appointment:

> I was overwhelmed, utterly delighted. I hadn't applied for the job when Sir Matt announced he was going to retire. I was just hoping that I might be considered. You dream that something like this might happen to you. And the way it has happened to me has been marvellous.

Any thoughts on what might be were pushed to the back of his mind. It wasn't until Sir Matt Busby pulled him to one side and told him to arrive at Old Trafford the following morning, smartly dressed in a collar and tie, rather than his more normal casual attire, that the feeling he was indeed in the running for the vacant post took on a completely new outlook.

It was perhaps a forgone conclusion that Busby's successor would come 'from within the ranks', as no major appointment at Manchester United had been made from outside the club. But was McGuinness the right man for the job?

At the age of thirty-one, he certainly fitted the criteria of being a younger man. As for experience, he had represented England at every level. He had made his United debut against Wolves in October 1955, having made his reserve team debut the previous March. However, a broken leg in December 1959 brought his career to a premature end, although a comeback was attempted in 1967.

He was appointed assistant trainer with the United Central League side, which later lead to the position of youth team trainer with England, later becoming manager, while also having a backroom role with Alf Ramsey's World Cup winning side in 1966. Certainly, there was a level of experience there, but was it enough to take charge of a football club and one with the pedigree of Manchester United? Was it enough to fulfil points two and three of Busby's criteria?

The answer must be no, as he was not a proven leader and his appointment was something of an experiment. Why else would he have been appointed for a probationary period?

The much-respected Arthur Hopcraft wrote in the *Observer*:

The conclusion is still inescapable. Sir Matt is not yet relinquishing control over the playing staff with the same finality that must have followed the appointment of a successor with an uncompromising title. Clearly the vital factor in resolving this predicament is going to be the personality of McGuinness.

Busby still held control over everything. However, not all thought that the appointment of Wilf McGuinness was a mistake, with his former teammate Denis Viollet quick to stress that the former half-back was not someone to mess with.

We used to split up into three training groups, and we all dreaded getting put into Wilf's. The team will find that if Wilf thinks something tough has got to be done, like dropping someone big, he'll do it alright.

Another who doubted the newly appointed manager's ability to succeed was Alan Gowling, who had made fleeting appearances under Busby.

I felt that the side which had done so well needed to be broken up, that other players who had been in the limelight less were in danger of being stifled, and their ambitions being killed. I think Matt Busby realised that it was a time for change all round and, this being so, he was prepared to give someone else the job of making a fresh start. He was due a break. He had earned the right to be able to relax a little.

As a coach, Wilf was well-liked, but he was still a contemporary of many of the stars. He had been their teammate on many occasions and some were more experienced than him. Or they at least considered themselves to be. But it was another thing altogether when he was given what amounted to the job of rebuilding the team.

With the unbeaten run having come to an end, as had Stepney's reign between the sticks, for the time being at least, United were once again left floundering when they visited St James' Park, Newcastle. However, in the penultimate league fixture of the season, with AC Milan waiting in the wings on European Cup business, they regained some of their poise and most importantly, winning instinct, with the 2-0 defeat of Burnley at Old Trafford.

So it was off to Italy and Milan, with the flight down through Europe allowing Sir Matt Busby some additional time to contemplate the semi-final tie, debating on what his team selection might be for his final joust at the ultimate football prize.

Indeed, he had much to think about. In goal, Jimmy Rimmer, who had taken over from Stepney against Newcastle, and prior to that, had only featured in two other league fixtures and one cup tie, had been given something of a rough time on Tyneside, requiring treatment on four separate occasions. Despite this, he had never played in a European tie. He had watched from the close quarters of the trainers' bench, but that and the physical approach of the Geordies was nothing compared to running out in the San Siro in front of 80,000 baying Italians.

Defensively, there were also other problems. Stiles and Fitzpatrick had been forced to play as stand-in full-backs in recent weeks. Brennan, however, had returned to the side against Burnley, replacing Stiles in the number three shirt with the England man reverting to his more familiar number six. Also in the line-up against Burnley was Bill Foulkes, the thirty-seven-year-old returning to the side in place of Steve James, after having spent the majority of the season on the sidelines. His performance against the Turf Moor side was certainly satisfactory, and his undoubted experience was unquestionable and would be more than valuable against the Italians, and added to that, Fitzpatrick and Sadler had minor knocks.

There was also the form of Bobby Charlton, who had featured in only two of the last dozen league fixtures and whose performances had been a matter of debate among the supporters and in the media. Having set himself such high standards over the years, any small blip was going to come under scrutiny after the initial shock that he was perhaps, after all, capable of turning in what could be considered 'ordinary' and even 'poor' performances. Sir Matt Busby said,

I am astonished that it has not happened to him before now. Bobby is a man who worries about his game, worries more than he should. There's nothing you can do to stop that. It's just his nature. And with the sort of strain he's been under playing all these games for us and getting to ninety caps for England, there was bound to be a reaction. Now that he is over thirty, people are inclined to ask if he can recover from a loss of form like this. I'm convinced that he can. He has gone through the odd phase like this in the past, one in particular about half a dozen years ago, and he has always come back better than ever. He is such a fantastic player, and he is still tremendously sound physically that I don't believe he won't start playing brilliantly again. I am confident that he'll do a great job for us again and that he can keep his place in the England team for Mexico.

There was never any possibility that an out of form Charlton was not going to face Milan – the occasion could just have been the necessary inspiration that he required to get him back on track. As United prepared for the semi-final in Varese, a mere 30 miles from Milan, Busby was quick to pencil him into his line-up. The United manager had also made up his mind on the other question marks in his team selection. Rimmer kept his place, as did Foulkes. Only Sadler missed out.

In the quarter-finals, Celtic had held Milan to a goalless draw in the San Siro. However, having done the hard part, they were defeated 1-0 in Glasgow, so Busby knew that despite having conceded only eleven goals in their twenty-six Italian League fixtures this season, they were not unbeatable. 'I know the crowd can be explosive, but most of our boys have seen it all before, and heard it all before and they are not likely to be upset', said a confident United manager. 'We have come here looking for a goal lead, and if we draw, we'll be very happy.'

His Milan counterpart, Nereo Rocco, did not share his confidence, saying, 'This is our most important game because I consider Manchester United to be one of the best teams in Europe.' Either way, it had the makings of a thrilling encounter.

Busby was certainly correct when he said that the Milanese crowd would be explosive; the San Siro was a wall of noise, with even United's emergence onto the pitch greeted by a crescendo of boos and a barrage of fireworks lighting up the dark Italian skyline. Desmond Hackett of the *Daily Express* was to write: 'In my world travels I cannot recall such bitter abuse, such an appalling avalanche of savage sound. This was the ugly mood of the Roman circuses, with 83,000 fanatics screaming for a soccer sacrifice.'

It was certainly like days of old, with United being the ones thrown into the lion's den. They were to find themselves under immediate pressure, conceding two corners in the opening 3 minutes, the sometimes ultra-defensive Italians abandoning such tactics, such was their determination to reach the final.

Rimmer flung himself across goal to push away a 20-yard drive from Sormani, following the second of those two early corners, with the confidence obtained from the save standing him in good stead; most of the action as the first half progressed had been played out in front of him.

United, while not exactly over-physical, did little to endear themselves to the home crowd, nor the opposition players, with some robust tackles. After committing a somewhat unnecessary foul, they almost conceded the first goal in the 10th minute, but Hamrin's free-kick went just over.

Action quickly swung to the opposite end and a Kidd header was saved by Cudicini. As Milan tried to catch United on the counterattack, Law caught Rivera with a kick to the ankle, forcing the midfielder out of the game. Further tackles from Brennan on Prati also incensed the Italians.

Rimmer once again came to United's rescue, denying Hamrin in the 25th minute. The 'keeper could do little to prevent the Italians taking the lead 9 minutes later, when the ball broke loose following a heading dual between Foulkes and Sormani on the edge of the United area, with the Italian reacting quickest, firing the ball past the United 'keeper who could do no more than get a hand to it. Sormani could have put the game beyond United's grasp seconds before the interval, but he headed wide of an empty goal.

If the first half kicked off a minute early, then United started the second 3 minutes late, as this was all it took for Milan to go two in front. Substitute Fogli crossed from the right, and Hamrin had the easy job of side-footing the ball past a helpless Rimmer.

The groans of despair from the United bench alongside the San Siro touchline were nothing compared to that of the 22,429, watching some 700 miles away on six giant 40-foot square screens on the Old Trafford pitch.

Having paid between 6s and 15s to watch the game as it happened, it sometimes felt that it was actually being played out live in front of them, such were the cheers and jeers that accompanied the action in Italy.

United seemed to awake from their slumber, perhaps sensing that their European crown was slipping away from them, but the Milan defence stood firm against whatever sent their way.

If their task at 2-0 down was considered a difficult one, then it was soon to be rendered as bordering on the impossible. With 14 minutes remaining and Fitzpatrick having come close with a powerful drive as the Italians back-pedalled, the Aberdonian found himself once again the centre of attention when he caught Hamrin with a kick when the ball was yards away. It was an incident missed by referee Krnavac, but spotted by his linesman, and indeed a large number of the crowd, leaving the Czech official with little option but to send the United man off.

Making the long and lonely walk towards the dressing rooms, Fitzpatrick was pelted by all sorts of objects and rubbish, from coins to empty miniature cognac bottles and fruit. To add to his indignity, he was to find the dressing room doors locked, and sat crouched tearfully in the tunnel as his teammates defended bravely in those final vital minutes.

The long-haired Scot could well be disappointed and disconsolate, as well as embarrassed having being clearly duped by Hamrin who continuously provoked the United man. When questioned if he had fallen for an age-old trick, he said nothing more than 'yes, that's true. I should know by now.' The sinned upon Swedish international simply offered the explanation: 'I tried to block his way, and he kicked me.'

Fitzpatrick's misdemeanour was not dwelt upon by his teammates, as the 90 minutes were debated in the dressing rooms deep in the bowels of the stadium. Nobby Stiles suggested 'their first goal was handball by Sormani. He just hit it down. The ball was too live for him to control.' While Sir Matt Busby was 'disappointed that Fitzpatrick was sent off. [I] did not see the incident, but players have been sent off for far worse than that. We will have to come at them in Manchester but I think we can do it.'

Twenty-two days separated the first and second leg of that European Cup semi-final, which should have allowed the United players the opportunity to recharge their batteries and allow for something of a rehabilitation programme to be put into place. But instead, for some unknown reason, the board sanctioned the playing of two friendlies in Ireland, against Shamrock Rovers on 5 May, and Waterford three days later. There would certainly have been some financial gain, but it is certainly doubtful if it was enough to jeopardise a place in the European Cup final should injuries have been picked up.

All but two of the regular first team players took part in both fixtures. The missing duo, Bobby Charlton and George Best, were involved in the more competitive and physical Home International tournament, with the former recharging his batteries with England, turning the clocks back with inspirational performances. If any Milan spies were watching, they would certainly have made a note in bold letters, as the Italian press had been quick to write him off after the first leg, wondering if he was now too old to play at this level.

Fortunately, all the players came through the two Irish fixtures unscathed, winning 4-0 against Shamrock and 3-0 at Waterford. Overcoming the Italians however, would be far from easy, but United were confident, with Sir Matt Busby proclaiming:

> They ought to know better, those people who have already written off Manchester United's chances against AC. It has always been a highly dangerous thing to do. Of course, with two goals lead, Milan will want to cling on to their advantage. They have proved themselves super strategists at defence, but in Milan they also showed that they have a flair for attack. We shall see what happens. We have to go at them, naturally. How we propose to do so is something I shall discuss with the players.

But, as had prior to the first leg, there were problems for the United manger when it came to finalising his team selection. Should he replace Bill Foulkes with Steve James while there was major doubt over Denis Law and his persistent knee problem? Although able to train, the Scot still required treatment twice a day. His appearance against the Italians would be in doubt until just before kick-off. One player who would not feature was John Fitzpatrick, suspended after his being sent off in the first leg. His replacement, Tony Dunne, although having recovered from a fractured cheekbone, had been surviving on a liquid diet and his match fitness was questionable. He was, however, expected to play.

The Italians on the other hand believed that they had done enough in the first leg to ensure a safe passage into the final. 'Obviously we feel more confident than we did when we came to Glasgow to play Celtic, because we have a good advantage', admitted coach Nereo Rocco to the assembled press on his team's arrival in Manchester. He also had no qualms about revealing how his side would play.

> We shall have five defenders, plus the goalkeeper. We shall have three more men midfield and two strikers only. Best will be marked by Rosato, Morgan by Schnellinger, Kidd by Malatrasi and Charlton by Lodetti. The rest will do what is necessary. If Manchester should get a goal, then we shall call off Rosato and replace him with Trappatoni at once, to try to recover that lead. The most important thing is to be calm before Manchester's opening attacks. And I am convinced that we could win if we use fast counter-attacks.

In the lull before the storm, Busby had one important job to do – to sit down and have a quiet word with George Best, as there was some concern regarding his behaviour during the season. Sent off against Estudiantes, he had been lucky not to have been sent for an early bath against Ipswich Town, mainly due to the referee's indiscretion. More recently, playing for Northern Ireland against Wales, he was reported as being 'irritable', while also considered to be 'looking decidedly mortal and tired'. United had paid dearly for Fitzpatrick's sending-off in the first leg. Losing Best in the second would be calamitous, more than likely resulting in their interest in the competition coming to an end.

On the eve of the match, the United manager pushed his thoughts on his line-up and his concerns about his Irish match winner to one side, and admitted,

> This is the crunch. For Wilf's sake, for the club's sake, I would like to hand over while we are still in Europe. We have only been out of it once in half a dozen seasons, and the boys in the team still going for the European Cup, it would be an ideal situation in which to hand over.

With no British side ever having knocked an Italian side out of Europe, it would indeed be difficult. 'Many accept that United could not play as badly again as in Milan', the United manager added. 'We have shown in the past we have the flair and ability to raise our game when the occasion demanded. Now we have never needed that ability more.'

From the kick-off, United's intentions were clear; not that they had any real alternative. Despite the determination to reduce their opponent's advantage as quickly as possible, the resolute Milan defence were rarely put under any real pressure, and looked calm and self-assured during those nervous opening minutes.

Playing in an all-white strip, Kidd came close to turning the volume up a few decibels in the 12th minute, rising to meet a Charlton corner, but his header went wide of the post. Hamrin had, moments before, completely silenced the packed stadium when he fired home, but to everyone's relief, it was disallowed for offside. As United took the game to Milan, even Foulkes got involved, attempting a re-enactment of his Bernabéu heroics, only to see his effort blocked by Cudicini. Unable to hold the ball, it fell tantalisingly for Morgan, but the winger's shot was smothered by the Italian 'keeper, aided by teammate Maldera.

The pace was frantic, there was a hint of desperation, but no goals. The tie was slipping away from United. As the second half got underway, it was almost grabbed inadvertently from their fingertips as emotions bubbled over.

Nereo Rocco hadn't waited for United to score before replacing Rosato (the world's costliest defender at £231,000), with Santin. As the substitute surged towards the United goal in the opening minute of the second half, the stadium erupted as Cudicini fell to the ground in the Stretford End goalmouth.

The referee immediately stopped play, with all eyes on the black-clad, prostrate figure in the rubbish-strewn goalmouth, felled by an object thrown from the heaving bank of United supporters on the Stretford End.

As the 'keeper received treatment amid the howls of derision, the referee was in deep consultation on the touchline. Soon an announcement was echoing around the packed stadium, warning the crowd that if there was any repetition of this incident, the official would have no hesitation in abandoning the game.

'Let us play in the proper manner' a voice boomed out over the loudspeakers, 'and give both teams a chance to do so.'

After his ordeal, Cudicini was to say, 'My legs trembled and I did not understand anything for 5 minutes or so. Every time the ball came near afterwards, something arrived from the crowd.'

Thankfully, as play resumed, there was no improper behaviour from either supporters or players, but still United toiled. Then, with 20 minutes remaining, Best turned on a sixpence before slipping the ball to his right towards Charlton. Pouncing on the ball, he went past a Milan defender before driving the ball past Cudicini from a tight angle.

Minutes later, Morgan headed over as the Italians showed a hint of panic for the first time in the match, but time was running out for United.

With 10 minutes remaining, a long throw from Crerand found Charlton who instinctively sent the ball into the Milan goalmouth. Law quickly flicked it towards goal and with Cudicini beaten, it rolled slowly towards the goal line. As the crowd held its breath, willing the ball over the line, it looked momentarily like United had somehow found that second goal. Law raised his arm in salute, as a joyous Kidd turned way to celebrate, the crowd erupting into a solid wall of noise.

Suddenly, out of nowhere it seemed, a Milan player appeared, blocking the ball and diverting it into the arms of his stranded goalkeeper. Some reports name the player as Anquilletti, others as substitute Santin. No matter who it was, they were in the right place at the right time, or from a red perspective, the wrong place at the wrong time. Frantically, the United players appealed for the goal, one that would throw the tie wide open, raising the already feverish atmosphere.

Everyone in a red shirt, wearing a red and white scarf or with the slightest leanings to all things United, claimed the ball was over the line. Watching on television, John Forbes was one who was not entirely convinced it had. 'I saw the "goal" once at normal speed and four times in slow motion', he confirmed. 'The more they showed the replay slowed down, the more I became convinced that the ball did not cross the line.

However, it was difficult to judge because the re-runs were rather blurred.' This was certainly not an opinion held by Matt D'Arcy, who also watched the drama unfold on television. 'Perhaps colleague John Forbes and I were watching on different quality sets, but on mine, there was no doubt that the ball rolled over the goal line. And the play-back confirmed it, showing the goal line appearing under the ball.'

Nearer to the action was *Manchester Evening News* photographer, Eric Graham. 'Because the police were standing throughout the second half, all the photographers moved closer to the goal. I was directly behind the goal, only a couple of yards from the goal line. Believe me, it was a goal.'

So, 2-1 in favour of a goal. But what of an alternative view? In the main stand was Keith Ward, another member of the *Manchester Evening News* staff. 'From my seat, I was on such an angle that the furthest post was hidden behind the nearest. So, I was ideally placed to see the ball appear well behind the posts, over the line. Yes, it was a goal.'

Despite the opinions of these four observers, it was the referee who had the final say – he simply waved play on, to the disbelief of the United players and the indignation of the home crowd.

Howls of derision vibrated from the terraces and stands, but nothing could alter the score line, leaving United with nothing to do but battle on for the remaining handful of minutes, in the hope that other opportunities would materialise and the game, that was now slowly slipping from their grasp, could be saved.

But there was to be no last gasp heroics, no twist in the tale. The disallowed goal had deflated United's hopes and dreams. That final step was simply one too big to take. The reign of the European Champions was over.

Although drained and disappointed, the United players lined up either side of the tunnel and shook the hand of the victors as they made their way off the pitch. Pat Crerand said,

> We stood there with the tears blinding us, and clapped them in. We felt like vomiting, but we clapped them in. Maybe it's a small thing, but it wasn't easy. Remember, there are a few of us in that team who aren't the greatest losers in the world. I thought the lads were marvellous.

There was, however, one final First Division fixture to fulfil against Leicester City at Old Trafford. Obviously, Sir Matt Busby's intentions were to go out with a win, but current League form, and the fact that the visitors required a victory to ensure their continuing presence in the top flight, meant such an outcome was far from guaranteed.

Leicester, despite their lowly, hazardous position, had reached the FA Cup Final. They had the ability, and players like one-time United targets

Alan Clarke and David Nish in their line up, to secure the necessary victory. If anything was against them, it was the fact that a United victory would see former club captain Noel Cantwell's Coventry City relegated. The Highfield Road club sat one point in front of Leicester, but had completed their fixtures. There was little possibility, however, that Cantwell's ex-team mates would take it easy, despite the looming European Cup semi-final.

Cantwell's reflection that his former teammates would 'go all out for him' disappeared in a puff of smoke as early as the 1st minute, when Clarke picked out Nish, who stepped in front of Stiles to side foot the ball past Rimmer. 'We must get the ball in the net as quickly as possible' Leicester manager Frank O'Farrellh said before the game. But even he was surprised by this early turn of events.

Sixty seconds later, however, Coventry were grasping at the First Division lifeline when the visitors allowed Best too much room and the Irishman hit the ball high and wide off Shilton for the equaliser. But no sooner were United level, than they were in front. Morgan's centre evaded everyone, and as Cross attempted to clear off the line, he momentarily lost control and the ball spun over the line as Kidd rushed forward to ensure its destination.

Leicester chased the game with a vengeance, knowing full well that United had their faults, hoping that prolonged attacks could exploit them, while only too aware that any counterattacks could prove fatal.

Three minutes into the second half, the outcome of the game, and Leicester's fate, was decided when Shilton attempted to fist the ball clear, only for it to land at Law's feet, who wasted little time in sending it beyond the 'keeper for United's third. There was now no way back for Leicester and Frank O'Farrell, who had only taken over the beleaguered club in December, saying that some had suggested that his team were 'too good to go down', saw the full-time whistle end their dream.

The final whistle also signalled a mass pitch invasion, as the fans swarmed over the perimeter fencing, congregating in front of the main stand, chanting Busby's name and being rewarded by the manager's appearance.

Although United had completed all their obligations on the playing front, with their League, and indeed FA Cup performances at times leaving much to be desired and sentimentality having cost the club dear, there were two outstanding confrontations to fulfil. On both occasions however, there was no hope of achieving a successful outcome. Both were guaranteed to end in defeat.

The events surrounding that penultimate fixture against AC Milan in the European Cup semi-final lingered on, having left a sour taste in the mouths of not only the United directors, but also UEFA; the actions of those individuals who threw coins, bolts and whatever else they had secreted into the Stretford End, were noted by their match observer. The report by Austrian Friedrich Siepelt, along with another from referee Marcel Machin, were presented to those who ruled the European game, and did not show Manchester United Football Club in a favourable light.

Prior to receiving either report, a UEFA spokesman said, 'we have handed out fines and cautions for similar incidents, but in those cases, no one was injured'; a clear hint that United could expect the book to be thrown at them for the actions of a minority.

It was reported in the media, prior to the investigation, that United were considering erecting 15-foot high fences behind the Stretford End goal as a deterrent to prevent supporters throwing missiles, possibly hoping that their own actions would lessen the blow from UEFA. It was something that did not work, as UEFA instructed the club to erect an iron fence, not just behind the Stretford End goal, but also behind the goal at the Scoreboard End. Following that news, Sir Matt Busby said, 'It is a great pity that the name of a great club has been dragged in the mud by a few hooligans. I will say no more at present.'

Rather surprisingly, objections were raised by the president of the Football League and several League clubs. At the directors' meeting on 22 July, it was decided by the United board to obtain further information to see if this instruction referred to domestic competitions or European competitions only.

Had United been involved in a European competition, then the matter of fences would have been enforced by UEFA. It was 1976 however, before the name of Manchester United would again appear alongside others on the continent, and by that time, due to trouble on the domestic front, fences were in place at Old Trafford.

The club's embarrassment was not simply confined to a few unruly supporters, as there were one or two other matters which came to light once the season had ended. One brought a summons to attend a joint Football League and Football Association Commission inquiry hearing over 'alleged irregularities' discovered in the club's books. This was to be headed by Dr Andrew Stephen, chairman of the FA, and Mr Len Shipman, president of the Football League, with Harold Thompson FA vice-chairman, Mr Alan Hardaker, secretary of the Football League, and a member of the Football League Management Committee. The big guns were out in force, and United were certainly in hot water.

But what had United done to land themselves in such a position?

Nothing more than providing Shay Brennan with a repayable loan of £1,000, without prior permission, which was considered an offence. They made a payment of £200 each to seventeen players in lieu of a club tour that could not take place due to a cluttered fixture list. As it was not a working tour and the money was in reality a gift, then it was regarded as a breach of Regulation 42. They paid £250 appearance money to eleven players who played against Estudiantes in the World Club Championship out with their contracts, as this bonus only came into effect had they been successful. Again, this breached Regulation 42. They made payments to club landladies of £5 10s for board and lodgings in relation to five apprentice players, when the Football League's Regulation 47 had set the figure at £4, and also paying board and lodgings for six amateur players, which contravened Regulation 25.

Hardly cardinal sins, but all were against the stated rules and regulations. Quite how Manchester United found themselves in such a position is something of a mystery as they were aware of such strict guidelines and had made no attempt to try and hide any of the payments made.

Club chairman Louis Edwards, secretary Les Olive and Sir Matt Busby all attended the hearing, speaking in the club's defence, but to little avail. They were guilty as charged, fined £7,000 and barred from playing any friendly fixtures outside England before next May, something that could cost the club around £15,000 per match. They were, however, allowed to fulfil their planned pre-season fixtures. No further comment from the club was issued.

Some felt that the fine, £2,000 more than Sunderland had been previously handed, and indeed the whole scenario was over the top and out of touch with the modern game. Why, they argued, should a club not be able to loan an employee money, as long it was legal and above board? If it was acceptable to pay players money in lieu of a club tour, which was cancelled due to an overflowing fixture list, and if written into their contract, then how could this not simply be accepted, as it would be impossible to foresee such a situation arising?

The payments to landladies were also up for debate, as the set figure had since been increased.

2
TESTING TIMES

When Wilf McGuinness officially stepped into his new role as chief coach, there was still the smell of pipe tobacco wafting along the Old Trafford corridors. Sir Matt Busby may have 'stepped upstairs', taking on something of an administrative role, but in reality, he had not moved an inch and still held claim to the key of the manager's office.

There was no pile of cardboard boxes waiting to be moved to a new home, or the name plate on the door needing to be unscrewed. Despite Wilf McGuinness commanding the senior role, he had to be content with the 'corner cupboard' that was Joe Armstrong's office; the chief scout having to take his notebooks and pens elsewhere. The new incumbent could, however, enjoy the trappings of a pay rise, as his salary more than doubled from £35 to £80, but still considerably less than Busby's, who earned more than double that.

And so the new man got down to work, wondering how he could make his mark on the players who were not so long ago his teammates and drinking partners. Yes Busby enjoyed a social life with a number of his players, but that was at his request and he had brought them to the club, not grown up alongside them. Busby was also 'old school', whereas McGuinness was becoming integrated in the 'new wave' of football management and coaching, with blackboards and miniature players and pitches, planning out moves and other tactics instead of the old 'go out and enjoy yourself' method.

Wilf McGuinness was on a ride to failure right from the start, and he perhaps knew that within himself. Although that European Cup success had only been twelve months previous, and it could be argued that United had been denied a second consecutive final appearance due to an incorrect refereeing decision, they were still a team on the decline. Fresh blood was required, whether coming through the ranks, or via the chequebook, which Busby kept locked in his desk drawer; re-enforcements were necessary.

With the new season on the horizon, and Wilf McGuinness itching to get his tenure up and running, he was given a massive boost by the news that Denis Law was fit and also eager to hit the ground running. 'I feel better than ever' the twenty-nine-year-old Scot said.

> I've had a good rest for once and it's made me feel great again. Obviously all the players are sick that we're out of Europe. And the public must feel pretty bad about it too. But it means we've got everything to fight for, including the League Cup, which has grown into wonderful competition.

The new season for Law and McGuinness, along with the rest of the United first team squad, got underway in North Wales, at the home of lowly Banger City, where the visitors faced a Welsh international eleven as part of the celebrations for the Investiture of Prince Charles as Prince of Wales.

Despite United having slipped from their lofty pedestal, they were still a major attraction and those unable to obtain tickets found advantage points from houses and trees on a steep hill overlooking the ground. The fixture was also perhaps an ideal start for the 'new United', as the Welsh players were under strict instructions to avoid any physical contact, as they were involved in another game a mere 24 hours later against a Rest of United Kingdom side at Cardiff.

A 2-0 victory got McGuinness off to a winning start, and the assumption by several members of the Welsh side that 'United seemed physically fitter than last season' was given further providence over the following week with a European goal spree when Copenhagen were defeated 6-2, and FC Zurich hammered 9-1.

The assumption by the Welsh players that United looked different than they had done during the previous campaign was certainly a correct one, as one or two of them confessed that Wilf McGuinness' pre-season training sessions had been tough, and that they had never experienced anything so gruelling. Although, they were also quick to confess that after the opening match in Bangor they had never felt fitter at the end of the game.

So what had McGuinness done that differed from Busby? Nothing more than attempting to combine the notable individual talent with a methodical team plan.

The *Manchester Evening News'* United correspondent David Meek, who watched the European goal avalanche first hand, was quick to praise the new man at the helm, writing,

> Manchester United mean business. You can knock the quality of the two continental teams that conceded fifteen goals as much as you like. I have seen enough to convince me that Sir Matt Busby's reorganisation of his management will launch the Reds into another era of success.

Chief coach Wilf McGuinness has slipped easily, confidently and enthusiastically into his new role of team boss. Already there is a rapport between players and coach. McGuinness knows exactly where he is going, and he will take the players with him. He and Jack Crompton are putting their men through their toughest ever pre-season preparation, including hard stints on the morning of their tour matches, yet there has been a freshness and zest about the football.

Bob Russell in the *Daily Mirror* was slightly more cautious in his assertion of the 'new look' United, wondering if the Danish and Swiss opposition were 'competent enough to prompt serious examination of United's prospects'. But he did go on to say that he believed United had to be regarded with the highest respect by those clubs who were going to challenge for the First Division title in the weeks ahead.

Those fifteen goals in two games had set United up nicely for their opening League fixture against Crystal Palace at Selhurst Park; the Londoners' first ever game in the top flight. On that August Saturday afternoon, the sun shone, a record 48,610 crowd, the highest of the day, had packed into the South London ground and United were out to re-establish those reputations of old with a manager who was keen to stamp his own mark on the club as soon as possible.

Palace were on a high, but would have started their initial campaign in the top flight with a defeat had it not been for the generosity of the United defence. In the 11th minute, Rimmer attempted to punch away a throw-in from Hoy, but Blyth got a head to it and Hynd prodded the ball over the line as Foulkes made a rather late effort to clear.

It took the visitors 12 minutes to equalise. Crerand and Sadler sent Morgan scurrying down the flank, his cross curling away from Jackson in the Palace goal, allowing Charlton to slide the ball home. This should have given United the impetuous to build on their superiority, but yet again the visitors gifted their hosts a goal just before half-time: Queen driving a Kember pass firmly past Rimmer.

United squandered opportunities, although they managed to pull a goal back in the 56th minute, Law beating Jackson to the ball and pulling it back to Morgan who scored at ease. But try as they might, a winner just would not materialise and they had to be content with one point.

McGuinness would most probably have settled for a point pre-match, knowing full well that Palace would be playing above themselves in their opening fixture in the top flight. Such a result in his early foray into the world of football management would sit favourably with him, leaving him content in his work on the training pitch and having felt that progress of a sort had been made.

On Wednesday 13 August, Old Trafford opened its freshly painted red gates for the first home fixture of the campaign, with Everton making the short journey along the East Lancs Road, a much sterner test for the new manager than newly promoted Palace.

Despite having gained access to the chalk and blackboard at the Cliff training ground, along with a pen and a sheaf of blank team sheets, Wilf McGuinness was not given a page, nor even a solitary column within the pages of the *United Review* – the club programme. Sir Matt Busby claimed the second page, usually reserved for the manager's comments. Although the former manager was club spokesman, McGuinness was the man in charge of team affairs, and it would have been of interest to the supporters to read his thoughts and plans. His brief appearances within the pages of the *Review* however were merely the odd photograph, as it was in that first programme of the season. No introduction, no profile of the new man at the helm. Nothing. He certainly knew his place.

'Wilf McGuinness has taken over the responsibility of team matters and team selection and he will have the full support of the directors, players and staff. I feel sure he will do a very good job and that the standard of football will continue to be of a high quality', wrote Busby in his column, while chairman Louis Edwards merely commented 'at the same time we have one of our own young staff men taking over as chief coach, a role for which we feel Wilf McGuinness well suited.'

A photograph of Wilf McGuinness and Matt Busby with the playing staff at the Cliff training ground was the best the new man in charge could do.

Everton were about as generous as the programme editor to the novice chief coach – a team far superior to the former European Cup winners – in their 2-0 victory, which stunned the packed Old Trafford, and left the often volatile support and those in charge of team affairs in no doubt that there was considerable work to be done if Manchester United were to climb once again to a lofty position.

'I've had a lot of letters' said the new man at the helm, 'and some of them tell me that we're over the hill. Some of these people have been brave enough to give their names and addresses. But I think we've got a side that can tear any other team to pieces on its day.' His early attitude was certainly defiant and could not be faulted, but he had to go out and impose his own character on the team. He still spoke of Busby as the boss, but it was his team now and he had to grasp the mantle and get the club back on track.

If the message wasn't clear enough that Wednesday night in Manchester, then it was certainly dazzling, shinning into everyone's eyes at 4.45 p.m. three days later.

As the United and Southampton players trooped off the pitch that Saturday afternoon, the heads of those wearing the red shirts bent low following a stunning 4-1 defeat, and the echoes of the boos aimed in the direction of one-time golden boy Denis Law still lingering around the stadium, the simplicity of the victory sent a shiver down the spine of even the most devoted supporter. The home defence had been torn to shreds by one-time United target Ron Davis, Southampton's Welsh international number nine, who claimed all four goals.

United had taken the lead through Willie Morgan after only 8 minutes, driving the ball past Gurr from close range. It was an advantage that was short-lived as the afternoon soon turned sour.

In the 12th and 16th minute, Southampton's outside-left John Sydenham slalomed past Shay Brennan, tormenting the Mancunian Irishman relentlessly and on each occasion delivered a tempting cross into the united penalty area, where Davies was on hand to head past Rimmer from within the 6-yard box.

Foulkes failed to offer any deterrent to the power of Davies, and 12 minutes into the second half, Brennan was again left mesmerised by Sydenham, as was Foulkes by Davies and the Welshman nodded home his third.

Davies claimed his fourth in the 77th minute, this time with his foot rather than his head, and the paying public, already showing their displeasure with slow hand claps, took their frustration up a level with the booing of the lacklustre Law.

The sluggishness of the United defence spread right across the back four, with Sadler the only one of the quartet to gain any plus points. As the game progressed, the indecisive play spread further up the field, with Arthur Hopcraft of the *Observer* writing, 'neither Best or Charlton made more than intermittent impact on the game, Best being intricate without being exciting, Charlton hitting diffident passes and running without optimism.' Of Law, he wrote that the Scot was 'barely able to make intentional contact with the ball ... was booed repeatedly and with specific venom'.

The treatment of Law was deplored upon by many, with the men in the press box in particular standing firmly alongside the seemingly dethroned 'King' of the Stretford End. 'The booing of Law was intolerant and shameful' penned David Meek, while Paul Doherty in the *People* kicked off his match report with, 'when they start to barrack "King" Law in his own domain, it's time to assess how intolerant United's fans are becoming with this sojourn from success.' Matt Busby was also quick to stand alongside one of his favourite son's. 'The fans here have been spoiled,' he exclaimed. 'They've had it so good for so long.'

Played three, lost two and drawn one – the worst start to a season since 1933/34. It was certainly not the start that Wilf McGuinness had envisaged to his career as the man at the helm of Manchester United. But it was something that he had to live with, as they were his decisions. On the eve of the return fixture against Everton at Goodison Park, he made what was certainly his biggest one to date – and quite possibly the biggest he would ever make – deciding to leave Bobby Charlton and Denis Law out of his starting line-up. Even those who had booed Law against Southampton were left open-mouthed, their uncouth treatment of the Aberdonian suddenly forgotten. You didn't drop players like Charlton and Law. But McGuinness did, and he went a step further by also pushing Bill Foulkes, Shay Brennan and Jimmy Rimmer onto the sidelines.

For Foulkes, who had endured a torrid time throughout the 90 minutes against Ron Davies, it was a time for reflection. The veteran defender decided that he had little inclination in being subjected to similar Saturday afternoons by younger, hungrier and more mobile centre-forwards, and the thirty-seven-year-old decided that it was time to leave the First Division stage and so hung up his boots.

Foulkes had been appointed reserve team coach in July in the wake of Wilf McGuinness stepping up to take over the first team. At the time, he had decided to continue playing, but with only three games of the new campaign having been played, he felt that it was time to go. He owed United nothing, but the club certainly owed him plenty.

Born in St Helens, Foulkes, like many others, found employment down the mines, but he was also blessed with a talent that took him away from those harsh conditions – he could play football. Even the lure of joining Manchester United, however, was not enough to make the talented youngster instantly forsake the coal face, as he was more than content to toil away between the two; money being the deciding factor in him working during the day and training at night, travelling back and forward at all hours.

He joined United as an amateur in March 1950, having previously played for Whiston Boys' Club, signing as a professional in August the following year. As the 1948 FA Cup winning side began to age and disperse, he found himself thrust into the first team at Liverpool in December 1952. National service, like his holding down of two jobs at once, was taken in his stride, and two years later, he was making his England international debut against Northern Ireland. Further international honours followed at under-23 and Football League level, but he was never to add to that solitary cap at full international level.

Obviously being a miner, he had the physical attributes to become a strong, no-nonsense defender, with his pen picture in the Scottish League v. English League programme of March 1955 describing him as,

A resolute, quick-thinking back who has gained distinction by his cool, accurate tackling and judgement in the pass. He rarely parts with the ball without endeavouring to place it to a colleague positioned to develop attack from defence, while he holds a close link with his goalkeeper.

Early appearances were as a full-back but, surviving the Munich disaster, he became the cornerstone of the 'new' United, being thrust into the limelight as captain, guiding his younger teammates through those dark days. In the early sixties though, he began to find the captaincy something of a weight on his shoulders, and asked to be relieved of the position. The move was a wise one, as his form returned to the level expected of him and he helped United to both FA Cup and First Division success.

A no-frills defender, Bill Foulkes was always there when required as well as being there when least expected, as transpired in the Bernabeu Stadium in Madrid in May 1968 when he went AWOL from his defensive duties and latched onto a George Best pass to steer home United's third goal in that dramatic 3-3 draw, which took Matt Busby's team into the European Cup Final.

Sadly, time had caught up with him after some eighteen years and 688 games. He deserved the rest.

Perhaps Bill Foulkes expected to be spending his Wednesday night in front of the television or catching up on a bit of gardening, but Messrs Law and Charlton certainly didn't foresee the humiliation of their own names not appearing on the team sheet for the trip to Goodison Park. It was the first time that Law had been dropped from a club fixture and only the second for Charlton; his last being nine years ago. The latter's omission did much to fuel the rumours that the best of the thirty-two-year-old's career was now behind him, and his effectiveness was clearly on the wane.

There was only one way that McGuinness could justify his widely considered drastic action and that was with a victory. His decision to reshuffle the pack, however, failed to conjure up any magic, with table topping Everton improving on their 2-0 Old Trafford victory, going one better this time. Their 3-0 victory should in reality have been more; Harry Catterick's team failing to pile further agony onto their visitors.

McGuinness had put his head on the block and the executioner's axe had fallen. He deserved credit though for being brave enough to make such a major decision, knowing full well that the 90 minutes on Merseyside could see his team remain fourth from bottom. The defeat did indeed keep United four places off the bottom, level on points with Ipswich Town and Sunderland and a mere point in front of bottom club Sheffield Wednesday. They had, however, played one game more than their fellow strugglers.

Charlton may have been out of form, but his guile was sorely missed. Paul Edwards, who replaced the aging Foulkes, was certainly more mobile and, despite having spent a considerable time on the sidelines through injury, showed promise. Debutant Don Givens, a forward by trade, was a little out of his depth in an unfamiliar midfield role, while Stepney returned confidently between the posts.

But the question was: where would United and McGuinness go from here?

The United coach backtracked on his decision to omit Law and Charlton from his team selection, reinstating both for the away fixture at Wolverhampton, with one other change coming in the shape of debutant Ian Ure, an £80,000 signing from Arsenal. Ure was not a McGuinness signing, he was Busby's. The man in charge of team affairs later saying of the new signing, 'I had seen quite a bit of Ian playing for the Gunners and I wasn't sure he was the man to improve our side in the long term. But Matt rated him highly. I respected his judgement and so went along with him.' At the time, however, it was something of a different story. 'Wilf's in charge of this one' said Busby. 'He has my wholehearted support and I believe Ian will be a fine acquisition to the club.'

No matter who said what, it was Matt Busby who had wanted to sign the rugged Ayr-born defender. Ure had formed the cornerstone of the Dundee defence when they won the Scottish First Division title in 1961/62, and reached the European Cup semi-finals the following year. A £62,500 fee had taken him south to Highbury in 1963, where he was to feature in over 200 games for the Gunners. 'It wasn't a panic buy' said McGuinness, adding that they had been looking at the player for some time and he was seen as the ideal man to add strength and security at the back.

Resembling a Viking invader with his mane of blonde hair, Busby had wanted to bring him to Old Trafford a few years previously, but no deal was forthcoming. Now he had got his man, but in the eyes of many, including Ure himself, it was something of a surprise signing.

Like Bill Foulkes, Ian Ure had suffered at the hands of the new wave centre-forwards, their mobility causing numerous problems compared to the old rough and tumble number nines, but the new signing had also suffered his fair share of injuries. His knee in particular caused him much grief. 'I had terrible knee troubles from about my second season at Arsenal' he was later to say, 'and I was swallowing pills just to keep me on the park'.

If there was such a prolonged problem with his knee, then why did United sign him and, more to the point, how did he manage to pass his medical?

The problem was not something that Manchester United were aware of and, according to the player, it was something that they both managed to keep under wraps.

At the time they were looking for a stopgap centre-half. Fortunately for me, but unfortunately for them, they didn't know how bad my knee was. The medical at Manchester United was a farce. They said to me, 'can you bend your knee?' I said, 'aye, watch . . . that was it. My knee was passed fit. I keep saying it; I wouldn't have signed me in the state I was in because of my knee, I'd basically been on the slide since the mid-1960s.

So, having passed his medical, or what had stood for a medical, Ure joined his new teammates, including Denis Law with whom he had enjoyed a bout of fisticuffs at Old Trafford in the not too distant past, and prepared for his debut against Wolves at Molineux.

Ure's first outing in the red of United did produce a few head-scratching moments during his 90-minute confrontation with Derek Dougan. The new signing added a touch of stability to the goal-leaking United defence, enjoying as much as anyone, the first clean sheet of the season in the 0-0 draw. A feat that was repeated four days later at Old Trafford, against Newcastle United.

Although it was only five games into the new season, there was already a divide between those who wondered if United were on the verge of going off the rails, or if it was simply a blip in form that would correct itself accordingly?

It was suggested that McGuinness, while not exactly wrong to drop Charlton and Law, did so too drastically and in a way uncharacteristically for a United manager. What would happen if Busby was proved wrong in choosing McGuinness as manager? How long could he stand back and watch, causing more problems the longer he tolerated them? They were testing times all around.

From conceding eleven goals in four games, to two consecutive clean sheets was certainly a vast improvement, and Ure must take some of the credit for this turnaround, although in Dougan and Newcastle's Wyn Davies, he was face-to-face with more of the old school style centre-forward. However, United had still not recorded their first victory of the season, and had only scored once in the last five outings, but with those two draws, perhaps the corner had been turned with a chink of light appearing through the cracks.

Having scored only three goals in six games was just as big a worry as those goals conceded. It was not too long ago that United scored goals for fun, and it was something that was expected due to the number of prolific goalscorers in the squad. Denis Law was still struggling with his seemingly continuous knee injury, while Bobby Charlton was, by his standards, having something of an indifferent season. But what of George Best?

In previous seasons his name would dominate the headlines, with the match reports repeating his name like a printer's error in every paragraph. In the half dozen fixtures of this campaign however, the casual observer would have had cause to wonder if he had indeed been involved due to his lack of a mention.

His summer had been spent soaking up the sun at his villa in Majorca, recharging the batteries. But while looking tanned and relaxed, his on-field presence projected a shadow of the impish Irishman. The man marking of Palace had kept him subdued, while his trio of creative opportunities in both fixtures against Everton had been easily dealt with by Gordon West. Against Southampton, he was there virtually in name only, and in the goalless encounters against Wolves and Newcastle, his name only appeared in the team line-ups of the following day's reports, such was his overall contribution.

Capable of turning a game in a matter of minutes, the 'Belfast Boy' was the one player that Wilf McGuinness needed more than any other as he fought to establish himself as a worthy successor to Sir Matt Busby. Even when not tantalising the opposition defence, his mere presence would always keep a couple of defenders occupied, creating space for his teammates. This season however, he had been subdued, but like a coiled snake prodded with a stick, he suddenly sprang to life and threatened all around him.

In 1897, American author Mark Twain wrote 'the reports of my death have been greatly exaggerated' following the appearance of an obituary in the *New York Times* when the man in question was very much still alive. As August 1969 faded in the autumn light, the demise of Manchester United from the forefront of English and European football slipped easily alongside that aforementioned quote, as Sunderland, second bottom of the First Division, a point behind United, arrived at Old Trafford looking for the opportunity to leapfrog their hosts and begin a climb to safety.

But it was as though United's previous fixtures, not including the goal strewn pre-season friendlies, had been little more than meaningless encounters, and finally having got the rustiness out of their system, it was all systems go with Sunderland.

George Best shrugged off the memories of the Mediterranean sunshine and whatever else he had enjoyed during the close season, and got down to business on the football front. 'George is back to his best', proclaimed David Meek in his *Manchester Evening News* summary of the match, as it took the Irishman only 7 minutes to breach the Sunderland defence, heading home a Kidd cross. Despite the promising start and Best's continuing menace, the visitors equalised 17 minutes later amid the audible groans from the Old Trafford crowd, who now expected yet another winless 90 minutes.

Thankfully, Sunderland's plight was worse than that of their opponents. Sloppy defensive play allowed United to take the lead 8 minutes into the second half through Brian Kidd, following fine work by Best. Then, 5 minutes from time, victory was assured when Don Givens scored his first goal for the club.

So sighs of relief around Old Trafford, with the first victory of the competitive season under the belt. There was still a long way to go however, as the following fixture, a League Cup tie against Second Division Middlesbrough, was to prove. This was a competition that United, when involved, seemed to struggle in no matter who the opposition was and it was only a solitary David Sadler goal, 15 minutes from time, that eased United through.

A 2-2 draw at Elland Road against Leeds United did much to restore the tarnished reputation, and they were now unbeaten in the last five outings. A true test of how much of an improvement had been made, and if the corner had indeed be turned, would be under scrutiny with the visit of league leaders Liverpool to Old Trafford on 13 September.

While sometimes lacking the glitter of previous encounters, United were not too concerned about the niceties of the game, as polished performances could come later. It was more about improved performances, points won and climbing the table to a more respectable position.

It was to be George Best who once again lifted United with a sublime second half performance, creating the only goal of the game for Morgan, having rattled the Liverpool crossbar just before the interval. In the heart of the United defence Ian Ure once again stood firm, the early season defensive frailties now a distant memory.

As if emerging from a cocoon or awoken form a trance, George Best was suddenly alive, once again turning in those virtuoso performances of old, tantalising defenders with his every move.

The hoodoo of countless trips across the Pennines to Hillsborough, Sheffield were exorcised in style. Best, performing more in an inside forward position than out wide, secured the first away victory of the season with two goals in a game, on a rain-sodden pitch, that was heading towards a 1-1 draw with 10 minutes remaining on the clock.

Creating the opening goal for Brian Kidd in the 10th minute, Wednesday drew level shortly before the interval in a match which devoted more to brawn than brain. Then, as the game reached its closing stages, Best took it by the scruff of the neck, tormented the home defence, and sent the red and white hoards back to Lancashire content in a 3-1 victory.

Pegged back a little in their march to mid-table respectability by a 2-2 draw against Arsenal at Highbury, Best again took on the role of saviour and inspiration, dragging United back single-handedly from the jaws of defeat with both goals when 2-0 behind.

The hard work on the training pitch was paying off. McGuiness had a spring in his step, Best was back to his brilliant, tantalising, majestic self and all things in the garden were looking rosy. However, there was still much work to be done as one man could not carry the weight of returning Manchester United to its glory days of the not too distant past.

The League Cup and the visit of Wrexham to Old Trafford removed any pressure of maintaining their current league form. The 6,000 followers from across the Welsh border, along with former United players David Gaskell, Ian Moir and Albert Kinsey, who were all in the visitors line-up, had to return home disappointed. United progressed to the last sixteen of the competition with a non-inspiring 2-0 victory.

Having taken something of a night off, George Best returned to his recent superior form and reclaimed the headlines in the 5-2 home defeat of West Ham United, with observing journalist Henry Matthews writing,

> That Irish wizard, George Best, condescended to grace this occasion with a twenty-minute conjuring cabaret act. It was his sole contribution to the ninety minutes play; for the remainder of the time he wandered to wherever the action wasn't … and there he daydreamed. But it was enough.

Ten games without defeat, and perhaps a little complacency, found its way into the mindset of the red shirts. If indeed some did let the current run of form allow them to think that victory was always within their grasp, or that one talented teammate would always rescue them from the jaws of defeat, they were given a wake-up call at the Baseball Ground where Derby enjoyed a favourable afternoon with a 2-0 win, perhaps riding their luck with a Fitzpatrick own goal and two disallowed United efforts aiding their success.

Last season's abysmal record of only two away League victories throughout the campaign was matched by mid-October, with the 3-0 success at Southampton and the 2-1 home defeat of Ipswich Town maintaining the momentum of the red revival. Both victories were again inspired by George Best, something that was becoming a regular occurrence. Brian Kidd was also beginning to create some attention, his goal in the 2-1 win over the East Anglian side was his third in four games, while another member of the squad was always leaving his mark on games, but for all the wrong reasons; the 0-0 League Cup draw against Burnley at Turf Moor, bringing John Ftizpatrick his fourth booking of the season.

Yellow cards today come as part and parcel of the modern game, but while the actual physical side of the game has been somewhat diluted from the tough, no-nonsense play of years gone by, a booking could be looked upon as something of a rare occurrence; a sending off even more so.

Visits to Burnley were usually feisty affairs and a cup tie even more so. This fourth-round League Cup tie certainly had an underlying edge to it, and as far as value for money entertainment went, none of the 27,000 there went home disappointed. But it was Fitzpatrick who captured the headlines.

Having kicked off the season with a fortnight's suspension, he was now overtaking Nobby Stiles as United's public enemy No. 1. His robust, sometimes over enthusiastic, sometimes downright nasty, confrontations with the opposition meant that match officials had one eye on him before the match had even started.

Warned twice for fouls on Steve Kindon, another desperate lunge was enough for the match official and he reached for his book. Some, like Ronald Crowther of the *Daily Mail* felt that the tackle was 'badly timed, rather than vicious', but nonetheless, it was simply one foul too many.

There was only one name on everyone's lips and that was George Best. Without him, Wilf McGuinness would have been in dire straits, probably staring relegation in the face, even at this early stage, with the wrath of the support echoing around his head.

A spectacular 46th-minute strike against Nottingham Forest in a 1-1 home draw, saw him latch onto a Charlton pass out on the left. He then jinked inside past Hindley, then drifting across the face of the penalty area before sending a searing right-foot drive past Hill without a change of pace or direction – a goal considered one of his best, even by his high standards. The Irishman then took United into the quarter finals of the League Cup, with the only goal of the Old Trafford replay against Burnley. On this occasion, nothing out of the ordinary; he simply kept his cool from the penalty spot.

While the name of George Best was on everyone's lips, that of another member of United's illustrious European Cup winning side had been erased from memory. Pat Crerand had not been considered for first team duty since the 2-2 draw at Elland Road, back at the start of September, and it was beginning to look as though his days at the club were numbered, with his number four shirt now the property of Francis Burns.

Having reached the age of thirty, his days at the top were certainly numbered, but he still had much to offer in both experience and ability, although stepping down a level, or indeed two, was not something that he had contemplated. 'It may seem corny, but playing for Manchester United is something very special' he was to say, 'and I don't think I would risk cheapening that part of my career by taking the readies to go to a small club'. Although professing his love for United, he was finding life as a Central League player hard to bear. His future however, lay in the hands of Wilf McGuinness. Or was it Sir Matt Busby, as many still felt that McGuinness was nothing more than a puppet, an acquisition he clearly denied.

> That's only said by other people. Matt refuses to tell me what to do.
> The most he does is suggest lines of thought. Since I took over, our
> relationship has been better than it was. As far as the team is concerned,
> Matt leaves everything to me. On match days he comes in and says 'all
> the best lads' and then we don't see him again.

Success in the League Cup would have provided a return route into European
football, something that a few weeks ago seemed little more than a distant
dream, while also giving Wilf McGuinness a firm foothold on securing the
title of team manager. League form suddenly became a little indifferent, with
only one win in three, a 2-1 victory over Noel Cantwell's Coventry City.
West Bromwich took both points in a 2-1 defeat at the Hawthorns, while
Stoke City left Old Trafford with a point following a 1-1 draw. The latter
saw the welcome return of Denis Law to the side, after a ten-week absence.

The return of one Aberdonian saw another nudged onto the sidelines,
not by injury or poor form, but due to on the filed misdemeanours. John
Fitzpatrick had already blotted his copybook, having been sent off in
Milan last season, his vicious approach to the game having also been noted
by match officials nearer to home. His fourth booking of the season at
Southampton brought an appearance in front of the Football Association
disciplinary committee in Manchester, but the original hearing ended
rather abruptly, with a question mark over the actual proceedings.

The reason behind the delay in administering justice was revealed, as
further enquiries were made, and it was suggested that United had been
ordered to suspend the player for a maximum of fourteen days, something
that they were reluctant to do when they themselves were unaware of
what punishment the FA would dish out.

Accompanied by both Wilf McGuinness and Sir Matt Busby, Fitzpatrick
made a brief twenty-minute appearance in front of the committee, before
leaving the room, being recalled for a further five-minute appearance
shortly afterwards. When approached by the members of the press upon
leaving that second meeting, the comment from one and all was, 'Sorry
gentlemen, there is nothing to add.'

When the case was eventually reheard over a fortnight later, Fitzpatrick
was suspended for eight weeks, due mainly to his previous record of two
sending's off and eight bookings over the course of four seasons – it was
perhaps not an unexpected decision. Had United, however, decided on
requesting a personal hearing for the player, then everything could have
been dealt with sooner and his suspension would have been served by the
time key games came around.

A fourth booking of the season against Burnley has seen a new file opened with his name in bold letters across the front. He was treading a fine line.

In order to inch closer towards that European dream via the League Cup, United had to overcome Derby County and their mudded enclosure, which they fobbed off as a football pitch. Already having tasted defeat, while having reverted back to their unpredictable form, few gave them much chance of reaching the semi-finals.

But it was their often beleaguered defence who received the plaudits in the hard-earned 0-0 draw. It saw Dave Mackay, Derby's granite-hewn half-back, stroll around the midfield area, collecting the ball at will and spraying passes across the length and breadth of the pitch. Precise openings, however, were few and far between, and not just for the home side, with some suggesting that United had come with the intention of securing a draw.

McGuinness was certainly more than able to organise his troops into encouraging defence more to the fore than the attack. Surprisingly, many still considered the United coach as no more than exactly that or indeed a mere trainer, with the *Daily Mirror* heading above their report of the League Cup tie proclaiming: 'Busby men stop slide to grab replay.' Others were undecided whether the man was able to take Manchester United back to the forefront of the English game.

For some, the be-all and end-all of United's season was defeating local rivals Manchester City. It was paramount that the Maine Road lot were put to the sword in both fixtures, as local pride mattered above all else. The cross-city trip to the blue environs on 15 November gave Wilf McGuinness the perfect opportunity to convince his doubters that he was more than capable of managing United, while at the same time getting his team back to winning ways. Neither happened.

City secured their first victory over their neighbours at Maine Road for ten years, a humiliating 4-0 trouncing, in a game they dictated from start to finish. Ninety minutes saw United reduced to little more than mere onlookers, overshadowed by a team over which they once held the upper-hand.

It was not simply a defeat, but a result that clearly emphasised that there was still much work to be done down by the Salford docks, and was perhaps best summed up by Denis Lowe of the *Daily Telegraph*.

For weeks, people in the game have stressed that United's over-reliance on Best's particular brand of magic had obscured many of the failings that marked their sad start to the season. Further evidence for this view was provided here, for with the Irishman under lock and key, United's attacking flair was non-existent. Law's contribution was negligible, and

the question of the Scot's future at Old Trafford is one of the problems
which face Wilf McGuinness.

It was an opinion echoed by another regular United watcher, Eric Todd of the
Guardian. 'This is perhaps no place for sermonising' he wrote, 'but Saturday's
events offered further evidence that United are not the team they were and
that henceforth, City will be Manchester's leading advertisement for high-
class football'. Although critical, he did add, 'On the other hand, I will not
accept either that United are "finished" in spite of the fact that reaction was
inevitable after they had attained their summit by winning the European Cup.'

Having been humiliated at Maine Road, some expected the doubt and
sorrow to continue when Derby County arrived in Manchester on League
Cup business. United had no fight for the replay, surrendering to the eager
and resourceful visitors, who on the first half alone looked the more likely
to march into the semi-finals.

But the United players had a conscience, a sense of guilt over their
performance against City, while at the same time having to prove to
the 57,122 who packed Old Trafford that they had not wasted their
hard-earned money in passing through the turnstiles to what was yet
another mediocre performance.

Derby should have scored early on, and if they had done so, would have
probably gone on to win. In a hard-fought encounter, which swung from
end to end with much regularity, it took only one goal to decide the eventual
winners: Brian Kidd with the match winner in the 65th minute.

Wembley was but two games away, although it was 180 minutes against
Manchester City that stood between Wilf McGuinness and leading out his
players beneath the twin towers.

Despite its desperate need for a makeover, Wembley still held that
magical appeal. Memories of that night against Benfica were still fresh in
the mind, but it was 1963 when United had last appeared in a domestic
Cup Final and a Saturday afternoon, or more so a whole weekend in
London, was certainly something to look forward to.

Victory over Derby had once again lifted the club from the doldrums
and it was smiles all round. Well perhaps not quite, as Willie Morgan was
far from happy at being left out of the starting line-up against Tottenham
on 22 November.

Having dislocated two toes playing against his former club Burnley, he
had failed to step back into the team upon his recovery, but with Denis
Law unfit to face the Londoners, Morgan thought he would be recalled,
only to see Carlo Sartori given the number seven shirt. A meeting with
McGuinness convinced him, for the meantime at least, that he still had
a part to play at the club despite his inclusion in the Central League side.

Two Bobby Charlton goals, a superb 18-yard drive and a free-kick from 4 yards further out helped to gain a 3-1 victory over Spurs, with the ageing England international also well to the fore in the 1-1 draw at Burnley. The timing was perfect, with Manchester City looming in the League Cup semi-final.

If there was an advantage to be had, then City, with their victory a handful of games ago, held it, but only by their fingertips. United, their faces still as red as their shirts for the embarrassing defeat, were out for more than revenge and local pride, and were determined to give their supporters some cheer in a season of performances as mixed as the Mancunian weather.

Their determination was supplemented with a vigorous performance, despite going behind to a Colin Bell goal in the 13th minute. The return of Nobby Stiles to the side against Burnley, following his summer cartilage operation, added some much-needed grit in a combative midfield.

City held their advantage until the 66th minute, having spent most of the second half on the defensive, when Bobby Charlton once again proved to be the player to inspire United. Under pressure, Tony Book headed a Brian Kidd cross to the feet of Charlton who drove the ball past Corrigan from 8 yards.

There were times that the tie looked like bubbling over, United content in employing a rather brutal and cynical approach. The game was well policed by referee Jack Taylor, although the official was to come in for some strong criticism with only 2 minutes remaining when he denied United the opportunity to go into the second leg on level pegging.

With full-time edging closer, Oakes found Lee just outside the United area. Surging into the area, Ure lunged at the City forward and as could be expected from the player commonly known as 'Lee Won Pen', down he went. The referee immediately pointed to the spot, amid frenzied protests from the United number five and his teammates.

Lee, having had plenty of practise, made little mistake from the spot.

'It was diabolical' exclaimed Ure, 'I went for the ball.' A sentiment which Wilf McGuinness echoed, 'I agree with Ian. The player got what he was aiming for. I thought we earned a draw.'

A draw would certainly have been a more favourable result for United to take into the Old Trafford second leg, but with another 90 minutes to play, it could still swing either way.

A 2-0 defeat at home to Chelsea was certainly not the ideal preparation for that second leg. If a lift was required however, then it came seven days later – at Anfield of all places – when Shankly's men were put to the sword with an emphatic 4-1 defeat. Liverpool, like United, had seen better days. This was their second successive home defeat, but they had beaten local rivals Everton the previous Saturday, while United had to re-juggle their team due to injuries.

Willie Morgan returned to the side, as did Pat Crerand, arguably the key to the victory, both doing much to consolidate their places with spirited performances in an 'I'll show you' aggressive prompting to the manager. Even Ian Ure got on the score sheet, but they were all, like everyone else, overshadowed by Bobby Charlton, with yet another goal-of-the-season contender.

Eight minutes remained, with United 3-1 in front and in no mood to sit back contentedly. Pushing forward once again, Charlton picked out Morgan. The reinstated winger nutmegged Wall, before slipping the ball back into the path of his teammate. Taking it in his stride, Charlton blasted the ball towards goal from some 15 yards, sending it soaring into the roof of the net past a helpless Lawrence.

It was a vintage Charlton strike, and one that saw not only the United contingent on the Anfield terraces savouring the moment, but a goal that saw the usually reserved Sir Matt Busby leap from his seat in the directors' box, something he was later to confess that he had never done before.

And so the players and supporters travelled gleefully back along the East Lancs Road, celebrating a notable victory in a season that had produced few, while dreaming of another similar victory four days later in the more familiar surroundings of home. Nothing could be better than beating City and reaching a cup final.

Having won the FA Cup the previous May, City were keen to make a return trip to Wembley and add the League Cup to their not too lengthy list of honours. United, although a goal behind, knew that they could triumph against adversity.

The game exploded into action in the 17th minute when Ian Bowyer gave City a 3-1 aggregate lead. Summerbee and Lee carved the opening initially for Young, but the City number ten's initial effort was blocked on the line by Ure. As Lee pushed the ball back towards goal, Stepney failed to hold it which allowed Bowyer to pounce and prod the ball home.

Stunned, but not deflated, it took United only 6 minutes to draw level, the goal coming from the unusual source of Paul Edwards, the twenty-one-year-old defender, with only five first team starts to his credit, ran onto a Crerand pass to score with a 15-yard drive.

Stepney kept United in the game, throwing himself across goal to stop a powerful Lee drive, with the same City player wasting another opportunity to re-establish his side's two-goal advantage. Bowyer then missed by inches, as the visitors kept their hosts under pressure and United hung on for the lives.

Having survived that first half onslaught, United regrouped after the interval and caught City out with a goal 14 minutes into that second period. Best, who had been somewhat quiet of late, brushed aside two challenges on the right before shooting for goal. Such was the power behind the shot that Corrigan failed to hold the ball and, before he could recover, Law pounced to give United the advantage on the night.

City were not about to surrender the tie, and soon had the United goal once again under siege. Edwards almost sliced Young's corner past Stepney, then Summerbee, when presented with an open goal, shot wide.

The game sat on a knife edge and, with 9 minutes remaining, was looking more than likely to be heading towards extra-time. City once again scurried towards the Stretford End goal defended by United, but Bowyer was halted in his tracks by Morgan some 20 yards from goal.

Lee lined up the free-kick and blasted it goalwards. Stepney failed to hold the ball and Summerbee skipped in to slip the blue into the net, and send the City support ecstatic. It was a goal that should never have been conceded as the free kick was indirect, and had Stepney simply stepped aside and allowed the ball to enter the net, the 'goal' would have been disallowed and the match restarted with a goal kick.

Had the United 'keeper not been aware of the referee indicating that the free-kick was indirect, or did he simply react as normal to a ball flying towards him? Either way, his actions cost United a place in the League cup final, as City held out for the remaining minutes of the game to seal a date with West Bromwich Albion at Wembley.

It was certainly not United's night. Gone was the opportunity for Wilf McGuinness to lay his hands on some silverware, only months into his new role had passed him by. Luck had certainly played a part in the outcome of the semi-final against City, but this was not the Manchester United of old, it was a team stuck in something of a time warp, amid a period of transition and perhaps uncertainty.

Wolves stood firm to earn a point from a 0-0 draw at Old Trafford on Boxing Day, with United looking devoid of ideas and only George Best looking threatening at times. This was followed by another dropped point in the 1-1 draw at Sunderland 24 hours later, which produced yet another lacklustre performance with the selected eleven seemingly content to absorb the home team's attacking thrusts, and then sit back contentedly instead of attempting to etch out a victory.

Two points and one goal from the two holiday fixtures was certainly not the best of form in which to end the year, but as the FA Cup beckoned it was time to step up it.

On 2 January, the Football Association suspended George Best for twenty-eight days and fined him £100 'for bringing the game into disrepute', after knocking the ball out of referee Jack Taylor's hands at the end of the Football League Cup semi-final first leg at Maine Road, having had his name taken earlier in the game for time wasting, an act that was considered 'immature' and 'petulant'. The booking remained on file as the charge was something that came under the jurisdiction of the Football Association, rather than being an offence within the laws of the game.

The decision came as a shock to both player and club, and all the Irishman would say following its announcement was that he was 'shocked by the length of the sentence. People break legs and get no more than this.' His disciplinary record could be considered commendable considering the amount of physical abuse that he had to endure week in, week out, with a mere five bookings and a sending, off over the course of seven seasons.

Losing £100 due to the fine and around £800 in wages would be no real hardship for the talented Irishman, with his many outside business arrangements, but his non-appearance on the pitch over the course of those eight weeks would certainly be missed by United, as not only had he been the inspiration behind the recent performances, there were important fixtures to be played in order to maintain a healthy League position while the FA Cup was about to get underway.

As Geoffrey Green wrote in *The Times*, 'Now he will be kicking his heels in a frenzy of frustration. He loves action and on his own admission "hates to hear the final whistle". He must now wish he had never heard it that December night at Maine Road.' Eric Todd of the *Guardian*, while not condoning the offence committed by Best, did feel somewhat sympathetic:

> No rational person would deny that the referee was right to report Best for his foolish action. But how many, like me, wonder whether Mr Taylor might have been inclined to overlook the incident or even to play it down if the game had not been televised. Television is an inconsistent witness at football matches, recording as often as not only what it thinks the public should see. Sometimes it is not even there. My own view is that if television is to be subpoenaed or used indirectly, either as a witness for the defence or for the prosecution, then it should present the case in full, not merely in extracts. Otherwise the referee, as the man in sole charge, should be left alone to administer the law as he thinks fit or, more important, as he is instructed so to do.

Before his lengthy lay-off, George Best had one final fixture to play: 90 minutes to ensure that United progressed beyond the third round of the FA Cup, a fixture in which he promised to turn on one of his more bewildering performances.

Best certainly turned it on and picked up the 'Man of the Match' award, but it was not the enigmatic Irishman, but David Best – the Ipswich Town goalkeeper, who put in a sterling display, defying United on numerous occasions. With full-time beckoning, it looked as though Ipswich had done enough to earn a replay, but their luck was to run out in those final seconds, with defender Mick McNeil achieving what United's forwards had failed to do.

Kidd gathered the ball and moved forward, as did Aston and Best, but the pass intended for the latter was a poor one and McNeil attempted to divert the ball back to his 'keeper, only to misjudge his effort and place it beyond his goalkeeper and into the net.

So, life without George Best began. For long periods during this season he had been the mainstay of the team, the man on which the hopes of Wilf McGuinness rested, but how would Manchester United cope in the Irishman's absence?

Perfectly well as it turned out, with Arsenal beaten 2-1 at Old Trafford the following Saturday, with the red number eleven shirt on the back of John Aston rather than George Best. Without the usual owner wearing it however, the attendance dropped by over 9,000 from the previous home fixture.

Without their talisman, many felt that United would struggle, developing a sense of insecurity, going on to drop points as well as league placement. The victory over the Gunners, however, was followed by a creditable 0-0 draw at Upton Park, where there was no drop in spectators, with a new ground record of 41,643 set – ninety-seven more than for United's visit the previous season.

A 3-1 victory seven days later brought widespread jubilation, not simply because yet another Best-less defeat was avoided, but due to the fact that it was against Manchester City and a cup tie to boot.

Best or no Best, there was never going to be an inch of free space in the Old Trafford terraces for this one. The stadium saw 63,417 click through the turnstiles, the majority of whom were hoping that lady luck would smile on the red shirts and that revenge for the League Cup defeat could be achieved.

City, who were FA Cup holders, were not so much beaten, but destroyed, in a game that possessed the usual edge that was so profound in local 'derby' encounters. The visitors lost Summerbee following a wild tackle from Burns in the 22nd minute, but could not really grumble as both Book and Doyle had plunged into reckless challenges with the game still in its infancy.

It was something of a surprise that it took United until the 43rd minute to open the scoring, such was their superiority and more so due to that opening strike coming from the penalty spot. Charlton had the ball in the net after half an hour, but saw his effort disallowed for offside. As half-time approached, he took up a throw-in from Edwards, drifted past two defenders before being brought down by Pardoe, Morgan beating Mulhearn from the spot.

If the game was screaming out for an individual to shine through, then he came in the form of Brian Kidd. Collyhurst-born like McGuinness, the twenty-year-old England under-23 international hit City with two goals in 15 minutes after the interval, to leave the visitors demoralised and defeated.

Five minutes into the second half, a long clearance from Stepney was pounced on by Kidd, who shook off a half-hearted challenge from Booth and raced through to put United two in front. Then 15 minutes later, a City attack broke down, Charlton cleared and once again Kidd scurried forward and as Oakes closed in with 'keeper Mulhearn advancing from his Stretford End goal, the local youngster lobbed the ball calmly over the 'keeper's head and into the yawning net.

'Hail Brian Kidd, the new King of Old Trafford', proclaimed the *Sunday Mirror*, a headline that a few weeks earlier seemed very unlikely when the hero of the moment had requested a transfer.

'If they had granted me a transfer when I asked for it I don't know what I'd have done' admitted Kidd. Explaining the reasons behind his request he continued,

> I felt I wasn't wanted after I'd been dropped and it made me so depressed that I wanted to leave. But what a difference has come over me since then. If there is any credit going for how I am playing at the moment it must, of course, go to Sir Matt Busby and Wilf McGuinness. But almost as much as them the Stretford End can take credit. They're the greatest. They make me lift my game. They can do no wrong for me. I feel on top of the world. And to think that a few weeks ago I was down in the dumps when I thought the club didn't want me anymore.

Victory was sweet, and for Wilf McGuinness it seemed as though a weight had been lifted off his shoulders, his remodelled and now rejuvenated team beginning to look the part. With the Stretford End finally giving their seal of approval by chanting his name, the United coach proclaimed that the victory was important to us, to prove we could beat Manchester City, but it is even more important to use this success as a springboard for the achievement of our ambition this season. And that ambition is to gain some material success with a place in Europe at the end of it.

European football had certainly looked a distant dream at one point, but with the City performance, undoubtedly the best the team had put together this season, a good cup run was a distinct possibility.

On the League front, United were sitting in eighth place on thirty-one points, only five behind third-placed Chelsea, but an uncatchable thirteen behind leaders Leeds United. Having crossed the Pennines on 26 January, the Elland Road side's arrival at Old Trafford heralded a coronation. It was not United crowning their Yorkshire rivals as champions elect though, but United supporter Norman Howarth scrambling over the Stretford End fencing, dashing onto the pitch as the United players warmed up and placing a 'crown' on Brian Kidd's head.

The local constabulary did not take too kindly to the impromptu coronation, and swiftly escorted Norman form the ground. Determined not to miss the match, he promptly queued up at the turnstiles again and re-entered the ground.

The visit of Leeds to Old Trafford would be an ideal test for United, enabling McGuinness to judge how far his team had come since that stuttering start. Over 60,000 were present to see the team who were chasing a domestic and European treble momentarily stopped in their tracks in a pulsating ninety minutes, which ended all square at 2-2.

Goalless at half-time, the opening 45 minutes had seen opportunities at both ends, with Kidd, Sartori, Jones and Lorimer all coming close. The game erupted into a frenzy of action 9 minutes after the interval, when Sadler gained possession 30 yards out and, without contemplating his options, drove the ball past Harvey and into the left-hand corner.

But it was a lead that United held for only 3 minutes. Sadler, again in the thick of the action, hesitated, as did Stepney, as a cross from Giles floated into the United area leaving Jones with an easy chance to equalise. On the hour, the visitors were in front; Giles picking out Bremner with precision and the diminutive red-haired Scot firing past a helpless Stepney.

Having gained the advantage, Leeds were happy to defend in numbers, soaking up the United attacks. But the red shirts persisted, and in the 77th minute it was to pay off. Reaney gave away a free-kick and the ball went from Burns to Charlton and then to Kidd. Continuing his fine run of form, the youngster despatched a 25-yard drive past Harvey to earn United a well-deserved point.

'This was the true test of our revival' said McGuinness. 'It was just starting when we drew 2-2 with Leeds on their own ground earlier this season, and tonight proved it.'

A 1-0 victory over Derby County at Old Trafford, mainly thanks to the performance of once again on-form Pat Crerand, saw United stretch their unbeaten run to ten games, with those early weeks of the season now nothing but a distant memory. Few would have imagined it possible at the turn of year with the suspension of George Best.

With Best's suspension at an end, McGuinness had no hesitation including the Irishman in his team for the fifth round FA Cup tie at Northampton Town on 7 February. Best had hinted that he would go out with a bang in his final game before the suspension took effect, but compared with his return to action, it was little more than a whimper. His return was like 5 November and New Year's Eve rolled into one.

By the end of the 90 minutes, the Northampton Town players, and even more so, their goalkeeper Kim Book, brother of City's Tony, were cursing their luck that the suspension could not have ended a few days later, as it turned out to be very definitely the George Best show. His name appeared on every headline, with his six goals in the 8-2 victory equalling the previous individual record held by Hillsdon of Chelsea in 1908, Rooke of Fulham in 1939 and Atkinson of Tranmere Rovers in 1953. Minter of St Albans had scored seven, way back in 1922, but it was in a qualifying tie and thus escaped the actual record books.

On a mud-splattered pitch, United managed to survive a couple of early scares, as well as losing Bobby Charlton with an ankle injury, prior to the first goal on the half hour, Best rising above Fairfax to head home. The same player added a second shortly before the interval.

A two-goal advantage at half-time was perhaps little more than could be expected, and few would have visualised that score line increasing to 7-0. Best adding number three, Brian Kidd number four, Best again with the fifth and sixth, and Kidd continuing his good scoring form with number seven. Even the Northampton support, who might earlier have begrudged paying £2 for a seat and 2s for a programme, realised that they were certainly getting more than their money's worth. They even got the opportunity to raise their voices, other than the moans that had echoed around the ground when Stepney saved Rankmore's penalty after McNeil pulled a meaningless goal back.

Impishly, the undoubted man of the match kept his best goal for his last, leaving the haunted looking Book lying in the mud as if he was relaxing on a sandy beach, as the Irishman ghosted past him to tap the ball home for United's eighth.

Frank Large added a second for Northampton and, when making his way back to the halfway line passed the referee, quipped 'still another seven to go', to which the match official replied 'better hurry then as you have only got a minute left'.

Sensing that that full-time was approaching, with a pitch invasion more than a possibility, Best edged his way nearer to the dressing room side of the pitch, and was first down the tunnel as the final whistle sounded.

Kim Book was obviously a little distraught at conceding eight goals, going as far as to ask the Irishman 'haven't you had enough yet?', as he walked past him after notching the eighth. 'It's the one goal they always seem to show', the shell-shocked 'keeper was to recall.

I remember thinking George was going to go one way, but he dropped his shoulder and went the other, and by then I was already on the deck. He was just too good for me. Every Friday, we would have a glass of sherry in the boardroom and our scout would go through the opponents and that week he said that if we nobbled Bobby Charlton early on, we had a chance. The trouble was that when he watched United, Best was suspended so he didn't mention him. My brother Tony was playing for Manchester City, and he rang me on the Friday night to warn me about Best, but we'd had a good week training and even though we didn't expect to win, we thought we would hold our own. We actually managed to kick Charlton out of the game early on, and at half-time I thought we were still in it, but then George put his scoring boots on. I have to hold my hand up for two of his goals but the rest were just brilliant. We were only Division Four players and not as fit as the guys are now. It's not a result I can see being repeated. A player like Best would be rested for such a game against a Fourth Division side today.

Scoring eight goals, no matter the opposition, was no mean feat and it was certainly beginning to look like United had found a new lease of life under Wilf McGuinness. Brian Kidd's fifteenth goal of the season earned both points at Ipswich, while his sixteenth, seventh in the last seven games, earned a point in a rather slovenly and casually approached 90 minutes against Crystal Palace at Old Trafford.

Had United not been so undisciplined against a Palace side so devoid of ideas, and taken both points instead of the one, they would have enjoyed the lofty position of fourth in the First Division, a point behind third placed Chelsea, but it was just as easy to say that had they not had such a poor start to the campaign, then they could well be challenging Leeds United for top spot.

Challenging for top spot they weren't, but there was a distinct possibility of silverware in the shape of the FA Cup, Middlesbrough standing between United and a place in the semi-finals.

McGuinness took his players to the cinema on the eve of the cup tie to watch *The Undefeated*, possibly in the hope that the title could inspire the visitors the following afternoon, but he always knew that it would be tough going against the north-east side, who although were in the Second Division, would be no pushovers.

Indeed, it was the home side that were the most impressive. They were disappointed to go behind to a deflected shot from Sartori in the 14th minute. Nine minutes before the interval however, they were level; Hickton, who had been leading the United defence a merry dance, scoring after mistakes by both Ure and Stepney.

'Boro hustled and bustled and closely marked the United danger men, with Tony Dunne forced to make a trio of last gasp clearances to keep the visitors in the game. Even Eric McMordie outshone his one-time travelling companion. Along with his teammates, they realised at full-time that they let United off the hook with a replay required to decide the tie.

Under the Old Trafford lights, Middlesbrough were undaunted by the task in hand, turning in a spirited performance, one that certainly signified what the FA Cup is all about. 'Not often have I seen United subjected to such relentless pressure from the elite of the First Division and of Europe,' wrote Eric Todd of the *Guardian*, 'let alone from a team, even a Yorkshire one, operating in a lower grade. Not often has a team suffered such agonies of frustration as did Middlesbrough. And not often has a team deserve extra-time at least and yet been sent away empty.'

It was a typical blood and thunder cup tie, the referee kept busy throughout, as was Stepney from the 2nd minute when he stopped a teasing shot from McMordie. His opposite number, Whigham, was also kept on his toes, twice preventing Best from opening the scoring.

But it was United who opened the scoring in the 26th minute. Crerand scurried down the left, knocking Downing aside before finding Charlton with an excellent finely measured cross. The latter's balding dome shining under the lights, meeting the ball in a packed penalty area to send it past the outstretched hand of the 'Boro 'keeper.

Unfortunate to be behind, the visitors sought the equaliser, but had to endure close calls from both Best and Sadler, while keeping their large and voracious support on tenterhooks until the 74th minute. The ball bobbled in the United goalmouth. McMordie's shot was blocked by Stepney, and as it rebounded, Hickton drove home.

Their elation was short-lived: a mere 4 minutes. Hickton, for some unknown reason attempted a 30-yard pass back, which was pounced upon by Kidd who was completely unmarked. The 'Boro scorer, attempting to make amends, sped back in pursuit, but his tackle sent the United forward sprawling and the referee pointing to the spot amid furious protests.

Morgan calmly side-footed the ball past Whigham. There was more drama to come, when Laidlaw 'scored' 10 minutes from time, only for the referee to disallow it, the 'Boro player fortunate to receive only a booking for pushing the official following his decision.

Speaking about the penalty, Whigham said, 'It was a terrible decision. There was no doubt in our minds that it was not a penalty, although I admit they should have had one earlier when Sartori was pulled down.'

Justice was perhaps done then, and United were in the semi-final of the FA Cup where Leeds United awaited.

Lady luck was certainly following United around the countryside. Perhaps that would be rephrased by some to say that the match officials were showing them a hint of favouritism, with yet another dubious penalty award going their way against Stoke City at the Victoria Ground.

United had gone in front through Sartori in the 13th minute, only to see Stoke edge their way in front through Smith and Burrows. Then, with 12 minutes remaining, Morgan raced through on goal. Gordon Banks dived at his feet and the United winger tumbled over the 'keeper's body and the referee pointed to the spot.

Earlier in the game, referee Harold Williams had twice denied Dobing a penalty when he was brought down by United defenders. Both tackles more worthy of penalty kicks than the decision made, which infuriated the England custodian and allowed Morgan to earn United a point.

So it was off across the Pennines to Hillsborough, Sheffield for the FA Cup semi-final against Leeds United, a contest between the First Division leaders and a team who, while not playing to their full potential, were enjoying a fine run of form. It was flair against aggression, skill against a purpose-built team who, although challenging for a unique treble, could not capture the imagination quite like United.

Throughout the game, there were a number of mini-battles going on in different areas of the ground: Reaney *v.* Best, Sadler and Ure against Jones and Clarke, Lorimer *v.* Dunne and Bremner, Giles and Madeley against Crerand, Charlton and Sartori. Odd points were scored, but none could combine to wrestle the advantage from the other and edge their team to Wembley.

An occasional tackle raised the hackles. Overall, perhaps surprisingly, it was a sporting 90 minutes that matched the occasion, with the Lancastrian United having the best of the opening 45 minutes, and the Yorkshiremen putting their opponents under severe pressure towards the end of the goalless encounter.

Before the two sides could meet again, United had two First Division fixtures to fulfil; first playing host to Burnley, where the exertions of three days previously were clearly visible as the visitors stormed into a 2-0 lead after only 5 minutes, a lead that had increased to 3-1 by the half hour.

But unbeaten in eighteen League and Cup fixtures, this was a United side full of determination. Despite the looming semi-final replay, as well as being without Stepney and Kidd, they hauled their way back into the game with

Law making it 3-2 in the 69th minute. Then, with Burnley thinking they had achieved a notable victory, up popped Best to equalise 3 minutes from time.

In the second of the two pre-semi-final fixtures, United travelled to London to face Chelsea in what could well be a FA Cup final dress rehearsal, the Londoners still having to overcome Watford in the other semi-final. This however, proved to be just one game too many for McGuinness's side, and the unbeaten run finally came to an end with a 2-1 defeat.

Villa Park waited to greet the two Uniteds for the modern day 'war of the roses' part two, and amid the mud and pools of water on the Midland ground, an epic encounter was fought out.

Once again, United enjoyed the best of the first 45 minutes and had numerous opportunities to settle the tie, with Kidd, Sartori and Charlton all coming close. As the second half got underway, Kidd headed narrowly over with Sprake beaten. Leeds did have odd moments of superiority, but it was almost all United with Sprake denying Morgan and Charlton shooting wide.

There was more an edge to this encounter than the first 90 minutes, with the Leeds players well aware that another 90 minutes would clutter up an already packed fixture list. As the game moved slowly towards extra-time, they looked to have the game won when Jackie Charlton rose to head home a corner. Their celebrations were quickly cut short as the referee disallowed the 'goal' for an infringement on the line by Clarke on Stiles.

Into extra-time it went and Denis Law, on in place of Sartori, should have secured victory 10 minutes into the additional 30, but headed wide from 2 yards out. Minutes later, Charlton was through on goal, but was again denied by Sprake.

Despite cramp beginning to tell as the game edged towards a second replay, the opportunities still materialised. Bremner raced through on goal, only to be brought down. Referee Jack Taylor waving away the howling protests of the Leeds players. Play quickly swung to the opposite end, but Best, like those before him, wasted a golden opportunity and overran the ball when clean through on goal.

The opportunities were many, but all failed to produce the solitary goal that would have been enough to claim victory. So the tie continued three days later with the next instalment of this thrilling trilogy, with what was virtually a home fixture for United, just a few miles along the road at Burnden Park, Bolton. But this third confrontation differed slightly from the previous two, with Leeds taking up the running from the start having had enough of allowing United to dictate the game from the first whistle.

It was a tactical decision by Don Revie which paid dividends, as after almost four hours of football, the deadline was broken in the eighth minute – 218th if you take in the previous two fixtures. Lorimer centred, and the ball was headed across the face of the United goal by

Clarke, hitting Jones on the knee. It bounced away from goal but not to safety, only as far as Bremner on the edge of the area and the diminutive midfielder rocketed the ball past Stepney.

Due to Revie's change in tactics, Cooper and Reaney were allowed to venture forward at will while Best was simply picked up by the nearest defender, allowing Leeds more flexibility in their play. Crerand and Charlton conducted United from midfield, but much of their good work came to nothing as both Kidd and Morgan were tightly marked.

Sprake in the Leeds goal was seldom tested, and it became clear that the opportunities that United had scorned in the first two games had been their best hopes for making the final. Law came on for Sartori just after the hour mark, but his only contribution was committing four fouls in 9 minutes for which he was booked.

It was disappointing to miss out on a second Final, but such was life and United had simply to get on with it and hope that they could finish in a high enough league position to qualify for the Inter Cities Fairs Cup. If those hopes were diminished slightly by the 2-1 home defeat to City and the 1-1 draw against Coventry City, then they went completely out the window with the 5-1 defeat at Newcastle. A 2-1 victory at Forest sandwiched in between the latter two fixtures mattered little.

If there was a lack of enthusiasm for the end of season fare, the news that Denis Law was up for sale at something of a bargain price of £60,000 certainly pushed Manchester United back into the spotlight.

Blighted by injuries over the past couple of seasons, many felt that the club had made the correct decision. Eric Toddof the *Guardian* wrote:

In his thirtieth year now, Law has been plagued by injuries and it must be accepted, I think, that he has passed his peak. The fact that in recent weeks he has been subjected to a series of searching fitness tests and has appeared several times as substitute surely were sufficient indications that United themselves recognised that they had had the best out of him.

The 'King' of the Stretford End had no inclination as to his dethronement:

It was disappointing news and a shock, but I am not resentful towards the club over this. Manchester United are a great club. I know many other clubs would not have seen me through injury patches as they have done. But it is ironic that the news should come just when I am fitter than I have been for some time.

I think £60,000 is a wee bit high, but this is the way transfer fees are these days. One thing is certain: I've not finished with football. I've a wife and family to think of. I've had some grand moments with United, probably the greatest was the FA Cup Final in 1963, and I hope there are some more to come with another club.

Law was not the only one heading for the Old Trafford exit door. Shay Brennan, who served the club over the course of eighteen years and for over 350 appearances, and will always be remembered as the scorer of two goals in that dramatic FA cup tie against Sheffield Wednesday immediately after Munich, was given a free transfer and a lifelong pension. Beginning in three years' time, Brennan would receive £15 per week and should his wife outlive him, she would be entitled to £10 per week for the rest of her life.

With nothing left to play for, many of the Old Trafford regulars found better things to do instead of attending the penultimate home game of the season, a mere 29,396 clicking through the turnstiles for the visit of West Bromwich Albion. Theirs was a foolish decision, as they were to miss a goal feast, with the Midlands side beaten 7-0.

Even less appetising for the supporters was the FA Cup third place play-off, two days later against Second Division Watford at Highbury on the eve of the cup final.

Taking the place of the England v. Young England fixture, only 15,105 bothered to attend, which United won 2-0 and at times was played at a leisurely pace. The pricey admission charges, which saw receipts of only £8,279, and the unappealing Friday night date kept many away.

The season drew to a close with a 2-1 defeat at Tottenham and a 2-2 draw against Sheffield Wednesday at Old Trafford, leaving United in eighth place. They headed off across the Atlantic for a close season tour that encompassed America, Canada and Bermuda, giving Wilf McGuinness time to contemplate the previous ten months at his leisure.

Finishing eighth in the First Division, eleven points behind champions Everton and reaching two domestic cup semi-finals, could be considered a more than favourable start for the novice 'manager'. Had it not been for injuries to the likes of Denis Law, Bobby Charlton's loss of form, lengthy suspensions of John Fitzpatrick and George Best, they could have secured a place in the Inter-Cities Fairs Cup. Who is to say that the League Cup would not have been won had it not been for Alex Stepney's semi-final error? McGuinness himself said,

> I was neither unhappy about my efforts during my first term in charge nor despondent about our long-term prospects. We had finished in eighth place in the First Division, three places better than had been managed by Sir Matt in 1968/69 and we had reached two semi-finals, both of which had been lost by the narrowest of margins. I thought too, despite

a few scurrilous rumours about dissatisfaction in the ranks, that we were a generally happy crew. Overall, it didn't seem too bad for somebody coping with a monumentally steep learning curve, and I was content with that, with two years of my contract left to run.

Everything in the garden, however, was not rosy. The roots of disarray and turmoil had already taken a grip. George Best more than anyone, had not simply dug the furrow, but scattered the seeds that would cultivate in the following weeks and months, entangling the club like a weed that nothing would deter.

It is difficult to say when the thorn first pierced McGuinness's side, but the public were certainly put in the picture regarding the Irishman's off-field activity in the middle of the Leeds United FA Cup trilogy. It was brought to their notice that on the afternoon of the first replay at Villa Park, instead of relaxing like his fellow teammates in their Droitwich hotel, Best was passing the time of day with an unknown female.

McGuinness, noticing that his star player was not with the others in the television lounge, began searching for him, discovering that he was in the room of his new 'friend'. Annoyed to say the least, McGuinness was in a no-win situation, with a dilemma over whether or not to play his main asset. Unable, or more to the point, simply not wanting to make the decision, he passed the buck to Sir Matt Busby. 'Play him' was his answer, although he was later to fine the player and warn him as to his future conduct.

Some members of the team considered this to be the wrong decision and were partly justified in their opinion due to Best's performance at Villa Park, where he looked far from his usual self, falling over the ball at one point when through on goal.

It was the beginning of the end.

3

THE REVOLVING DOOR IS IN MOTION

The summer of 1970, much to the confusion and dismay of the United supporters, saw no activity on the transfer front, despite the lack of firepower upfront and the sometimes fragile defence. A handful of the promising youngsters from the Central League side – John Connaughton, Tony Young, Willie Watson and Tony Whelan – were taken on the close season tour, due to Stepney, Kidd, Stiles and Charlton all missing the World Cup, and not because they were considered money-saving stars of the future.

One would have thought that the last thing any of the players wanted was a tour that took them away from home from 24 April until 19 May, taking in seven fixtures, two against representative X1's in Bermuda, followed by fixtures against Bari, Celtic and Eintracht Frankfurt in Canada and the States, but the financial side of things was more important than the playing staff's recuperation from a long hard season.

The tour was also to produce a mini-riot during the game against Bari in New York, with the referee taking both teams off the pitch for 20 minutes due to a pitch invasion by unhappy Italian supporters following Sartori's controversial winner in the 2-1 victory. There was also the on/off substitution of Francis Burns in the fixture against Eintracht Frankfurt in Los Angeles. Starting the game in the number four shirt, he was substituted by Steve James in the 35th minute, only to come back on eleven minutes later to replace Paul Edwards. With 20 minutes remaining, he was again replaced, this time by Willie Watson; then with 10 minutes to go, he came on for Pat Crerand.

The meeting on 11 May between Celtic and United in Toronto was to take on a much bigger mantle than a simple close-season meaningless friendly. Unbeknown to Wilf McGuinness, rather lengthy talks had taken place between Busby and Jock Stein as regards to the Celtic manager moving south to take over a similar position in Manchester.

Lengthy meetings were held between the two Scots and rather surprisingly, it was not a well-kept secret as Stein's assistant, Sean Fallon, and the Celtic players were well aware of what was going on and were far from happy. Celtic historian Steven Sullivan was to add:

I think Stein was fed up with a few things in the summer of 1970. There was a bad atmosphere after Celtic losing the European Cup final. The United job was certainly something that had instant appeal to Stein, as there was something of a strained relationship in the east end of Glasgow at that particular time, following the club's European Cup final defeat by Feyenoord. With his mind in turmoil as regards the approach, he actually packed his bags and left the tour, returning home to Glasgow to talk things over with his wife and family. The offer to manage Manchester United was to remain on the table indefinitely.

There was interest from both sides of the border regarding signing Denis Law, with one or two clubs reportedly toying with the idea of taking him off the Manchester United payroll. But niggling away at the back of everyone's mind were the knee injuries that had prevented him from racking up more appearances in a red shirt. Law himself was unperturbed by the lack of interest, and simply got his head down to some pre-season training. His teammates were on the opposite side of the Atlantic, and keeping himself fit for whichever club was paying his wages during the coming season, he saw his determination pay off with a place in the United side for the Watney Cup tie against Reading.

Elm Park was a far cry from some continental destinations for a pre-season warm-up, but there was once again some financial gain to be made from the inaugural, brewery-promoted competition, which saw the two top-scoring clubs from all four divisions invited to participate. For the clubs in the top flight, it was limited to those who had not qualified for one of the European competitions. United's sixty-six goals were actually the fourth best in the First Division, only four behind third-placed Chelsea. A trip to Reading would also work out less expensive than taking a squad to the likes of Denmark, more so when they had just returned from America a couple of months previously. But having made a profit of £48,700, the highest since 1957/58, money wasn't exactly a problem, something Wilf McGuinness was hoping would aid his planned rebuilding.

Against Third-Division Reading, with Denis Law back on the United side and looking faster and sharper than he had done for some considerable time, United overcame the attack-minded home side. Reading happily played with only four established defenders in their line-up and had no real hopes of progressing to the semi-final stage, so much so that they had organised a friendly against Glentoran that same night.

Goals from Paul Edwards and a Bobby Charlton double saw United go through by the odd goal in five, although there was never any fear of a shock result in the warm summer sunshine. The victory produced a semi-final tie with Hull City at Boothferry Park.

Hull, never overawed by their opponents, took the lead in the 11th minute. It was not until 13 minutes from time that Denis Law equalised, pushing the game into extra-time. With no further scoring and a place in the final to be decided, the 34,007-strong crowd were treated to the first ever penalty shoot-out at senior level in domestic football.

Robert Oxby of the *Daily Telegraph* wrote that it 'must be rated a resounding success. The suspense as five players from each side fired alternatively was almost intolerable.' For whom, he didn't say, but goals from the spot by Best, Kidd and Charlton were equalled by Neill, Butler and Houghton before Law saw his effort saved by McKechnie.

With advantage to Hull, Wagstaff fired wide. Morgan restored United's lead and the outcome now balanced on the final kick by McKechnie. Face-to-face with his opposite number Alex Stepney, the Hull 'keeper saw his shot cannon off the crossbar and bounce over. United were in the final.

Having enjoyed lower league opposition in the two previous fixtures, United now came face-to-face with fellow First Division side Derby County, who had finished fourth and eight points better-off the previous season, although having scored two goals fewer.

This particular 90 minutes, still deemed as a friendly rather than a competitive fixture, was seen as more of a challenge for United. It was one that they failed miserably, losing 4-1 in an embarrassingly one-sided game, with headlines screaming 'McGuinness has more problems.'

Those problems were not simply due to their 'unimaginative' play, with their performance considered as a 'contender for the worst opening ever'. McGuinness also had the added worries of injuries to Morgan, Stepney and that man Law again – his hamstring this time rather than his knee. All were considered a doubt for the opening fixture of the season against Leeds United.

As if they had not seen enough of the Yorkshire side in the previous campaign, a better and indeed easier start to the League campaign would have been wished for. Even more so following the solitary goal defeat, during which United constantly lost possession due to careless and wasteful passing, with a number of players failing to show any real conviction.

Starting a season with two home fixtures, a full quota of points would or should be expected, but one point was all United had to show for their first 180 minutes of football at Old Trafford, having drawn the second fixture of the new season against Chelsea 0-0.

Back on the ground where they had lifted the FA Cup four months previously in the most physical display of football ever witnessed at the ground, in their confrontational replay against Leeds, the Londoners did in the end hold on for a draw, but without a goal in their opening two games, United had much work to do.

The lack of goals was clearly worrying, with a move for Southampton's Ron Davies once again being touted. A fee of £180,000 was earmarked for the twenty-eight-year-old and a deal seemed within touching distance. It fell through at the last minute due to what was given as 'financial problems'. Closer to home, it was suggested that Busby 'dissuaded' his successor against making a firm offer, telling him that it was a lot of money for an old player.

Davies would have been welcomed with open arms by McGuinness, but the man who was now considered 'manager' rather than simply 'coach' had a preference for Luton Town's goal machine – twenty-year-old Malcolm MacDonald, a player he had been to watch in disguise from the terracing towards the end of the previous season.

'I was mightily impressed' said McGuinness and, following his detailed report to the man with the chequebook, Matt Busby and Jimmy Murphy also did an undercover job to watch the player.

According to McGuinness, an approach was made to Luton and United were given first refusal on the player. Something he found strange and was to say,

> This mystified me because that April we allowed four of our players, including Jimmy Ryan and Don Givens to join Luton. I don't know why United did not twist their arm over that package deal by telling them that they could forget signing our quartet unless they sold McDonald to us. If I had been a bit more experienced I'd have pushed harder for that, and even to this day I can't understand why Matt didn't go in a bit harder if he truly rated the player, as he assured me he did. Certainly it is fair to suggest that Malcolm McDonald would have been a sensation in a side that contained the likes of Best, Charlton, Law, Kidd, Morgan and Crerand.

But what of the player in question? Was he aware of United's interest and why did no deal materialise? Looking back, he related the following:

> In the latter months of the 1970/71 season, while playing for Luton Town in the Second Division, I was very aware of interest in me from the higher division clubs generally. But interest specifically came to me on the Easter Sunday in the centre circle of Kenilworth Road. We had a promotion chance until the Good Friday and Easter Saturday matches ended in defeat (Bristol City 3-2 Luton Town, then Millwall 4-0 Luton Town). We were in for light training on the Sunday with a match, Leicester City at home, the following day.
>
> After a few final sprints, coach Jimmy Andrews told the squad to head for the dressing rooms and to have a good soak in the steaming plunge bath and get a massage if you wished.

Manager Alec Stock then appeared from the tunnel and motioned for me to about turn and follow him. He stopped in the centre circle of the pitch in the echoingly empty Kenilworth Road ground and looked constantly over his shoulders and mine as well, to ensure we were not going to be overheard.

He said, 'Well you see, old son, promotion is now out of the window with these last two defeats. Easter always catches the weak out, and we weren't quite there for the run-in, were we? So that leaves the club in its usual financial plight and the only solution at a time like this is that you have to sell your prize asset to survive to the following season, and that, old son, is you. Now the news I'm going to impart must stay strictly between you and I and you must not breathe a word to anyone, ok?'

I nodded assent.

Good. Now, old son, there are three serious contenders for your signature ready for next season. They are Manchester United, Chelsea and Newcastle United. All you need is to keep sticking it in the old onion bag until May, got it?'

Harry Haslam, my old mentor from Tonbridge, Fulham and now Luton Town had told me some months before that Manchester United were checking me out quite thoroughly, and were liable to put a private detective on me to see what my living style away from football was.

No worries there, I was young, married, a father and had a three-bedroomed detached house in a lovely village in Bedfordshire, and of course a mortgage to pay. The odd night out following a match would be to Caesar's Palace in Luton, where my wife and I, along with teammates and wives would be welcomed in to a terrific cabaret table.

We saw wonderful acts such as Bob Monkhouse, Bruce Forsyth etc. A couple of pints of beer would be sufficient for the night.

Alec Stock had said to keep sticking them in the onion bag, and that's precisely what I did. He had given me a target of thirty goals for the previous season. I apologised to him at the end of the last match, having only got twenty-nine.

This season, however, with four games less, I was given the identical target to hit. Come the final league match of the season, Cardiff City (fifth placed) at home (with us immediately after them) and us needing to beat them by two clear goals to go into the Watney Cup instead of them, I was one short of the target set me of thirty.

Also, Alec Stock had made it abundantly clear this would be my last game as a Luton Town player, but, I was still sworn to silence. I did detect a couple of knowing glances from him as we prepared to exit the dressing room.

In the dressing room after the final whistle everyone was delighted. We had beaten them 3-0 and qualified for the Watney Cup. I went across to Alec Stock and said well there you are, boss. I got your thirty goals, plus one that I owed you for last season and there's an extra one for luck, I had scored a hat-trick in my last appearance for Luton Town.

Alex Stock looked at me and said you'll need some bloody luck where you're going this summer. Come and see me 10 a.m. on Friday, I might have some news for you.

I was there at the same time as he arrived from the Great Northern Hotel, King's Cross. 'I've just agreed the final deal for you; £185,000. Go and see Joe Harvey at King's Cross and sting 'em for every penny you can get. Good luck, old son'.

There was never a further mention of Manchester United after that Easter. I would have had to be pushed hard to consider Chelsea, being a Fulham fan. So Joe made the early move and it paid off.

Manchester United did all the early front running, but when it came to doing the business they went missing. And their demise that followed in such sad fashion in the following three seasons made me appreciate Newcastle United all the more.

Putting him on the spot, I asked 'If United had made an offer for you, would you have considered it and eventually moved and would you have picked them above Newcastle?'

'I certainly would have considered any approach made by Manchester United whilst I was at Luton Town.'

Malcolm replied.

If it had been an offer similar to Newcastle United I would have considered it, certainly. But there was one thing that Joe Harvey did that convinced me absolutely that a move to Tyneside was right. He warmed me to the history of the 'number 9' scoring and captivating hearts. I'm not so sure that Manchester United have ever been a club to state to a prospective signing, 'You will be in the first team and everything built around you.' That's how Joe had made it feel for me, and he lived up to his word. Would I have picked Manchester United in front of Newcastle had it been a straight choice? I think I would have to say no. My consideration is that, at the time, they were in a bit of managerial upheaval after the retirement of Sir Matt.

So no Ron Davies, no Malcolm MacDonald, no Mick Channon (who had also surfaced on the radar), and no goals for a third consecutive game as the trip to Arsenal saw United left reeling on the ropes with only three games of the new season played. Goalkeeper Alex Stepney suffered a dislocated shoulder just before half-time, with the score 2-0. He could not be faulted for Arsenal's third just after the break despite his injury, and he was eventually replaced by David Sadler who went on to concede the fourth. All this, however, took nothing away from the home side's dominance and the visitors' abysmal afternoon in north London.

Frank Butler in the *News of the World* asked if it was 'too early in the season to ask is this the end of an era?' adding that he had 'never seen a Manchester United side so devoid of energy and the quality to fight back'. He went on,

> They had come to Highbury, the scene of many past triumphs and brought a galaxy of stars. There was Denis Law back at inside left to partner George Best, the most feared winger of them all. In the middle was Bobby Charlton. And Nobby Stiles, Pat Crerand, Ian Ure and Alex Stepney were in the big parade. It was like putting on a first night on Broadway with all the stars names up in lights. Then someone forgot to switch on. The battery was dead. There was no spark in the side and we watched, instead, a side of ghosts.

Butler's opinion was shared by many, with one unnamed Arsenal player, although not wanting to dismiss United as challengers, adding 'they have so many brilliant players that it was astonishing to see them give the ball away so often. We are not complaining, but it was a little sad to find them so disordered. It isn't a team I would like to be playing in.'

It was certainly troubling times on the banks of the Manchester Ship Canal, and an influx of new blood into the system would almost certainly have had a massive effect, lifting both team and support. Respected journalist Ken Jones commented that the recent interest in Ron Davies had much to commend it, but he pulled no punches in his assessment of the team.

> While opponents have begun with a fair measure of fitness and cohesion, United have seemed to acquire these things through their opening games. First Division managers have had good cause to bless the computer when it has sent them to Old Trafford in August rather than April.
>
> United have begun badly again – struggling to arrange their individual talent into a comprehensive and influential pattern. The faults are familiar but it's now becoming increasingly harder to put them right.
>
> In their efforts to establish a definitive pattern of play, United seem torn between deploying their men in a practical fashion and playing to the strength of highly skilled individuals.

Even allowing for Law's threatening willingness in the air, their attempt at playing with three and sometimes four forwards is immediately devalued by the absence of a tall, strong and mobile target, who would increase the permutations available to their midfield men.

But perhaps the most disturbing feature of their game is the refusal of experienced players to accept that the real antidotes to poor form are graft and determination.

Where do United go from here? There is little conviction that they can do well this season, although the possibility of them ending up in trouble is immediately dispelled by their skill and spending power.

Despite their expansive style, little comes out of Old Trafford, which Manchester United do not want made public, and the elements of doubt must be pieced together from muttered complaint.

The player who says, 'At the moment we need four footballs to play with', may not be far from the point. But there is no eagerness to elaborate, no conscious attempt to blame any one player for the team's shortcomings. On the other hand, there seems little eagerness to put things right. Some might worry over their individual form. Others might live with the conviction that things will change as they have always done. It's not bound to happen that way.

And this was only the third game of the season!

A trip to Burnley followed. A short coach journey from Manchester, but one always viewed with trepidation. With the jury out, debating their verdict on the current United side and their recent performances, they viewed this fixture with close intensity and came back with an overall majority vote of 'not guilty'. Any presiding judge, however, would have resisted the option of letting them off scot-free and instead putting them on probation for a short period of time.

It was Denis Law who restored faith in the mediocre United side, claiming both goals in the 2-0 win. The employment of Fitzpatrick and Stiles in midfield, the former moving back from the inside forward position he had recently filled, and the latter replacing Pat Crerand, added an extra dimension to United's play.

Against West Ham United at Old Trafford, a Fitzpatrick goal earned a point, but it was the re-emergence of Denis Law that gave United a glimmer of hope that the early season cobwebs had been blown away, with a superb vintage display by the Scot inspiring a 2-0 home victory over Everton.

Anfield was next up for the revitalised United, and it was a satisfied Wilf McGuinness who left the Liverpool stronghold with a well-earned point. 'We are not getting too excited' proclaimed the United manager, 'but I think we can feel pleased with the way things are settling down.' Law was another who left Merseyside with a smile, saying 'at last I really am 100 per cent fit. It's great to walk off the field, not limp off it and not have to worry, even if you feel all right then, what the Monday medical will bring.'

But, as in the past, just when United seemed to be back on course and ready to compete on the domestic front, the past came back to haunt them.

There were warning signs in the League Cup second round tie at Aldershot, where they scraped through 3-1. Although this was considered as nothing more than the Fourth Division side lifting their game against the 'big boys', but the 90 minutes against Coventry City at Old Trafford, a 2-0 victory, kept the signs of recuperation well to the fore.

Although not getting his name on the scoresheet, Denis Law continued to impress. A shadow still hung over his United career though, as his availability was still something for debate. He still carried a £60,000 transfer tag around his neck and although Wilf McGuinness enthused about his performances, saying after the victory over Coventry, 'brilliant … brilliant. He's playing in matches as he did in training last season', there had never been any official announcement as to his future.

His name remained on the available for transfer list and all that Sir Matt Busby would say was 'just forget he was ever available', with McGuinness adding 'he remains a United player. No one has had the courage to ask about him.' But surely now, having proved his short-term fitness at least, United would not sell. The club, with two men in the driving seat, still seemed unwilling to clear up the mystery surrounding a player vital to their future at the present time.

Suddenly, due to their on-field performances, United found themselves back under the microscope, with Ipswich Town tearing them apart at Portman Road in a 4-0 blitz. A performance that showcased everything that was bad about the current United side – an unstable defence, non-combative in midfield and a completely ineffective front line.

Blackpool arrived at Old Trafford on 26 September, placed second bottom of the First Division. They gave United a frustrating afternoon though, so much so that the home support felt inclined to slow hand clap and jeer their incompetent team as they struggled to hold onto a point in the 1-1 draw. McGuinness had rung the changes in an attempt to boost his beleaguered side, bringing in Willie Morgan, Steve James, Willie Watson and Francis Burns in place of Stiles, Ure, Edwards and Dunne, but the performance was still erratic and cohesive and the slide continued at Wolverhampton seven days later, losing by the odd goal in five.

A solitary 1-0 win over Portsmouth saw progress on the League Cup front, but Bobby Charlton's 500th League appearance at Crystal Palace, followed a week later with his record breaking 199th league and cup goal, brought little cheer from a 1-0 defeat. In the space of a month, United had plummeted from eighth to seventeenth.

It had certainly been an indifferent start to the season, so much so that it would have seen many others (having endured a similar couple of months) plunge into the transfer market in an effort to improve both performances and playing personnel. At Old Trafford however, there was something of a reluctance to do so, with Sir Matt Busby asking for patience at the annual AGM, while hinting at an excellent crop of youngsters coming through the ranks, with seven having been sent to the England youth trials. Unfortunately, there remained something of a blinkered view regarding the club's youth system, with the quality of those moving through the ranks being far removed from the halcyon days of old. Of the seven, Tony Young, Tony Whelan, Eric Young, Brian Greenhoff, Billy Fairhurst, Tommy O'Neil and Kevin Lewis, only one would have a lengthy and productive career at Old Trafford, while Lewis would certainly make the headlines, almost claiming a niche of his own in United's history, but unfortunately not in the way Busby envisaged.

Numerous players and clubs, who were finding life difficult at the wrong end of the League table, looked upon cup ties as a break from the norm, a chance to play at a more relaxed pace, without the fear of defeat nudging one's team closer to the brink. Victory of course was always paramount, a craving necessity, another step on the road to silverware, but unless it was in the semi-finals or the final itself, defeat was a little easier to accept. There was also something about a cup tie under the floodlights, something a little more magical, with the ground taking on a completely different look while creating an atmosphere that Saturday afternoons can't re-create.

Such was Old Trafford on the night of 28 October 1970, when Chelsea journeyed north for a League Cup fourth round tie, playing their part in one of those games that stay in the mind for a lifetime. Though perhaps not the entire 90 minutes, just a few jaw-dropping seconds of individual brilliance.

A Bobby Charlton goal in the 29th minute gave United the lead, following one of those runs that look designed to hit a brick wall, but instead produced a drive from all of 25 yards, through the smallest of gaps, that left Peter Bonetti grasping in thin air as 'we're going to Wembelee' vibrated from the Stretford End.

Six minutes later, Chelsea were level with a goal of equal panache, John Hollins controlling a loose ball, before firing past Stepney. A minute before the interval, the visitors thought they had scored a second, Hutchinson prodding the ball home, but referee Keith Styles deciding there had been a push by a blue-shirted player prior to the ball crossing the line.

Luck was certainly not on Chelsea's side, as they were denied a penalty on the hour when Steve James brought down Hutchison, but there was no luck involved in what materialized 10 minutes later.

John Aston collected a pass midway inside the United half and moving forward, he held the ball until George Best broke forward, who perfectly measured the pace of the ball as it rolled into the Irishman's path just inside the Chelsea half. The 40-yard race on goal was now on. Best, with his red shirt flapping in the night air, pursued by three Chelsea defenders.

As he neared the edge of the penalty area, with Ron Harris inching closer with each stride, the Chelsea defender suddenly lunged at Best from behind. The tackle momentarily knocked the Irishman off his stride. Regaining his balance, he stepped to the side of Bonetti before slipping the ball between the post and a static Marvin Hinton on the goal line. His momentum kept him moving towards the packed Stretford End, before sinking to his knees, arms aloft, savoring the moment in front of those who worshipped him most.

Weller rattled Rimmer's crossbar in the 77th minute. Try as Chelsea might, they could not breech the resilient United defence, the home side holding on to claim a place in the last eight.

It was a result that simply papered over the cracks.

Off the pitch, Alex Stepney handed in a transfer request, having lost his place to Jimmy Rimmer back in August, the young 'keeper being one of the next generation of players that McGuinness visualised as the future. Stepney's request was politely rebuffed, but would be reviewed again at the end of the season according to Busby. While on the pitch, Newcastle added to the problems with a 1-0 victory at St James' Park.

But still United bounced back: a point in a 2-2 home draw with Stoke City, followed by the first away win in the league for three months at Nottingham Forest. The 2-1 victory brought some much-needed relief to Wilf McGuinness, as did the 4-2 quarter-final League Cup win over Crystal Palace. A Wembley cup final appearance was now only one step away.

But United had already got their hands on silverware a fortnight earlier, although it was a trophy that would not appear on the Old Trafford role of honour, never mind looking good on Wilf McGuinness' CV. The *Daily Express* National Five-a-Side trophy just did not have that special ring about it.

Today, such a tournament would see fringe players sent to what was then known as the Wembley Pool. Despite a packed fixture list, the quest for points in the fight for survival and the threat of injury, the six man United squad read Stepney, Fitzpatrick, Sartori, Sadler, Charlton and Best.

Defeating Celtic 4-3 on penalties, a young Kenny Dalglish scoring for the Glasgow side and an equally young Lou Macari missing his spot-kick, the second round match against Ipswich Town also ended level and again went to penalties. It required two rounds, the second phase of sudden- death kicks being taken from further out than the first. This did little to deter United, and Charlton's kick was enough to put his team in the semi-finals.

Crystal Palace, as in the League Cup, were determined to halt United's progress. George Best took centre stage, and his two goals plus another from Sartori saw United through to the final where Tottenham Hotspur lay in wait.

Best however, was now on-song, and although this was no major venue, or indeed competition, he was still the maverick producing moments of magic. Knowles gave Spurs the lead, only for Best to equalize with an audacious effort, kicking the ball off an opponent's shin before firing home the rebound. He then took things a step further, running out of his own half, past Knowles, wrong-footed England, before shooting past Hancock. The 8,000 spectators rose as one to acclaim the goal.

The dependency on George Best was huge. Before, it would be the goals of Denis Law that would more often than not see United through, but the 'King', his injury problems seemingly behind him, had been eased back into something of a midfield role. But Best alone, despite his brilliance, could not carry United forward.

Each 90 minutes of league football seemed to push the former European champions further down the table, dropping three places in three weeks, the defeat at Southampton and the home draw against Huddersfield doing little to ease the sense of turmoil around the club. And it wasn't only the league position that was on a downward slide, as Old Trafford attendances had also suffered with 59,365 having watched the opening-day encounter with Leeds United, dropping to 45,306 for the recent visit of Huddersfield Town.

For too long the support had stood firmly behind the team, but there were now rumbles of discontent. 'There's nothing wrong that a couple of signings would not put right' proclaimed Sir Matt Busby, to which was echoed, 'then why have they not been made?' Names had been mentioned, as they had been last season, but nothing concrete had materialised, with Wilf McGuinness (and Sir Matt Busby?) seemingly living in the hope that a new crop of young players would surge through the ranks to grasp first-team places. Strong the likes of Paul Edwards, Steve James and Alan Gowling may have been, but such youngsters could not be expected to carry an ailing team.

It was certainly not a question of money, as a profit of around £100,000 had been made for the past four seasons, around half of which had been lost in corporation tax each year. For a club such as United to be somewhat reluctant spenders was something of a mystery, splashing the cash on only three occasions over a six-year period. A mere £230,000 on Alex Stepney (£50,000 in September 1966), Willie Morgan (£100,000 in August 1968) and Ian Ure (£80,000), was pocket money for a club of United's standing.

There was therefore little doubt that sometime very soon, a considerable sum of money would have to be paid out, as seven members of the team, Bobby Charlton, Denis Law, Pat Crerand, Nobby Stiles, Ian Ure, Tony Dunne and Alex Stepney were all aged between twenty-eight and thirty-three; not past it by any means, but certainly now in the twilight of their careers. Many sensed that there was reluctance for the club to actually open the chequebook.

Despite the trials and tribulations, the players kept their own counsel, with little making its way over the walls of the Cliff training ground. Perhaps the nearest any of the squad came to voicing their opinion and any direct confrontation was through Bobby Charlton, the United captain using his regular column in *Goal* magazine, where his contribution was little more than 'a general piece about all clubs, players and aspects of the game'.

But for once he diverted off the straight and narrow, and under the headline 'Stop knocking me and Manchester United', he wrote the following:

I hope you will forgive me if I devote the column this week to answering critics who have been having a go recently at my club and myself. To hear some of these people talk you would think that Manchester United were on the skids.

Just because we're not up there among the first three, these critics are saying it is going to take years for United to get back to the top – if they ever manage it at all.

We all know at Old Trafford that we haven't exactly set the world on fire with our soccer so far this season. We have been too inconsistent to present a challenge for the title. But against teams we should be beating – Blackpool, Ipswich, Crystal Palace, and I mean them no disrespect, we have fallen badly.

This inconsistency has been our biggest problem, and a lot of it has stemmed from injuries to key players.

Alright, we won't win the League this season, but I am more convinced than ever that the future of this club is bright. People have moaned that United haven't gone out to buy players to help ease the situation. To that, I say, what is the point of wasting money on players who are no better than the ones already on the staff. The great players are simply not available.

To the doubters and moaners, I say, be patient, Manchester United will come again. There is too much ability on the staff for us to fade away.

Strong words in defence of the club, but his comments would leave many supporters scratching their heads in bewilderment, although the 2-2 draw against third-placed Tottenham at White Hart Lane went as far as to emphasize everything that was good and bad about the modern-day United. Law and Fitzpatrick added to the excitement by squaring up to each other during the game.

Despite United's failings, they were still a top attraction; 55,693 flocking to north London for the confrontation with Spurs. However, few would have clicked through the turnstiles to see the likes of Fitzpatick, James and Aston, while no one outside the away support, with some of them being equally ignorant as to who Watson, the red-shirted number two was. The man they had handed over their hard-earned money to see was undoubtedly George Best.

Best was the idol of thousands, a modern-day footballer in every sense of the word, an individual who had the world at his feet and opponents in the palm of his hand. He lead those defenders a merry dance, as he did with the United management, but at times he still required an arm around his shoulder and guidance along what was often a bumpy road.

Having outgrown the lodgings of Mrs Fullaway in more ways than one, he plunged some of his ever-increasing bank balance into property. For him, it was not to be a house hidden away behind high walls and gates and even higher trees, but what was in effect a goldfish bowl.

Custom built, at a cost of £35,000 in Bramhall, Cheshire, his new home was basically a flat: three large rooms over a double garage and a games room, a sunken bath, a large 'L' shaped living area where the television would appear down the chimney, a small compact kitchen and two bedrooms. Strangely, the same orange-coloured carpet could be found in every room.

The architect behind it all, Frazer Crane of Building Design Unit had watched Best play and confessed:

When I sat down to prepare my sketch schemes for the house, I concentrated on his performance. My interpretation of his football is simple and clean yet with extremely complex undertones, which I hope my critics will feel I have achieved, at least in some way, in the building I have designed for him.

The house on its own would have attracted much attention due to its modernist look, but it was common knowledge as to who owned it, with it quickly becoming a magnet for children and adults alike, all hoping to catch a glimpse of the United superstar. But for one young United supporter, he was to get more than just a glimpse of the outside.

As a child growing up in Salford, a 10-minute walk away from United's Cliff training ground, Paul Anthony (many years later to enjoy a spell as a presenter with MUTV), was always going to be a United fan and his love for the club and George Best in particular was to provide him with an unforgettable experience.

During the school holidays I would spend pretty much every day at the Cliff, standing at the gate waiting for the United players to arrive for training. In those days you were allowed into the training ground to watch as the players were put through their paces. My idols were there for all to see: Denis Law, Bobby Charlton, Paddy Crerand, Brian Kidd, David Sadler, John Fitzpatrick, Nobby Stiles and of course the unmistakeable George Best, all training under the watchful eye of Matt Busby.

Then after training, we would hang around the car park waiting for the players to emerge so that we could get their autographs. They always obliged.

Of course Bestie was the star man. He was the superstar both on and off the field, opening his fashion boutique in Manchester and had started a 'fan club' for his adoring fans to get to know even more about him.

The monthly newsletter and magazine had pictures of 'Georgie' in action, in his shops or standing by his car, as well as a personal letter from him, and every so often there would be a competition which offered his followers the chance to win some fantastic prizes, such as a pair of Stylo Matchmaker boots with laces along the side, just like he wore, a signed replica Manchester United shirt, small size, a year's free subscription to the George Best fan club and even a VIP visit to watch United in action at Old Trafford.

I remember entering every competition, including the one that had a prize that money could not buy. On this particular occasion, the first prize was a visit to George Best's futuristic luxury home in the leafy suburbs of Bramhall, Cheshire.

To this day, I still remember the question I needed to answer – 'Where does George Best originate from?'

I couldn't complete the entry form quick enough; '16 Burren Way, The Cregagh Estate, East Belfast, Northern Ireland.' I'm sure that wasn't the answer they were looking for, as either Belfast or Northern Ireland would have sufficed, but hey, if you know the answer, then go for it.

The entry form was duly posted and I waited, along with hundreds of others, to see if I would be lucky enough to win this awesome prize.

Four weeks later, a letter arrived from the George Best Fan Club, addressed to me personally and signed by the fan club secretary who I think was called Anne.

'Dear Paul, Thank you for your recent competition entry and congratulations, I am pleased to tell you that you have won one of the first prizes. We will be in touch shortly to arrange the dates and times for your visit to Chez Sera. Congratulations once again, Anne'

At first I thought it was my dad winding me up. He was a big City fan who, when I had entered the competition, told me that entering was a waste of a stamp, but it couldn't have been him: the postmark on the envelope was from Cheshire.

Sure enough, two days later I received another letter telling me that I had indeed won the first prize and, along with two other members of the George Best fan club, I would be spending a day at his house and would be meeting the man himself.

The day arrived, I know it was a Monday because I had to get special permission to take a day off school with instructions from my teacher, Mrs Twiddle, that I had to write a project about my day, when I came back into school.

A car came to our house in Wellington Street, Salford, and I was whisked off to Stockport where we picked up another fan club member and fellow winner, I think his name was Gary, but I can't remember. From there it was on to Bramhall and to Bestie's house.

We arrived at about 11 o' clock and was greeted by Anne, the fan club secretary. She invited us in and took us both to the living room, which I remember had huge windows that went from the floor to the ceiling. There were wooden floors and a giant, white sheepskin rug. The furniture was very futuristic, orange chairs that I remember thinking looked like giant oranges with a piece cut out to sit in. There was a big TV, much bigger than the one at home, and lots of pictures of George, some with his mum, dad and sisters and others with what I suspect now was his girlfriend, who at the time I think was Siv Hederby, although at the time I wasn't sure as he had so many.

While we were being shown round, Anne told us that George was at training, but that he would be meeting us when he had finished.

We were shown into the kitchen where there were sandwiches and orange juice set out on a big glass table. Both me and Gary were invited to sit down and help ourselves while Anne told us about the fan club.

As we were eating the salmon paste sandwiches the doorbell rang and Anne promptly disappeared to come back a minute later accompanied by Moira, the third winner who had arrived from Belfast, she obviously knew the answer to the competition question. It later transpired that she lived two streets away from the Best family home. If she didn't know the answer, nobody did.

Because Moira had missed the initial tour of the house, we were shown around again, back into the living room and then to the bathroom which had a huge bath and a shower, something of course that we never had at Wellington Street. A bath shared with my brothers was as much as I got.

We were then shown downstairs to the underground garage that housed George's E-Type Jaguar. It was big enough for two cars and I remember seeing a punchbag hung up in the corner and a set of weights lying on the floor. Bestie obviously kept in shape at home as well as at the Cliff training ground.

We sat and chatted for what seemed like ages and then the moment arrived. As if by magic, George Best appeared at the door of the living room. I remember to this day he was wearing purple flared trousers, a black polo neck sweater with a medallion and a black leather bomber-type jacket.

This was awesome, here I was a young kid from Salford in George Best's living room just feet away from the great man.

As if he needed to, he introduced himself, 'hi I'm George', as if I didn't know. Anne then introduced us to him: 'this is Paul, Gary and Moira'.

George shook our hands as we were introduced and started asking questions, 'Where did we live?', 'How long had we been members of the fan club?' 'Had we ever been to Old Trafford?' and ' Who was our favourite player?' – bet you can't guess who we all said?

Then we had another tour of the house, this time it was George doing the guided tour telling us how long it had taken to build, how he had enjoyed staying in lodgings with Mrs Fullaway, how he had always known he was going to be a footballer, but never missed school, how his father 'Dickie' had always encouraged him to play and how he missed home when he came to Manchester. He spoke about United being the greatest team in the world, he mentioned Bobby Charlton and Denis Law, but said his best friends at United were Paddy Crerand and David Sadler and said Matt Busby looked after him like his dad.

While he was talking, we went downstairs to the garden which was pretty big and had goalposts with a net at one end. Needless to say, George decided that we should kick a few balls into the net. We all took turns in goal while Bestie took penalties against us, not one of us saved any. Then it was our turn against George; three penalties each, the winner would get a special signed prize. Gary went first, the first one went in, the second was saved and the third went wide. Now it was my turn: first one was saved, the second went in and the third was saved by George. Now it was Moira: first one went in, the second went wide and the third went in with George standing there laughing.

Moira, the girl from Belfast, had beaten the boys and had won herself the football we had been playing with and it was duly signed by George.

Me and Gary protested that it had been a fix, 'no way' was the reply from the goalkeeper.

All too soon the day was over. George thanked us for being members of his fan club, we all had pictures taken with him before he gave us a pack which contained signed pictures and a copy of the *George Best Fan Club Magazine* along with a certificate to show that we were competition winners and had been to his house.

As we were shown to the door, he again shook our hands and bade farewell before we were chauffeured back home to reality.

It was a day I remember vividly and will never forget, apart from Gary. George was a brilliant man who had taken time out of his playboy lifestyle to meet some of his younger fans. My only regret is that after leaving school at the age of fifteen to join the Army, I never kept any of the mementos from the day, but I have the memories and for me they will be there forever.

There's nothing quite like a local 'derby' encounter to put a spring in the step and banish all thoughts of what has gone on before – well for 90 minutes at least. The eighty-third meeting between United and City at Old Trafford was, however, not one for the red faction of Manchester to dwell upon as it was a shameful encounter, tarnished with petty fouls, niggles and nastiness. It also did little to waylay the home support's opinion that their favourite's current form was, as Bobby Charlton had suggested, little more than a blip with the corner soon to be turned.

City were superior in every department and well worth their 4-1 victory. There are often crumbs of comfort in defeat, but on this occasion for the vanquished there was nothing.

Francis Lee was responsible for most of the damage, claiming a hat-trick in a 16-minute spell; Mike Doyle, who detested all things red, having given City the lead with only a quarter of an hour gone. Brian Kidd grabbed what could be very loosely termed a consolation in the 74th minute, but the main talking point occurred in the 25th minute when Best and Pardoe went for a 50-50 ball, which the United player won. However, it left his opponent in agony on the mudded ground, with what was to turn out to be a double fracture of his right leg. Best was booked for the tackle, following a lengthy chat between the player and the match official. Many felt the decision was harsh. Others considered it lenient.

It was certainly all doom and gloom, with power cuts causing much upheaval across the country due to industrial action by power station workers. Everyone was inconvenienced. Hospitals had to cancel operations, journeys to and from work were made in the dark, while sales in candles hit a post-war high. Whatever small glimmer of light they offered could do nothing to dispel the huge dark shadow that hung over Old Trafford.

December 16 allowed United the opportunity to redeem themselves in the eyes of the British footballing public, while reigniting the belief that their own supporters held in them, with the visit of Aston Villa to Old Trafford for the first leg of the Football League Cup semi-final.

Their opponents, once fellow First Division stablemates, but now languishing in the depths of the Third Division, offered a clear indication and timely reminder as to how far and how quick a team could actually fall.

Victory in the League Cup would ensure entry into the Inter-Cities Fairs Cup. Something of a backdoor into European football, but one that was ajar and would certainly not be laughed at nor ignored by United. Even against a team from a lower division, United's confidence was low, although their performance was certainly an improvement on that of four days previously, but it still fell short of what was required. Villa on the other hand, with little to lose, showed enthusiasm and industry in abundance.

The visitors had the ball in the net after only 5 minutes, Lochhead heading home an Anderson corner, but the referee judged Rimmer to had been impeded. As for United, the closest they came to scoring was when Fitzpatrick shot against a Villa defender, as the United forwards attacked only spasmodically while the defenders performed in an erratic fashion.

Then, 4 minutes before the interval, Old Trafford was stunned when Andy Lochhead, who always had the better of Steve James, gave Villa the lead. Hamilton pushed the ball into the area and the Villa number nine forced the ball home. It was a short-lived lead however, as with the first half moving into stoppage time, Sartori crossed into the Villa penalty area and Kidd met the ball in mid-air, scoring with a spectacular scissor kick.

United desperately tried to gain control in the second half, but there were no further goals. The general view was that having done the hard part, the Third Division side were now favourites to progress into the final.

'The decline and fall of Manchester United continues at an alarming rate' penned journalist Alan Hart following the 3-1 home defeat by Arsenal, as the crisis around Old Trafford deepened. Sharing that same press box was Bill McFarlane, not one of its usual occupants as he was more adept in scribbling about the likes of Rangers, Celtic or Heart of Midlothian for the Scottish *Sunday Post*. An unbiased viewpoint would therefore be more than welcome here.

McFarlane began by stating that one of his objectives for journeying south was to find out 'what had gone wrong with the great Busby Babes', not, please note, Wilf McGuinness's team. During his journey by taxi to the ground, he admitted that his driver, himself a United supporter, had told him that 'United are still a great bunch of individuals, but no longer

MANCHESTER UNITED
DIVISION ONE
1973-74

Back row (left to right): ARNOLD SIDEBOTTOM STEVE JAMES ALEX STEPNEY JIMMY RIMMER JIM HOLTON PETER FLETCHER
Middle Row: SAMMY McILROY IAN MOORE TREVOR ANDERSON ALEX FORSYTH MICK MARTIN MARTIN BUCHAN
Front row: WILLIE MORGAN TONY YOUNG LOU MACARI GEORGE GRAHAM GERRY DALY BRIAN KIDD RAY O'BRIEN

Alex Forsyth. Scottish international signed from Partick Thistle in December 1972 for £100,000.

Alex Stepney. Top of the United goal scoring chart with two penalties during 1973/74.

George Best rounds
the Sheffield
United defence at
Old Trafford in
October 1971 before
scoring one of the
outstanding goals of
his career.

Action during the
Daily Express
five-a-side tournament
at Wembley in
November 1970.

Left: George Best
scores against Spurs.

Below: Best again
in action, this time
taking on Celtic.

Ian Storey-Moore. Signed from Nottingham Forest via Derby County for around £225,000 in March 1972.

Iam Ure. Former Arsenal defender who was to team up with his ex-sparring partner Denis Law at Old Trafford, in August 1969.

Jim Holton. He wasn't 6 foot 2, neither were his eyes blue, but following his transfer from Shrewsbury Town in January 1973, he was to soon become a cult hero of the Stretford End.

Jim McCalliog. Yet another Scot who joined the Old Trafford tartan army, but sadly his goals in April 1974 failed to prevent relegation.

September 1972, and Ian Moore heads home in United's 3-0 victory over Derby County, the team he almost signed for.

Left: Denis Law turns away after scoring 'that' goal for Manchester City at Old Trafford in April 1974.

Below: A jubilant Lou Macari after scoring on his debut against West Ham United in January 1973.

Right: Lou Macari. His Old Trafford career was almost over before it got started.

Below left: Malcolm Musgrove, Frank O'Farrell's assistant during his brief stay at Old Trafford.

Below right: A trade card showing Mick Martin, a £25,000 signing from Bohemians in January 1973.

Another of those best from Best goals. This time at Old Trafford against Chelsea in the 1970/71 Football League Cup.

United's Daily Express five-a-side winners – David Sadler, Alex Stepney, George Best, John Fitzpatrick, Bobby Charlton and Carlo Sartori.

Pat Crerand. The former half back was to become Tommy Docherty's assistant manager.

What every well-dressed Stretford Ender was wearing in 1973.

Sammy McIlroy scores on his league debut against Manchester City at Maine Road in November 1971.

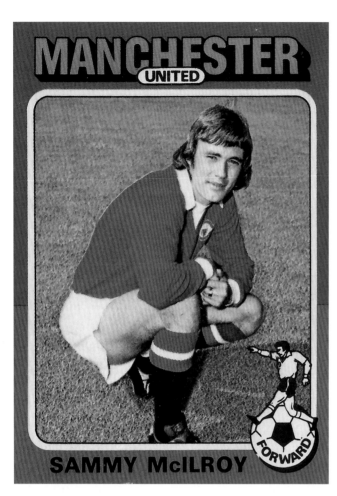

SAMMY McILROY

Left: A trade card showing a young Sammy McIlroy.

Below: Alex Stepney scores from the penalty spot against Birmingham City in October 1973.

STEVE JAMES

STEWART HOUSTON

Trade card showing defender Steve James.

Trade card showing full back Stewart Houston in the unfamiliar yellow jersey.

Ted MacDougall celebrates after scoring against Liverpool in November 1972.

United go down

Law sinks Reds: Saints, Brum win: WH draw

Colin Barrett of Manchester City (left) does a good job of marking United's Jim McCalliog as he covers the back of Manchester City goalkeeper Joe Corrigan in the derby game.

Dozens ejected

Manchester Evening News headlines following the 1-0 home defeat by City in April 1974.

Tommy Docherty. A man of many words.

Ted MacDougall signs on the dotted line. A £200,000 record fee from Third Division Bournemouth.

The goal that never was against AC Milan in the European Cup semi-final second leg at Old Trafford, May 1969.

Tony Young. Urmston-born youngster who made his league debut as a substitute against Ipswich Town in September 1970.

Trevor Anderson. If you weren't Scottish, you had to be Irish, the twenty-one-year-old joining United from Portadown in October 1972 for £20,000.

Above left: Wilf McGuiness who had the unfortunate job of succeeding Sir Matt Busby.

Above right: Wyn Davies became one of the few players to represent both Manchester United and Manchester City when he signed in September 1972.

Left: Willie Morgan. Former Burnley winger who joined united in August 1968. He was later to have an infamous row with Tommy Docherty.

a great team.' McFarlane was to quickly admit that he had not tipped the man enough, exclaiming,

> How right he is. From start to finish, Rimmer, Watson, Crerand, Morgan, Best and Sartori were tremendous performers. And, although each of them turned on what was little short of sheer poetry, a layman would have thought he was having his leg pulled when told of United's ignominious league position.

Summing up his visit, and United, the Scot penned, 'I never thought the day would dawn when a Manchester United side would be slowly hand-clapped from Old Trafford, but yesterday was the day. One final thought for United, is Bobby Charlton now a luxury they can no longer afford?'

David Meek thought that there was now a nervousness about playing at Old Trafford, with opposing teams no longer venturing to the Stretford area of the city with emphasis on defence. They were now happy to attack, knowing that a result could be achieved. As this was something the home support was unfamiliar with, their apathy was picked up upon by the players with Pat Crerand saying that he 'didn't think the fans appreciated them much these days and that attitude was hardly inspiring to the players'. Alan Gowling added that he thought expectations were too high at Old Trafford, and less trying away from home. Excuses?

If a casual observer could detect the faults surrounding Wilf McGuinness and his team in a random visit, then within the corridors of Old Trafford those same faults must have been painfully obvious for some time.

Stepney had already hinted at a move, with teams such as West Ham, Everton and Cardiff all keeping an eye on things. Stiles was a target for Hull and Middlesbrough, while Morgan was another who, while languishing in the reserves, could be prised away for the right fee.

Stiles was soon to make the agonising decision to leave United, saying,

> I have been considering this move all season. Even thinking of leaving Old Trafford after fourteen years is like cutting off my right arm. But I have made my decision now. I told Wilf I quite saw his point of view in dropping me for the Arsenal game and he knew that my decision does not hinge on this. I have felt that I have been losing my enthusiasm through being in and out of the team, and I enjoy football too much to be stuck in the reserves for long spells.

Nobby was asked by McGuinness to hold off with a written request until after the cup ties were out of the way, but the player was adamant that he wanted to leave. 'I am determined now. I have lost enough sleep over making the decision, but there will be no going back. It is not a case of leaving a sinking ship because everybody knows I would give my last drop of blood for United.'

Stiles remained a United player until the close of season, before stepping into the Second Division with Middlesbrough.

Few would have travelled to Villa Park for the second leg of the League Cup semi-final with confidence, but when Brian Kidd put United in front with only 14 minutes gone, hopes of Wembley were rekindled. Perhaps the five changes McGuinness had made to the team from the first leg were going to make that vital difference, with Crerand, Ure, Morgan, Sadler and Law all hoping to restore some pride and prestige.

Dunn in the Villa goal saved from Morgan as United pressed forward, but 8 minutes prior to the interval, the home side equalized. A one-two between Godfrey and Bradley on the right carved the opening and Lochhead beat Ure in the air to head home.

Kidd again put United in front 3 minutes into the second half, only to be denied by the linesman's flag. Rimmer saved well from McMahon as the game flowed from end to end, Villa slowly chipping away at their visitors defence, their persistence paying off in the 72nd minute when Lochhead flicked the ball to Anderson and from the former United player's cross, McMahon headed the ball past a helpless Rimmer.

United were down and out.

Boxing Day saw United at Derby County, where they were a goal behind after only 4 minutes, then two behind 17 minutes later. Surprisingly, Law pulled a goal back in the 55th minute, then Best equalized 2 minutes later. Law struck again in the 59th minute, but Hector once again leveled the score in the 67th minute. Gemmill scored Derby's fourth 3 minutes later, only for Kidd to score a fourth for United. Wilf McGuiness proclaimed,

> I was pleased with the way we played in the second half, and the way the lads came back after being two goals down suggests to me that the spirit is right.In fact, if we can fight back like that in one match, we can fight our way back from our disappointing run of recent weeks. When Derby went ahead I thought it was going against us again, but after the interval we opened up and played the right way, both tactically and in our attitude in the game.

Pleased he might have been, and his hopes of something of a resurgence in recent form were well intended. Three days later however, Wilf McGuinness was no longer the man in charge of Manchester United.

There had obviously been discussions at board level regarding the current situation the club found itself in. Performances would have been analysed, as would the training and the overall capability of Wilf McGuinness as manager of Manchester United. For Sir Matt Busby, it would have been somewhat tormenting, as not only was McGuinness a former player of his, it was his decision to have the former reserve team coach appointed as his intended successor.

The newspaper headlines of 30 December were bold and brash. 'McGuinness Is Sacked' were the three words that they all carried, and although one or two others were added in the various titles, none were really required as those three were simply enough.

For a brief four months McGuinness had held the title of manager, but at 11.15 on the morning of Tuesday 29 December, the following statement was released at the Old Trafford by Sir Matt Busby:

The directors had a special meeting last night to discuss the performances of the team and decided to release Wilf McGuinness from his duties as team manager. As he did not wish to leave the club, and as the club felt he still had a part to play, he was offered his former position as trainer of the Central League side, which he has accepted. The board have asked me to take over team matters for the time being and until a new appointment is made in the close season. Things haven't quite worked out the way we would have hoped. We were looking for continuity but unfortunately it has not worked out. I thought that all these team worries were behind me now, but it is that club that counts. And, the situation is now that I shall do anything I can to get results going our way again.

Somewhat strangely, Busby added, 'I think perhaps Wilf is still a bit raw and young. But it has been good experience for him.'

Although the headlines had screamed that McGuinness had been sacked, they were wrong, as he had merely been demoted back to reserve team trainer. Many would have walked away from Old Trafford, heading up over the railway bridge and onto Warwick Road, making off into the distance to pastures new. But McGuinness was red through and through and announced:

There was so much I had hoped to do, but it was not to be. Obviously this is a disappointment to me. But managers have to be judged on results. I still feel I have a part to play with the club and I am happy to stay. This is going to be a great club again and that is all that matters in the long run.

The man who covered Manchester United for the *Daily Mirror*, Derek Wallis, was one of many journalists who added his opinion to the headline-grabbing story.

I say that Sir Matt Busby must not hand over again until the club have been steered clear of the collision course with disaster they were on already when he relinquished control in the first place. I do not suggest that Sir Matt deserted the ship with the bridge already awash at the end of a twenty-year reign in which United won everything worth winning.

I do suggest though that at the time of his part-retirement, deficiencies in the team were obscured by hysterical acclaim of their European Cup triumph against a Benfica side that later event showed were also on Skid Row.

The shortcomings, which began to erode the shell of the team, spread alarmingly. But ambition had been achieved and there appeared to be a certain complacency about Manchester United ... almost as if everyone at Old Trafford believed they had a divine right to football's major prizes.

This then was the inheritance of Wilf McGuinness, a beginner at the management game in which the throw of the dice depends not so much on the way up it lands as the ability to switch it when your opponent is momentarily distracted.

He never had a chance. As he prepared for his first season in charge, I wrote 'now United must stand trial. And into the dock with them goes Wilf McGuinness. I do not envy him his job. If he is successful, he will have achieved nothing new. If United fail to make an impact then he too must fail in the eyes of the public utterly spoiled by success. Manchester United have not failed because McGuinness failed, but because McGuinness was appointed too soon. Before he was ready and more important, before the team were ready.'

Even the placid, uncontroversial weekly publication *Goal* could not keep the goings-on out from among their full page photographs to the stars of the day. Its editor, Alan Hughes wrote,

Matt Busby is a prisoner of his own success. While Matt is at Old Trafford, how can Busby United become Manchester United?

United can argue for as long as they like that McGuinness had complete control. But that was theory. In practice, the ship had two captains, and between the pair of them almost everything – and that includes discipline – fell apart.

Hughes went on to point a finger at the current squad saying,

United have never had so many players as they have now who have made no significant progress in the last two or three years ... players like Aston, Burns, Sartori, Fitzpatrick, Gowling, James. But they stay on at Old Trafford because United have failed to produce any better.

He also added that because the flashes of genius from the likes of Charlton and Law were now infrequent, it was clear that there were too many average players at the club, that the transfer market had not been exploited and that there was a problem with George Best.

In the *Sun*, Frank Clough added his two-pence worth:

> I believe McGuinness's problems started when he decided to drop Charlton for an away match at Everton last season.
>
> They were close friends since boyhood and, rightly or wrongly, some of the players believe that McGuinness sacrificed that friendship to hammer home to all the players that he was boss.
>
> There have been too many rumours of resentment and rifts between McGuinness and the players for all of them to be lies and unfounded gossip.
>
> For weeks the football grapevine in Manchester has buzzed with a persistent story that the players had signed a round robin asking the club to relieve McGuinness of his job. When this was put to Busby, he said: 'I cannot and will not, answer that sort of question. I believe that too few senior players had faith in his tactics, his ideas of how the game should be played, his thoughts on team selection and on team discipline.'

If others could see the problems, then why could those closer to centre of things not do likewise?

Did McGuinness get a fair crack of the whip then? Brian Kidd is quoted as saying to his teammates, when the squad was told the news, 'It's you lousy bastards that have got Wilf the sack.' One Collyhurst lad looking after another. To what he referred to is unknown, but it was rumoured that some of the players were too close to Sir Matt Busby, while others claimed that Wilf had a poor relationship with a number of those under him. 'He had never been anywhere' and 'he was a no-hoper' were just two of the quotes from those under him.

Alan Gowling spoke more of 'Wilf's inexperience', going on to say, 'When initially offered the job, one he was never going to refuse, his lack of managerial experience was always going to tell.' But given more time, did he think Wilf could have turned it around?

> I don't know, George, I suppose didn't help, but I think some of the senior players felt threatened in some way, as they were getting on in years and they were not able to cope with the change. No one likes change.
>
> While not criticising Wilf in any way, Sir Matt was charismatic and had the backing of all the players, who were in effect his players and Jimmy Murphy's players, and when Wilf was attempting to change things, there was an uncertainty with people who were unsure as to what would happen.

An atmosphere was created and in the end, I am convinced it was player problems that caused the axe to fall on his head. He couldn't overcome those which had arose with the senior players.

From a fan's perspective, London Red, Alan Tyler, followed the club home and away, penning the match reports for the newsletter of the *London Fan Club,* and viewed the McGuinness reign as follows:

Managers come and go with varying levels of success and longevity, but Wilf McGuinness was different. Following Matt Busby's retirement, his appointment as head coach in the summer of 1969 at the age of thirty-one was, in management terms, almost as bold a move as the introduction of the Busby Babes. How appropriate for someone who himself had been one of those Babes.

From his debut as a seventeen-year-old in October 1955, we had followed his career with interest. At first, as an enthusiastic defensive wing-half, he seemed destined to be an eternal understudy for Duncan Edwards and when United signed Stan Crowther after Munich, he seemed set to play a similar role. However, the following season, he established himself in his own right and won two England caps before a badly broken leg in a reserve game against Stoke in December 1959 appeared to have ended his playing career and he was appointed to the coaching staff.

Amazingly, more than six years later, he attempted a comeback, playing more than thirty games for the reserves, but the closest he got to first team action was as United's substitute at Leicester in November 1966. Sadly, he wasn't called upon and that particular dream ended, but we then remembered his fist pumping encouragement to the team at Wembley prior to extra-time against Benfica in the European Cup Final. We knew that Wilf McGuinness was a fighter and felt he was one of us. We viewed his appointment with optimism and his departure eighteen months later with the 1970/71 season with real sadness. So, what went wrong? The first half of the 1970/71 season displayed many of the same characteristics as the one which preceded it. Writing in November 1970, I described the month as seeing 'the continuance of United's Jekyll and Hyde form, but fortunately most of the Hyde was restricted to the League performances.

Throughout his time in charge, many of United's older established stars struggled against injury or loss of form: Crerand, Stiles, Charlton and Law included. Even Best had his off days, though, in the main, he remained the team's shining star. At the same time, some of the youngsters struggled to establish themselves as chances were given to Paul Edwards,

Don Givens, Carlo Sartori, Steve James Alan Gowling, Jimmy Rimmer, Tony Young, Willie Watson and Ian Donald. McGuinness made only one major signing, Ian Ure from Arsenal, but he was to prove inconsistent and at times hapless.

That is not to say that it was all bad. When on song, United's attack remained a match for anyone but defensive frailties, particularly in the air, often let them down and the team seemed to lack confidence in going forward for fear of what they would leave behind them.

Having reached the semi-finals of both the League Cup and the FA Cup the season before, most of United's best performances were again in cup competitions. Their League Cup campaign started rather shakily at Aldershot and was followed by a scrappy home win against Portsmouth. However, things improved with a spirited home win against Chelsea, including the famous Best goal as 'Chopper' Harris attempted to separate his legs from his torso and a fine quarter final win against Crystal Palace. Two pulsating and memorable semi-final matches against Aston Villa followed before United went down 3-2 on aggregate. Not too bad you might think, but the problem was that Villa, at that time, were a Third Division side and for much of the two games, outplayed United.

In other cup competitions, United won the National five-a-side Championships at Wembley on one of the best evenings I have ever spent at a football event, with Best the star of the final. They also reached the final of the pre-season Watney Cup before losing 4-1 to Derby. Perhaps the fact that McGuinness locked the players in the dressing room afterwards for a post-match inquest should have given us some inkling of what was to come. Sadly, whatever he said, if the team's performances in the League were anything to go by, they weren't listening.

Though poor starts in the League were also the norm during Busby's reign, United were into their fourth game before they managed to score a goal and there were some truly awful performances, notably 4-0 losses at Arsenal and Ipswich and defeats at home to Crystal Palace (1-0), Manchester City (4-1) and Arsenal (3-1).

Their best performance was probably the 2-0 defeat of the previous seasons champions Everton at Old Trafford (though Everton came into that game with even fewer points than United). When United then followed this by taking the lead in their next game at Anfield, it looked as though things were improving. Although they emerged with a draw, United's second half performance left much to be desired and they struggled to hit the heights thereafter.

McGuinness' last game in charge at Derby on Boxing Day was at least memorable. Three weeks earlier, we had had something of a preview in a thoroughly entertaining 2-2 draw at Tottenham on a very muddy pitch.

At Derby the score was doubled and the pitch was even worse! In many respects, this game typified McGuinness's time in charge.

On a Christmas pudding of a pitch, United reached half-time two goals down after Ure had given away an unnecessary free-kick on the edge of the penalty area, which Dave Mackay smashed home, and an attempted clearance by Law had been returned with interest by Wignall. Gloom all round.

After another suicidal back-pass from Ure had almost cost a third goal, United threw caution to the wind and what a game we had. Two goals from Law and one from Best in the space of just 4 minutes put United ahead. Back came Derby with goals from Hector and Gemmill to lead 4-3, before Kidd levelled again. Wonderfully entertaining but littered with mistakes.

Three days later, with United fifth from bottom, McGuinness stood down to the genuine disappointment of most United fans; not because we felt he had been particularly unfairly treated ... in truth the team showed no real progress during his time in charge and, towards the end, appeared to be disintegrating alarmingly ... but because we had so wanted him to succeed. It felt a little like a death in the family.

The press was awash with the change of leadership at Old Trafford, trying to predict who would take over and why McGuinness failed. Some went as far as to point the finger at Busby for the club's current plight. Brian Clough, never one to shirk an issue, wrote,

This week's events at Old Trafford merely emphasized the one occasion when Sir Matt failed. For all the wonderful service he had given United, he could have had a crowning moment of brilliance if he had gone gracefully out.

There was no need for him to nominate a successor. He could have bowed out quietly, but because he didn't do so, the blame for the fiasco United went through then, and are going through now, can only be laid right at Sir Matt's door.

It is a long time since we offered sacrificial lambs in this country, but McGuinness was virtually one. From the day he took over he never had a chance.

Another journalist, Alan Smith, added,

No one can run United while he [Busby] sits just along the corridor. No matter what position or title he takes within the club, only he will be regarded as boss. There is only one way in which any manager can follow

Busby, and that way is for Busby to lock his door, hang a sign on it 'Gone Away' and let the new man do the job the way he sees it has got to be done.

Jimmy Ryan had been at the club in those halcyon days when the League and European Cup were won, but had left for Luton Town towards the end of the previous season. He recalled,

> I'd had a feeling for a year or so that maybe I should leave. The thing is, it's a very difficult thing to break ties with a club like United because they have always been very much a family type of club you know, and it's a great place to be. I think really that I should have left a year before that. So when finally Luton came in, we went down, me and another player called Don Givens, who joined together, we were impressed with it. We were impressed with what they said, we were impressed with the little club, and even got that kind of homely feeling that you got at United. So it was a relatively simple decision to make.

But what did he make of his former manager's sacking?

> I had moved to Luton and was more concerned with my own problems, adjusting to a new club, buying houses etc. My feeling is that the fantastic team that had won the European Cup was breaking up and the contrast in age and experience between Wilf and Sir Matt made it very difficult for him to create his own team. He certainly lacked the gravitas of Sir Matt, and perhaps the difference in personality was hard for the players and the board to adjust to.
>
> Also, although this may seem very simple, it may just have been that Wilf was not cut out to be a manager. He was not particularly successful in any of his subsequent managerial jobs and it may be that his talents were best suited to the development of younger players! This sort of thing happens quite a lot in this country and many good youth coaches are victims of their own ambition!

'We shall again advertise the position of a new team manager at the earliest opportunity' announced Sir Matt, but it had not been advertised previously. No sooner had the newsprint dried on the 'sacking', than the press was full of speculation as to who the new manager would be. 'People are tied up with contracts at the moment' the new short-term manager added, 'but obviously it will be an outsider this time' and there were plenty of candidates put forward.

The early favourite was former club captain Noel Cantwell, the current manager of Coventry City, who had also been to the fore prior to the appointment of McGuinness. A former member of the West Ham school of football, he was highly regarded by many, as was another former Hammer, Frank O'Farrell, who had cut his managerial teeth with Weymouth and Torquay before moving to Leicester City. Another former United player, Ian Greaves, now with Huddersfield Town, was also a front runner, as was Bill McGarry of Wolves, Don Howe of Arsenal and Burnley's Jimmy Adamson.

But Matt Busby was once again the man in charge, for the short-term at least.

> I didn't want to have to take charge of the team again – but my directors asked me. At my age, I feel I have had enough of managerial worries at team level. It means becoming involved again and getting with the players.
>
> I shall be at some of the training sessions and maybe put a tracksuit on occasionally. It's something I think I am still capable of doing for a while – but I would have preferred that we weren't in this situation. It is unfortunate that things haven't worked out. I feel very sorry for Wilf, who was appointed on my recommendation.
>
> I see my task very simply, very clearly. I have to make Manchester United look like Manchester United again, a team who play football, not only because they get paid for it but because they love it and their personalities demand that they play it a certain way. United aren't finished by any means. We can be back – and soon.

Rather surprisingly, Sir Matt Busby made no changes to the United line-up for his first game back in charge: the Third Round FA Cup tie at Middlesbrough on 2 January. Wholesale changes were not expected, but if this was the best available, then McGuinness was possibly dogged by bad luck as much as anything, or were the players, like Kidd had apparently suggested, not playing for the manager?

As it turned out, not only was the team the same, but so was the performance on the rock-solid Old Trafford pitch. United had the best of the first half, but just could not break down the Second Division side's defence. After the break however, the visitors came into their own and were unfortunate not to progress into the next round. Rimmer saved United on more than one occasion, while Hickton hit the post 20 minutes from time when he should have done better.

From an ice-bound Old Trafford to a snow-covered Ayresome Park three days later, United's troubles intensified when they became the first big name casualty of this season's FA Cup. Goals from McIlmoyle and Downing, in the 7th and 74th minute, added to United's fast fading reputation, with George Best's last-minute goal not even worth considering as a consolation.

Sir Matt Busby had only been back at the helm a matter of days, with his unwanted problems intensifying with the cup defeat at Middlesbrough. As if he did not have enough on his plate, his problems were soon to intensify one-hundred fold with something that had been slowly simmering away undetected for some time, only now for it to come to the fore and signal the beginning of the end.

With United due to visit Chelsea, George Best's phobia of railways and train stations once again forced him to miss his third train in a month. The Irishman had missed training on the Friday morning and had not met up with the rest of the United party for the 1.30 p.m. train to London. He later flew south, despite being told by Sir Matt Busby 'not to bother', with the United manager adding,

> Best will not now be playing against Chelsea. He has been told not to travel to London and the matter will be dealt with by the directors later. George didn't report for training this morning. Naturally I'm unhappy about it. To be frank, the boy has not been doing it for us in recent weeks. I just don't know what's wrong with the lad. Something seems to have upset him. Perhaps his life outside football has got something to do with it. I just don't know.

On 5 December, Best had missed the train to London for the match at Tottenham, but had played in that particular fixture. Then, as recently as four days before his latest misdemeanor, he had been three hours late in turning up for a disciplinary hearing, again in London, after missing not one, but two trains to the capital. He had also missed training on Christmas morning and been fined £50.

At the FA disciplinary committee hearing, where he was in trouble for having received three bookings in the past twelve months, he was fined a record £250 and given a suspended six-weeks sentence. His explanation of turning up late due to not feeling well was accepted by the committee.

Against Chelsea, the Best-less United, but with Stepney and Stiles back in the side, perhaps inspired more than deflated by the Irishman's absence, turned back the clock and recorded their first win in eleven games with a 2-1 victory. The Stamford Bridge side, with only one previous home defeat, were no match for the visitors and had even taken the lead, but United fought back with a Morgan penalty and a second from Gowling to take both points.

Having travelled to London, Best avoided the team hotel. Instead he made his way to Islington and the flat of actress Sinead Cusack, where he remained for the rest of the weekend, practically under siege once the media discovered his whereabouts, as did children from a nearby school, with around 100 of them actually managing to force their way into the block of flats, hastily followed by television crews, only to be forced outside again by the police.

Best was adjudged to have said that there had been no intentions of either catching the train, or playing against Chelsea and he wanted a showdown with the club, although he was not going to ask for a transfer. His problems, he insisted, were all football-related and he wanted to meet with Sir Matt, and if necessary, apologise for his actions.

On the Monday, Sir Matt Busby spoke of the ongoing problem.

I haven't heard from George all day. I'm upset and feel terribly let down. We have always had a father and son relationship. I thought I could confide in George as much as he would confide in me. It seems to have been a crazy day. I had to sit back down and remember he is a grown man and not the soccer 'babe' I introduced to United. I am disappointed and tired. But now I am firmer than ever. George must come to me, I will not go to him for talks. He must get to grips with himself and come to me as a man before I can discuss his future.

Busby later released a club statement which read, 'George Best did not turn up for training this morning and we have had no contact with him. I have been in contact with my directors over the telephone and we have decided to suspend the player for fourteen days as from today.'

Despite the olive branch from the United manager, Best's business partner, Malcolm Mooney, added coal to the fire before setting off for London in order to bring his wayward friend back to Manchester to face the music.

Sir Matt Busby has taken the easy way out and made the Best headhunters happy. I think the public and the club are pushing George too far. He is on the verge of a nervous breakdown. During the past few days he has been turned from an ice-cool man into a highly emotional wreck. He is sick of criticism. He is sick and tired of being blamed for Manchester United's poor form. He has every justification to hang up his boots. He has enough interests outside the game to keep him happy financially for the rest of his life.

Following his four days in exile, Best returned to Manchester to face the music, and following a 50 minute meeting with his manager, he told the waiting press that,

It was completely wrong and I know it. I have apologized to Sir Matt and the United club for the way I have behaved. I came to see the boss today and I have told him everything. The problem is private and personal. I won't tell anybody. The only person I can speak to about it is the boss. I think the problems are on the way to being sorted out. They are problems only two people know about, and the boss has very kindly let me have two days to have a rest and start all over again. I'll never be a naughty boy again. Now I am going to change my image. I have decided the jet-set life and soccer don't mix.

But he was also to add that the team's loss of form had been part of the problem. He continued,

I was playing well at the beginning of the season but my form has suffered since and I have blamed myself for not being able to help the team out of the doldrums. I have been stupid in trying to make my protest this way. I hope my teammates don't think I have been testy – I know some of them have been quite concerned about the way I have been behaving. All I want to do now is to get away for some peace and quiet. Then I can put my heart back into the game again.

So life went on and United struggled to get a point against bottom of the table Burnley at Old Trafford, the brightness from the win at Stamford Bridge once again dimmed. A 2-0 victory in Ireland over Bohemians, although nothing to be excited about, did produce one hint that perhaps there was a future at the club, following a 45 minute cameo appearance by sixteen-year-old Sammy McIlroy, who scored United's second with a fine 12-yard drive.

Suddenly, the shackles were removed and with United having struggled to grasp odd points here and there over the past few weeks and months. The return to the fold of George Best brought a marked improvement to the side, or at least something did.

Huddersfield were beaten 2-1 at Leeds Road. Tottenham, by the same score line at Old Trafford a fortnight later with George Best scoring with a precisely measured chip over the heads of five defenders and into the net. Next came a defining 5-1 victory over Southampton, also at home, where Alan Gowling took the plaudits with four of the goals. But with the Old Trafford crowd having been lukewarm to recent home displays, and justifiably so, the demolition of the south coast club was watched by only 36,000, almost 13,000 less than had turned up for the previous home fixture.

Matt Busby was by now growing fed up with his position as stand-in manager, wishing the season would hurry up and finish so that he could get his life back to some sort of normality and more so that the club would finalise the appointment of a new man to take over the day-to-day running of the club.

Jock Stein's name had been widely mentioned in the press when McGuinness was demoted, although none were aware that he had been approached several months before. But with the season drawing to a close, United once again sounded out the Scot as to whether or not he wanted the job, with the actual position now available, putting greater pressure than before on the Celtic manager.

By now the Celtic board was well aware of United's interest, and began to put pressure on Stein to make up his mind once and for all. Despite everything he had done for them as a manager, they were quite forceful in their method of persuasion.

At a board meeting, talks of the manager's position was high on the agenda with the minutes reading: 'It was agreed to put out to the manager that he was being paid a very high salary, that loyalty to the club should play a very important part in his thinking and that "we were not prepared to enter into an auction"'. They also stated: 'The chairman, who was not present, was very much in agreement and very disappointed that he should be so tempted.'

Such were the concerns within the Glasgow club, that Celtic captain Billy McNeill approached his manager, wanting a reassuring response that the rumours regarding Manchester United were nothing more than that. McNeill left Stein's doorstep, stunned by the admission that his boss had indeed been approached and offered the Old Trafford job and not only that, was considering accepting the offer.

Filling the Old Trafford managerial position was of utmost importance and, with half a dozen games of the season remaining, Pat Crerand was given the job of contacting Stein and according to Stephen Sullivan who spent a number of years writing for the Celtic website and club magazine,

> Matt Busby, having made his initial approaches through Pat Crerand, met the Celtic manager at a motorway service station near Haydock on 14 April 1971. Terms were discussed and, seemingly, agreed. But within 48 hours, the deal was off. As Crerand explained: 'later that week', Matt said to me, 'that's some pal you've got'. He took the job and then 'phoned me this morning to say he's not taking it after all.' I was surprised because I knew Jock definitely fancied coming to United, although I knew Jean (Stein's wife) didn't want to leave Glasgow.

Although Busby was surprised that Stein had rebuked the offer, there was a suggestion that the pair had disagreed on the matter of the Celtic manager bringing his backroom staff from Parkhead to Old Trafford. According to Stephen Sullivan,

George Stein (Jock's son) suggested that this was in fact a critical issue on which Busby and his father did not see eye-to-eye.

Initially I was sure that he was ready to accept, but gradually, though, the more he talked, the more the doubts filtered through. Not about my mum's feelings, because he knew that she was reluctant to move, but about the job itself ... He was insisting that he wanted to bring in his own back-room staff so that he had his own people round about him. But Sir Matt had his own loyalties.

Stein eventually decided that the job wasn't for him, whether due to his own indecision or his wife's reluctance to move south, it matters little. The position of Manchester United manager was still up for grabs.

As for matters on the pitch, the corner had certainly not been turned as the inconsistency continued right up until the final match of the season. Confidence had certainly returned, Best was back to his old self, the possibility of European football had resurfaced, but always lurking in the background was those ignominious and erratic displays of the past, with the mistake-strewn displays against West Ham and Derby County destroying the belief that Busby had managed to get United back to normality, with the defeat at Coventry City destroying that perhaps outlandish hope of European football. Then the 5-3 victory over Crystal Palace, when George Best did catch a train to London, made a mockery of the whole season.

The interim manager, despite his status, was not immune to criticism with a 'disillusioned' Brian Kidd giving the manager who gave him his initial break both barrels. 'He has washed away all my feelings for this club' the twenty-one-year-old said.

Things are going from bad to worse for me here and I don't want to be considered a Manchester United player a minute longer than necessary. I've been made to feel more like an outlaw than a United player. All sorts of people have asked me if I have got into trouble with the boss. The only trouble as far as I'm concerned is the way I've been treated. My face doesn't fit with Sir Matt Busby and I will ask for a transfer. I want to leave as quickly as possible.

A hastily arranged meeting between the two parties soon brought a change of heart from the player, but there was one high profile departure.

Wilf McGuinness having toiled and kicked his heels in charge of the Central League side finally called it a day, and turned his back on United, despite not having a definite job to go to. Several offers had come his way and he had decided to take some time out to think them over.

'It was difficult for me to accept the new situation having been team manager, but the decision to leave was made by me', was all he had to say.

For Sir Matt Busby, the curtain came down on his managerial career in perfect fashion, amid a seven-goal thriller at Maine Road. Fortunately that grand finale had not been four days previously at Bloomfield Road Blackpool, where supporters caused havoc before the match and Pat Crerand was sent off, along with the Seasider's Craven midway through the second half, following an exchange of punches.

Perhaps surprisingly, it was a peaceful 'derby' encounter that brought the curtain down on the season, with United storming into a 3-0 half-time lead mainly thanks to a vintage display from Charlton, Law and Best. City, to their credit, fought back with Hill reducing the score line and Stepney reducing Lee, Young and Mellor to tears with a trio of outstanding saves. Best restored United's three-goal advantage, but with the game bordering on testimonial tempo, City pulled it back to 4-3, but failed to get that equaliser which few would have denied them.

So, that was it. Busby had completed his unwanted period as stand-in manager, securing a presentable eighth place in the First Division (although they were twenty-two points behind champions Arsenal), before stepping once again out of the immediate spotlight.

I do not want to pack in my relationship with the dressing room, but common sense tells me that I must. This is a young man's game. There is not a chance of me ever coming back again to run the side. It was wonderful when I could get out in a track suit and a pair of boots and kick about with the boys. But there comes a time when you cannot do it. The pressure is intense, there are always people to see, phones to be answered, problem to sort out. Thank heavens my wife Jean has been such an angel, putting up with all this. I'll still be general manager of course, but I will not interfere. I know people say I might have not been able to leave the team alone – but I will. The new boss will have entire control over team selection, tactics and the buying of players. The directors want me to be general manager and there certainly is a need for one. The demands are so great. We talked about four or five men for the position of team manager at the last meeting. The sooner we get someone appointed the better. It will be a great load off my mind.

There is no record of who the 'four or five men' actually were, and it would be foolish to guess even now, but why not? Telephone calls had been made 'from Manchester' to Ronnie Allen, the former Wolves manager currently in charge of Bilbao, while there would of course have been the number one choice Jock Stein and then United old boy Noel Cantwell. Dave Sexton, Tommy Docherty and even Manchester City's Malcolm Allison were most probably the others in the mix. But no matter who was about to step into the hot seat, the shadow of Busby would still be looming in the background, despite the promise to keep way.

4
NEW MAN AT THE HELM

In choosing the next manager of Manchester United, there had to be no margin for error this time around. The directors could not make an appointment, or perhaps be similarly influenced by Sir Matt Busby as they had been for the appointment of Wilf McGuinness. This was one that they had to get right if the long-term future of the club was to be stabilised and guaranteed.

Of course, who was a good manager today might not be one tomorrow, coupled with the fact that Manchester United was simply no ordinary football club, making the appointed individual a man who had shown a number of the qualities required to take the club to a new level and further success. National five-a-side winners did not sit comfortably alongside European Cup winners, League Champions and FA Cup winners.

But between the last ball being kicked at Maine Road against City, or against Grasshoppers in Zurich if you throw the three-match end of season tour into the mix, it took the directors a mere thirty-four days to name Frank O'Farrell the new manager of Manchester United.

It did of course take longer, as the search had begun as soon as Wilf McGuinness had returned to his reserve team duties, or even before. A list was compiled and kept in a locked drawer, away from prying eyes. Each name was scrutinised and debated time and again, until that one name remained. The forty-three-year-old Irishman from Cork was handed the poisoned chalice on 8 June 1971.

An 'iron fist in a velvet glove' was one description of the new Manchester United manager and one-time apprentice engine driver, whose career as a player took him from Cork to Weymouth via West Ham United and Preston North End, cutting his teeth as a manager at non-league Weymouth before moving on to bigger and better things with Torquay United and Leicester City.

His CV was not trophy strewn, neither on nor off the pitch, with promotion from the Third Division to the Second with Torquay, relegation from the First to the Second, and FA Cup runners-up with Leicester City all that stood out. But he was a member of the famed West Ham United team of footballing scholars who spent afternoons in a café beside the Upton Park ground, debating tactics with the aid of salt and pepper pots and sugar cubes. He had studied well and was more than keen to improve.

The appointment was not entirely clear-cut however, as the United board were certain that they could persuade Stein to come south. Rebuffed, they had to begin a second search. 'It was becoming a nightmare' admitted Busby. 'We dared not work in the open. We were afraid that some people would use an approach by United to put pressure on their own clubs, and that we were making life embarrassing for the man who eventually would say yes.'

So, the whole thing took on something akin to a spy novel, a cloak and dagger scenario.

After the 'thanks, but no thanks' reply from Stein, it was decided by the United board that the other names on the shortlist would be telephoned by someone having no visible club connections, with the conversation drifting round to the possible manager being casually asked if, in the unlikely circumstances that they were offered the United job, they would accept?

It has been stated that O'Farrell was top of the list, bar one of course, and the initial approach to him was made a month before his appointment, with the telephone caller asking the Leicester City manager how he was fixed. Mistakenly, O'Farrell began going on about his team's chances back in the First Division and what positions he had to fill before the start of the new season. The bait was not taken. O'Farrell was none the wiser as regards the back door approach, and the caller believed that it had all been a waste of time and O'Farrell was not interested in the job.

Others on the list were interviewed by the mystery caller, but nothing materialised. Then, out of the blue, it came to light in the national press that O'Farrell and Leicester City were at loggerheads over a bonus he was apparently due after leading the Filbert Street club to promotion. The antennae at Old Trafford began twitching. Leicester panicked and offered their manager a new contract.

The chase was on, and in order to speed up the process, there was no underhand methods employed with the Leicester City board approached directly on Friday 4 June during the annual dinner of the secretaries and managers' association at the Park Lane Hotel in London, where O'Farrell was the main speaker.

Following the meal and speeches, Louis Edwards and Sir Matt Busby made a beeline to Leicester City chairman Len Shipman in a quiet bar elsewhere in the hotel, and asked for permission to talk to his manager about the possibility of him becoming United's next manager. He was unhappy by the approach, but in the circumstances felt that he could do little more than allow the United duo to pursue their interest.

So the United equivalent of Batman and Robin set off to find O'Farrell, but in such a large hotel, and with over 600 guests at the dinner, it proved impossible. Determined to grab him first thing in the morning proved to be equally elusive, as the Leicester manager and his assistant Malcolm Musgrove had checked out at 7.00 a.m. and headed home as they were due to attend the wedding of inside forward Rodney Fern.

Telephone calls went unanswered, with O'Farrell moving from the wedding to opening a garden fête at his daughter's school, so it was decided that the best option was for the Leicester chairman to speak to his manager first thing on the Monday morning. United had to sweat over the weekend.

Shipman spoke to O'Farrell, notifying him of United's interest, but requesting if he would postpone any meeting with United until the following weekend, as Leicester had a board meeting planned for the next day. Perhaps hoping that if they could get the proposed new contract finalised and presented to O'Farrell, they would force United's search for a manager to continue elsewhere. But O'Farrell, having been flattered by United's interest, realising that it was a once in a lifetime opportunity, took the bull by the horns and contacted Busby.

'He told me that he wanted to step back from managing Manchester United' said the softly spoken Irishman.

> The team had been together too long, some players were getting old and the team needed to be rebuilt. He said it was a five-year job and that he wanted me to take it on. I asked him what the terms of the contract would be. He said, 'five year contract, so many thousand bonus if you win the league, so many thousand if you win the cup, so many thousand for the European Cup and so on and a basic pay of £12,000.' I thought it was a little stingy as I was expecting an offer of £10,000 from Leicester. I was confident in my own ability. OK, the club was bigger than I was used to. But I was experienced and the object of the exercise is the same wherever you manage: you want to win. I said I'd think about it over the weekend, talk to my chairman at Leicester, and get back to him on Monday. I spoke to my chairman and he wasn't happy about it, but I had not signed a new contract so agreed I could talk to United. I then arranged to meet Matt Busby and the Manchester United chairman, Louis Edwards to discuss the matter again.

'We couldn't take the chance of being seen together in public' continued O'Farrell, 'so I couldn't even invite him to lunch.' Instead, the clandestine tryst took place in a lay-by on the B5020, just outside Mackworth in Derbyshire, suggested by Busby and an ideal spot halfway between Leicester and Manchester, away from prying eyes.

In the back of the chairman's Rolls Royce, O'Farrell admitted that there were not many questions to be asked, or even very much for him to say, except to go over the proposed terms of employment in case there was anything that the chairman wanted to add.

Busby repeated the terms and that the salary would be £12,000, but immediately Edwards jumped in saying: 'Oh no, Matt, that's wrong, it's £15,000.' O'Farrell claimed,

> That got us off on a bad note, me and Busby. He knew that I knew he wasn't playing it straight. The trust was damaged from the start. From that moment, I didn't trust him. It certainly left a bad taste, and a few years later, after I had left the club, I was talking to Jimmy Murphy and he said he knew the story to be true because Matt told him he could've got Frank for £12,000 but 'that big stupid bugger told him it was £15,000.'

Before agreeing to join United, O'Farrell wanted to talk it over with his wife and, as she had no objections for moving to Manchester, he telephoned Busby at 8.00 p.m. on the Tuesday night and accepted the job. During the call, Busby said 'Frank, don't expect miracles at Manchester. We won't. Given time, I know United will be great again, and I know you can make them that.'

Having spoken with the new manager, Busby then released the news to the press saying,

> I am very glad the position has been resolved and am very happy with the appointment. Regarding my own position, I have decided to retire from all management of the club and the board have invited me to become a director which I am pleased to accept.

'I aim to continue United's tradition as one of the brightest and most entertaining teams in football' said the new man in charge. 'I am going to ask the United fans to be patient. Let me find my feet. I have been told there is a lot of money available for new players. It will stay in the bank until I have decided if any are needed.'

For Frank O'Farrell, it was a huge step up, but he was confident that he could handle the challenge in front of him. 'I shall have full control at Old Trafford' he confirmed, 'I have been given that assurance. Sir Matt Busby will be on the board and I shall be manager in every sense of the word.' That, however, was only partly true, as Busby, once again attempted to belittle the new manager.

O'Farrell explained,

When I first arrived, Matt was still in the manager's and there were workmen constructing a new small office for the new manager, me, down the corridor. I politely suggested to him that it didn't seem right if he continued to use the main office and he eventually did move out. Even Jimmy Murphy, his former assistant, asked me how I had managed to achieve that.

Installed in the manager's office, O'Farrell set to work, adding his Leicester City number two, Malcolm Musgrove, to his back-room staff, before making George Best the club's top earner, as he had been anything but with a wage of less than £150 per week. No sooner had O'Farrell arrived in Manchester than he was beset with a problem, finding a stadium where his team could play their opening two league fixtures.

During last season's home game against Newcastle United on 27 February, a knife was thrown from the Stretford End, narrowly missing the visitors full-back Ron Guthrie, an incident that had seen the club hauled before an FA commission back in April. This had been adjourned as United requested a personal hearing, while also clearing an area at the Stretford End, clearing a 20-yard area around the vicinity of the goal, which reduced the capacity from 63,000 to 58,500. Despite this, there was little that United could do to avoid punishment, even although it was an individual rather than the club, who had sinned. They were, however, stunned when the verdict was announced.

Having considered all the evidence, the commission is satisfied that a spectator threw a knife on to the pitch at the match between Manchester United and Newcastle United. The commission recognises the fact that Manchester United have taken steps to prevent crowd misbehaviour, but the club is by rule responsible for the actions of its spectators. It has been decided that the Manchester United club ground be closed for the playing of matches for the period 14 August to 28 August inclusive, and that the club be ordered to compensate any club due to visit the Manchester United ground during the period of the closure for any loss incurred by the club in the event of their share of the gate being less than it would have been had the match been played at Old Trafford – the amount due, if any, to be based on the average gate of Manchester United home matches during season 1970/71. In reaching its decision, the commission took into account the club's previous record of spectator misconduct. Having asked for a personal hearing, the club is ordered to pay the costs of the commission.

Eric Todd of the *Guardian* added,

> The Stretford Enders cannot rightly complain at the FA's decision. Many
> of the occupants of that part of the ground are loyal and well-behaved
> supporters; the rest have been living on borrowed time. Frequently, they
> have been asked by Sir Matt Busby to behave themselves. The club and
> the police have added their support to that plea. Part of the Streford
> End has been made inhabitable so that while obscenities may be with
> us forever, the end of the missile throwing may be in sight. If not, United
> know what to expect.

The evil shadow of hooliganism that had continued almost unabated since
the mid-sixties had latched on to United like a ball and chain, much to
the club's continual disgust and annoyance. No matter how many column
inches Sir Matt Busby and his fellow directors had given the subject in
the club programme and the media, it had seemingly gathered momentum
with each passing match. Some went as far as to see it as nothing more
than part of their normal match-day routine.

There had been numerous unsavory incidents in and around the ground,
with a clash last season between United and Liverpool supporters in the
nearby Dog and Partridge pub (which stood yards from where the Bishops
Blaize stands today) possibly one of the worst.

'It was like the Wild West' commented a passer-by, with at least fifteen
people taken to hospital and countless more injured, when windows,
tables and glasses were all smashed and bottles flew through the air in the
incident which saw 'hundreds involved'.

So how would anyone want to play host to an invasion akin to a cross
between the Vikings and Genghis Kahn's lot?

Having to play at least 12 miles away from Manchester, early names
banded about were Blackburn, Burnley and Preston, but after much
consultation, Liverpool's Anfield would host the fixture against Arsenal,
and Stoke's Victoria Ground the second 'home' fixture against West
Bromwich Albion. Wembley had also been approached to host the Arsenal
fixture and although interest was shown, it was to be a no-go as the
stadium still hosted speedway events, which would have clashed with the
proposed fixture. Old Trafford meanwhile stood dormant, with those in
the Stretford End soon to find themselves punished for the action of one,
with the immediate area behind the goal barricaded off.

Frank O'Farrell got down to work, making his first team selection for
the fixture against Third Division Halifax Town in the Watney Cup; ninety
minutes that would have proved a real eye opener for the new manager,
as even with Best, Law and Charlton in the line-up, his newly acquired

personal could not progress in this minor competition, losing 2-0 with a hapless performance. Certainly not the best of starts.

Friendlies at Luton Town (won 2-0), Fulham (lost 2-1) and a 3-1 home win against Coventry City in the week before the stadium ban took effect allowed O'Farrell to cast his eyes over what he had inherited before kicking off the First Division season in earnest at Derby's Baseball Ground.

Derby manager Brian Clough had been another name linked with the United job, but had replied when asked about the position: 'Would I have taken the job at Old Trafford? I'd have walked up the M6 to get it! But I wouldn't have gone 100 miles of it with Sir Matt there.' Honest and to the point as always.

Taking a 2-0 lead in the first half, everything looked perfect, but for some unknown reason, the visitors sat back and allowed Derby back into the game and to snatch a point. 'Too many captains, too many individuals and too little team work' was one early observation.

If playing two home fixtures at neutral venues was not enough of a drawback early in the season, then George Best's sending off at Stamford Bridge as United grabbed both points with a 3-2 win, gave O'Farrell an additional headache.

Instilling a new 'get tough' approach, referee Norman Burtenshaw dismissed the Irishman in the 40th minute following Chelsea's opening goal. Many adjudged Osgood to have pushed a United defender prior to Baldwin heading home, and Morgan was booked for his protest. Best then approached the referee. With the game waiting to restart, and after an exchange of words, the official pointed to the tunnel. Best sunk to his knees in disbelief before being lead off the pitch by Charlton and Dunne.

United equalised in the 68th minute and took the lead soon afterwards, before going 3-1 in front 8 minutes from time with a Charlton blockbuster; Chelsea grabbing a second in the dying minutes.

But despite the early headaches, O'Farrell's start could be considered more than favourable, with the two 'in exile' fixtures both producing 3-1 victories. A point was dropped at Wolverhampton, with the unbeaten opening sequence coming to an end at Goodison Park in a 1-0 defeat, but it was back to winning ways in the first actual home fixture with a narrow 1-0 win over Ipswich Town.

The new manager had mapped out a rigid 4-3-3 formation, with the players readily adapting to not simply the challenge, but the expectancy to play in somewhat unfamiliar positions. Prime examples were Willie Morgan and Alan Gowling moving out of the front line and into midfield; the former, often erratic as a wide man became more involved in the game, while Gowling had actually volunteered to take over from the suspended Crerand.

With George Best having a suspended sentence hanging over him, it was little more than a forgone conclusion that his recent dismissal at Stamford Bridge would earn him yet another spell on the sidelines. But thanks to a defence plea by PFA Secretary Cliff Lloyd, who put forward the case that the player had not directed his words at the referee, the commission announced, 'After hearing all the evidence we are not satisfied beyond reasonable doubt that George Best directed the words (you're a ****ing disgrace) to the referee.'

A case or two of wine should have found its way to the PFA offices as a token of thanks, as the wayward Irishman, having secured both points with his goal against Ipswich prior to the hearing, demolished West Ham United five days after the hearing, scoring a hat-trick in the 4-2 win.

'Now that Pelé has retired – for the last time – the genius of George Best is unrivalled in world soccer' penned David Miller in the *Sunday Times*.

Two of his three goals at Old Trafford yesterday were indication of his astonishing control and reflexes. Having given the FA the slip last Monday – on the slenderest technicality – Best now applied himself to West Ham's destruction with a virtuosity which is undiminished.

The victory took United to within two points of early leaders Sheffield United, a 2-2 draw at Liverpool pegging them back slightly, but with the leaders due at Old Trafford the following Saturday, ground could certainly be made up.

For those who managed to get into Old Trafford before the gates were locked, they were to be treated to something special, extraordinary even, one of those 'I was there' moments. But for an estimated 10,000, they could certainly say they were there, but they were not inside the ground as the game got underway due to the chaotic scenes around the stadium at 2.30 p.m.

The 51,735 inside was almost 2,000 less than had watched the West Ham match a fortnight earlier, and was well short of the 54,000 capacity. With the construction of the new stand at the Scoreboard End though, along with the safety aspect outside, the police were left with little alternative but to tell United to close all the turnstiles.

On a sun-kissed pitch, the visitors were soon to prove that they deserved their lofty position, while United scorned ideal scoring opportunities, and as the game progressed, it began to look as though the points would be shared in a stalemate. Then with 6 minutes remaining, mouths dropped open and heads were shaken in disbelief, following a goal – still considered as one of the finest ever scored at the ground – that changed the course of the game.

Collecting the ball some 30 yards from goal with little hint of impeding danger, George Best casually glanced at a penalty area filled with white shirts. Moving forward, he suddenly turned to his right, running parallel to the goal, waltzing past imaginary tackles of three bemused defenders. Into the penalty area, conjuring up a gap through which he slipped the ball under the advancing Hope, who had none. 'Best jinked, changed pace, beat three men and created with magic one of the great goals of any lifetime' was how Frank McGhee of the *Sunday Mirror* saw it. No one argued.

Alan Gowling added a second, and United were inching closer to that top spot, grabbing it with both hands seven days later at Huddersfield. Again, it was a Best inspired victory, scoring once in the 3-0 win, continuing his superb run of form with the only goal of the game in the following two fixtures against Derby County and Newcastle United, consolidating that top spot, while having kept a clean sheet in the past four league outings. Had the corner at last been turned?

Stopping Best was perhaps the only way you could prevent a United victory, a sly trip, an elbow to the ribs, or a foot raised perhaps a little too high could all be employed to stop the Belfast Boy. Some however, wanted not simply to put him out of the game for a few weeks, but for good, to the point of ending his life with a bullet.

George Best was born a Protestant in Belfast. For many on one side of the Irish Sea it mattered little, for others back home he was the enemy. Suddenly, he was a marked man off the field with an IRA death threat hanging over his head. In the run up to the Newcastle fixture, police cars occupied his drive and on the day of the game he was given special police protection. Neither put him off his game, although he later admitted that he seldom remained still during the 90 minutes.

He was also to admit that he was enjoying his football more than ever:

> I think everything has improved. Frank O'Farrell must take a lot of the credit for what he has done at United but I think his assistant, Malcolm Musgrove is terrific too. My own game has certainly developed because the team is doing well and I have the encouragement I need. I am strictly a front man now. They don't want me going back into my own half. Scoring goals or at least having a hand in them is what it has always been about for me, so I am going well.

He also remained a kid at heart.

> I still find a special thrill in playing with goalposts that have nets. When we are training and there are no nets, I feel like going in the huff and refusing to play. I still get that special charge when the ball makes that whirring noise as it hits the net.

The appointment of Frank O'Farrell could certainly be considered as a step in the right direction, as football on the whole was attack-minded. Having achieved First Division leadership, everyone was happy – for the time being at least.

There was however, the huge dependency upon that one individual, with any ultimate success relying heavily on not simply George Best maintaining his current form, but on his continual peace of mind.

O'Farrell had perhaps contributed to this upsurge in Best's form when he adjusted his wages, although the player's off field endorsements more than adequately covered any shortfall in his earnings at club level. Putting his name to an annual saw an initial print run of 20,000 at £1 sold out within three days, leading to overall sales of around 120,000. He used to joke that he wanted to be a millionaire. It was now no longer a joke.

The first reversal since the 1-0 defeat at Goodison Park came against Leeds United at home on 30 October, three days after a hard-fought 1-1 League Cup draw with Stoke City. Ipswich and Burnley had been disposed of in earlier rounds, the latter after a replay, and it was to take a further two encounters with the Potteries side before interest in the competition came to an end.

In recent weeks, Best had seldom been overshadowed, even for a brief spell during a match, but it was another 'Belfast Boy' who was to grab the headlines in the first Manchester 'derby' of the season: seventeen-year-old Sammy McIlroy grabbing the spotlight from his fellow countryman with a debut goal in the 3-3 draw at Maine Road.

'It came as a great shock to me to discover I was playing. I knew I was in the party, but thought it was just for the ride' said the youngster, who was totally unfazed by the occasion, with his 39th minute goal picking up a loose ball when Best was obstructed by Book, giving United the lead. Kidd made it 2-0, but City fought back to draw level. Within minutes though, they found themselves yet again behind. Only 3 minutes remained when City yet again equalised for a share of the spoils.

McIlroy struck again in the 3-1 victory over Tottenham and again a fortnight later in the 5-2 hammering of Southampton at the Dell, sandwiched in between two 3-2 victories against Leicester City and Nottingham Forest as United consolidated their position at the top of the First Division, enjoying a five-point lead over Derby, City and Leeds.

If everyone considered George Best to be the only 'problem boy' within the ranks, then they were wrong, very wrong. Perhaps Kevin Lewis didn't have off-field problems, but he had more than enough on-field ones.

In November 1969, the seventeen-year-old had been fined £25 for receiving three cautions. Then in April 1971, he had been suspended for the remainder of the season and fined £30 following a sending off in a

Lancashire FA Youth Cup tie against Burnley, as he was already on a four-week suspended sentence. He also promised the commission that he would study the laws of the game. Either he didn't bother with the latter or it made little difference to him, as on 10 December he was banned for the remainder of the season and fined £50. His offence on this occasion was having tripped an opponent and was about to get booked, he was alleged to have sworn at the official and then attempted to assault him. Had it not been for an appeal by Frank O'Farrell, then Lewis would have been banned sine die.

Although top of the pile, a position that delighted everyone connected with the club with Sir Matt Busby proclaiming that O'Farrell was the 'best signing I have ever made', not everyone considered United to be worthy of their lofty position, particularly Malcolm Allison and Brian Clough, assistant manager of third place Manchester City and manager of second place Derby County respectively.

Following his side's 3-1 defeat by second place Derby County, the outspoken Allison said, 'We've no need to worry when there's a bad team at the top. Derby County, Manchester City and Leeds United, all on twenty-seven points, are the three teams in the race.' With the equally outspoken Clough adding, 'I am surprised Manchester United have stayed the course for so long.' O'Farrell refused to be drawn into the debate, simply saying that he was happy to let the team's record speak for itself, but the comments from the two critics were soon to be proved correct and not simply attempts to unsettle a team and its manager.

Three consecutive draws should have derailed the title challenge, but it merely reduced their leeway to three points, although there was a clear warning sign from the performances against Stoke, Ipswich and Coventry that something was amiss. The well-oiled machine of previous weeks was not running smoothly. 'Disjointed' was how they were described against Coventry, salvaging a point in the 2-2 draw with a rare Steve James goal 5 minutes from time. The point in the 0-0 draw against Ipswich was considered 'lucky', with one headline proclaiming there was 'Panic in the Air'.

On 1 January, a new year and surprisingly a new United, as 1972 got off to the worst start possible with a 3-0 defeat at Upton Park. Many observers felt that there was not three goals between the two teams. Nevertheless, it was a setback to their ambitions and a ready reminder that there was still a lot of work to be done if they were to make a serious challenge for the championship. Previously, United had sprung back from such reversals, but not this time, with Frank O'Farrell about to have his managerial credentials severely tested.

Seven days after the defeat by West Ham, United again conceded three; Wolves leaving Old Trafford with both points on the back of a 3-1 win.

This result was perhaps not unexpected as United and O'Farrell had suffered an agonising week in the run up to the fixture.

George Best, more than anyone, had been instrumental in United's meteoric climb to the top of the First Division. His demons of the recent past seemed to have been exorcised. He was enjoying his football and had a smile on his face. However, his peg in the dressing room at the Cliff training ground had been empty since Monday. Instead of appearing in front of his ardent admirers, lining up with his team mates to face Wolves, he was at Heathrow Airport, seeking sanctuary in the vast sprawl of the capital.

Not only had O'Farrell the onerous job of getting his team back on track, he now had the added responsibility of dealing with his wayward genius.

When the news first broke that Best had failed to turn up for training that Monday morning, it was first rumoured that he was unwell, before progressing to concerns about his family in Belfast, caught in the middle of the sectarian troubles and such concerns had seen the player fly back to Ireland. Given his earlier death threats, this should have been instantly dismissed as nonsense. But even so, Frank O'Farrell went out of his way on the Thursday to make an unscheduled stop in Belfast on his way back to Manchester from Dublin, hoping to speak to his player, only to be told that Best had not been over the water since the previous October.

Sympathy was now in short supply for Best as he was slowly becoming something of an embarrassment and an unwanted distraction. 'If he has been in Belfast, we might lean over backwards to make an allowance' said one teammate. 'But general feeling is that the story about him being worried about his family is just a load of rubbish. George has just gone and done it again.'

It left O'Farrell with no option than to make his plans for the weekend fixture against Wolves without the player, offering the media the excuse 'he has not been picked because he is not match fit. He has not trained this week.' Sensing a major story, the press began turning over every stone looking for anything with a link to the man who had gone AWOL.

His teammates were rightly annoyed by his disappearance.

Listen, if George was that worried about his parents, he'd only to send them their fares. They could have flown to England next day ... You have to understand that he's popular. Except at times like this. Then the lads are bloody angry. There has been a lot of muttering this week. He wouldn't have got too many cheers if he had turned up on Friday.

Comments were also made about the club rule that said all single players must live in 'approved digs', and the club had only allowed Best to build his infamous home in Cheshire as long as his parents joined him in England.

Some doubted that they had ever even seen the place.

'Going adrift this week of all weeks' moaned another teammate.

> He's been part of the decline and he should have been there to help us put it right. We have worked our guts out this week trying to find out what we are doing wrong. And he didn't even show up. By the end of the week some of the lads were saying 'Right, we can do without him' and they didn't just mean for one game.

So where was George Best? Having arrived in London, he disappeared. Many thought he was with his latest girlfriend, Carolyn Moore, but she denied all knowledge of his whereabouts. Then in a statement, the truant said,

> I have an explanation for what has happened. But I can't say what it is until I've seen the boss. I was sick when I heard of my team's 3-1 defeat on Saturday. Frankly, from what I saw on TV, I doubt if it would have made much difference to the outcome if I'd played.

A huge shadow was cast over the club, as there was a possibility that player and club could go their separate ways. The former could well ask for a move, as he had openly said 'I'm going through one of those lean spells that can hit a player. Nothing seems to be coming off for me. And the harder I try the worse it seems to get. It's hard to put a finger on what's going wrong.' The club, on the other hand, could take the gamble and put him up for sale.

If Best returned to Manchester expecting sympathy and an arm around the shoulder from his manager, he was very much mistaken. Though O'Farrell had to tread carefully, despite having the backing of Sir Matt Busby. Best was his prize asset, the player on whom his hopes of success depended. He had however, to show a firm hand and stamp his authority on the player and the club as a whole. Anything else would immediately prove disastrous.

Almost immediately following Best's return, O'Farrell handed 'the lonely boy' his punishment – fined two weeks' wages, thought to be around £400, ordered to train every afternoon as well as mornings for a week, ordered to forfeit his day off for the next five weeks to make up for the training he missed, and finally ordered to leave his home in Bramhall and return to his former digs with Mrs Fullaway. The manager added,

> George's habits were already formed by the time I got to Old Trafford and it was something I took on. Matt had signed him on as a boy and he couldn't handle him, so what chance did I have? He was just a wayward

person. He was always threatening to give the game up. The other players would moan when he failed to turn up for training and I would punish him with fines, but it was only a slap on the wrist. He hinted at times that Manchester United didn't need a new manager, they needed new players, and he was right. I think he was concerned that the United team was not good enough.

'I deserve it, I'll take it' said the problem boy, who was immediately reinstated into the team for the FA Cup tie at Southampton, but served up little of note in the 1-1 draw. The replay four days later however, was a completely different matter, as Best stepped back to his irrepressible best, conjuring up two goals in the 4-1 extra-time success.

But controversy remained lurking in the background, as a two-fingered salute from the double marksman was seen by many at the game and on television. The gesture, he was to reveal, was directed at the critics in the press box who had sniped at his friends and to the 'cranks' who had sent sick letters to his new landlady. Thankfully, the matter blew over quickly.

The whole episode, although now closed, had deep repercussions and an immediate knock on effect. There was now a divide within the camp although it was to remain on the outside.

Chelsea's 1-0 victory at Old Trafford knocked United off top spot; the home side's performance forcing one correspondent to write that 'they looked as if they had never even been there'. The headline above the report in the *Guardian* suggested that 'Old Ghosts Gather at Old Trafford – Funeral Bells Toll', with Alan Dunn commenting,

> There is little room for sentiment in professional football, but there was a sadness about the way Manchester United surrendered their three months' tenure at the top of the First Division. Defensive failings are all part of the old, old story at Old Trafford where forward flair is expected to be the compensating factor.

West Bromwich kicked United when they were down, winning 2-1 at the Hawthorns, while a 2-0 FA Cup victory over Preston at Deepdale gave them some reprise, the best of the action taking up all of 4 minutes on television. But the tolling bell was about to break clear of its fittings and fly out of the belfry.

Newcastle United made it five league defeats in a row and eight without a win, with a 2-0 victory at Old Trafford; totals that were increased by one the following Saturday in Yorkshire, the bleakest afternoon of the season to date with a 5-1 hammering from Leeds United. From first to seventh in a matter of weeks.

'Getting back into form is something that will just happen' said the beleaguered United manager, 'at the same time I am sure that a win or two would bring the confidence back. Perhaps if we could score an early goal you would see a big difference in the team.'

The FA Cup again offered a brief escape, an outlet gratefully grasped, although it took two attempts to dispose of old foes Middlesbrough. Prior to the initial Fifth Round tie, David Meek emphasised that O'Farrell had persisted with more or less the same eleven that had underperformed against Leeds, because he had little option as too many of the players were operating below their normal level. The United correspondent writing 'one man out of form and the answer is easy – a reserve gets his place. But I would say that the reds have had more than half the team one degree under.'

Earning a 0-0 draw in Manchester, 'Boro were confident that they could secure victory on their own ground, but three goals without reply took United into the quarter finals, a disappointing result for 'Boro goalkeeper Jim Platt.

We'd beaten Manchester City and Millwall, both after a replay, two extremely tough games, more so as we were drawn away for the initial fixtures. Then we got United at Old Trafford. Strangely, I don't remember much about the match, except that I was in awe of the place, as it was my first visit, as well as being in front of the biggest crowd I had ever played against: 53,850. Not only that, I was up against George Best.

Nobby Stiles was our captain that day and it was his first return to Old Trafford since joining us. We drew 0-0, so I must have done ok.

I do remember the replay though, as it was played in the afternoon because it was the time of electricity strikes and the FA, I think, ordered us to play it then as there might be a strike on the night and it could happen in the middle of the match. If I remember correctly, the electricity board, as it was then, didn't give you prior notice and in which part of the country it would turn off the supply. Anyway we lost 3-0 in front of 39,671 fans. Ayresome Park only held 40,000 in those days. To this day people tell me that they took the day off work/school to watch the match. Morgan scored a first half penalty and Charlton and Best got the others.

That 3-0 replay victory however, offered manager Frank O'Farrell little comfort amid his search for the reinforcements, a matter that was now something of a priority. Back at his old club Leicester City, full-back David Nish was available, although around £200,000 would be required to prise him away. 'I would certainly not be afraid to spend big money now if I thought the man I was getting was the right player for the side', while adding that he had a concern about his players regaining something of their earlier form. 'I hate naming names, but take George Best because he is a good example. George was brilliant earlier this season. But since he did his moonlight flit, he's hardly had a good game, except against Southampton in the cup.'

£225,000 changed hands for Nish, but it was Derby not United who were prepared to break the bank, as O'Farrell continued to cast the net far and wide. Some interest had been shown in Aberdeen's twenty-two-year-old captain, Martin Buchan, but this had cooled somewhat of late. On the eve of the Middlesbrough cup replay though, a United contingent travelled to a hotel on the outskirts of Shotts in Lanarkshire to speak to and hopefully sign the Aberbeen defender.

Buchan, who had captained Aberdeen to Scottish Cup success in 1970, was already a full Scottish international and had many admirers within the game and O'Farrell did well to claim his signature ahead of Everton, having to pay £125,000 to secure the player. 'I'm delighted to get the boy' enthused the United manager. 'He will play a big part in my plans. We have watched him several times and I myself have watched him twice.'

The player himself added:

It's a dream come true for me and although I know it is a big challenge I accept it. I've been very happy with Aberdeen, but I'm a professional and I must accept this great chance to improve myself. Football to me is job to be done. I enjoy playing it, and I aim to do it to the best of my ability. I know I am not an especially skilled ballplayer. That's why I prefer playing in the back four to midfield. I have adjusted my style to suit what ability I have. Off the field, I don't care much for the showbiz side of soccer. How could I turn down an offer like this? Manchester United are a great club – one of the greatest in the world. They say the English First Division is the best in the world. Naturally I want to try myself against the very best. This is a great opportunity.

Buchan recalled,

I could have gone to either Liverpool or Leeds, but they had Tommy Smith and Norman Hunter, while I knew that David Sadler at United was carrying a knee injury so they were obviously the best option. But having said that, Eddie Turnbull taught me everything at Aberdeen and I was confident in my own ability and know that I could have gone and played anywhere in the world. Sir Matt, Frank O'Farrell, John Aston and Les Olive all travelled up to Bellshill to meet me and my manager Jimmy Bonthrone and I actually telephoned Eddie before signing, just to sound him out. United offered me £110 at week, compared to the £40 I was on at Aberdeen.

Although a player of extreme promise ('an exceptionally gifted player' was how his Scotland team boss Tommy Docherty described him), it was a high order to expect Buchan alone to reverse the recent losing trend. O'Farrell admitted that he was still perusing the marketplace, but also stated that he would not be panicked nor pushed into any deals due to the transfer deadline looming.

Buchan made his United debut at Tottenham on 4 March, but could do little to avoid yet another defeat, the home side winning 2-0, although the new recruit was widely praised for his performance in North London. It was a game that was to quickly disappear into the record books, comments on the defeat vanishing off the back pages as if written in invisible ink, as there was another story clawing for the headlines.

The debutant however, was not exactly impressed by what he found at Old Trafford saying, 'They were a strange mix, three superstars and one or two players that would not have got a game with Aberdeen reserves.'

On that same afternoon as Spurs were inflicting yet another defeat upon United, Derby County had paraded Nottingham Forest forward Ian Storey-Moore as their new signing, with the Monday morning papers proclaiming 'Derby sign Moore for record fee', going on to report that Brian Clough had paid out £225,000, a British record fee, to take the winger the short distance from Nottingham to Derby.

The transfer was bad news for United, as O'Farrell had shown more than a passing interest in the player and had been convinced the previous day that Moore would end up in Manchester, having left the player in a hotel to think things over and imagine a future at Old Trafford. Clough however, had other ideas and hijacked the deal by offering the player better terms. How the Derby manager knew what United had offered no one knew, but he had turned the player's head and it was a smiling Ian Moore who was paraded at the baseball ground that Saturday afternoon and had confessed that he regarded himself as a Derby County player.

'It was done by the book' said Brian Clough. 'Forms have been signed by the player and we are now giving them to Forest to sign.'

As we saw earlier in the season, United were fair game for everyone to take a potshot at, with Brian Clough and Malcolm Allison both being critical of the club and Allison once again got his two-pence worth in saying,

There should be no surprise that Ian Moore wanted to join Derby County rather than Manchester United. They have had a marvellous run. They still hold the imagination of the floating fan up and down the country, so that their away gates better those of Leeds and other vastly superior teams at the moment.

But they are living on yesterday's glamour, yesterday's triumphs and what Ian Moore sees today the fans will see tomorrow. That is unless Frank O'Farrell is able to work an overnight revolution.

He is going about major construction and he got close to one of English football's most dangerous forwards on Friday night. Naturally he is disappointed. United, with tremendous resources, must have been able to match Derby's terms. What seems to have happened is that Moore has asked himself a very simple question ... 'which side am I more likely to win with?'

On this season's showing there could only be one answer to that. The decision does shatter the impression that whenever United move in for a big player he is ready to leap into a red shirt.

It used to be the case of course, but it is nearly four years since performance matched the reputation and that defeat in a Nottingham hotel was more significant than the one which followed at White Hart Lane.

Allison's opinion was certainly not based on bias, as Jackie Charlton had also recently commented on the slump, saying, 'Manchester United are rather living on past glories and reputations.'

Unlike some of his players, O'Farrell did not know when he was beaten. Despite Forest and Derby agreeing on a fee, no paperwork had been signed and Moore remained, for the meantime at least, a Forest player, with his club furious at Derby having paraded him before the deal was concluded. O'Farrell went on to say 'our transfer negotiations did not break down, they were just interrupted. I am now waiting to hear from Forest so that we can continue where we left off.'

It is more than likely that Forest contacted Frank O'Farrell and informed him that he still had an opportunity to sign Moore, in order to jeopardise the move to the near neighbours and getting a sniff that a deal could be back on, the United manager and Sir Matt Busby travelled to Moore's home where, following a short conversation, the player said he would be happy to move to Manchester.

Having concluded the deal, a jubilant United manager said,

There may have been some misunderstanding, but I've got the player and I don't wish to comment on those misunderstandings.

We were in the process of negotiations last Friday night when we were interrupted. Brian Clough came on the scene and things happened on which I cannot comment.

I've got a top-class footballer. The best available and only the best is good enough for Manchester United fans.

Amid all the confusion, some sources state that United got the player for
£200,000; £25,000 less than was reported as the fee Derby had agreed
to pay Forest. Others give the fee as £225,000, but mention that it was
£25,000 more than O'Farrell had offered on the Friday. No matter what,
this was certainly nothing to do with the player, whose only comment was

> I am sorry that the weekend situation arose, but it was not really my
> fault. Everything got out of hand and I was carried along with it. Thank
> God it is all over. I have no intention of trying to explain all that has
> happened during the past three days. Frankly, I want to forget all that. It
> might seem strange, but I have always wanted to join United.

Derby County were later fined £5,000 by the Football League for 'flouting
the accepted rules and procedures in the negotiation of transfer deals. Their
action was of a nature likely to bring football transfer deals into disrepute.'

Having added Moore to the squad, United had certainly extended their
attacking options, while increasing pressure on the other players to step
up a gear. But one individual admitted he did not feel threatened by the
new arrival, and that was George Best, his comments being picked up
upon by David Meek who wrote that this was a rather arrogant approach.
Meek summed up the feeling among the senior players that everything
would come right on its own accord that contributed so considerably to
the team's slump in League football. Meek went on to add that O'Farrell
was creating a strong squad, and, for the first time since his arrival, he had
room to manoeuvre to cover loss of form, injuries and perhaps even more
importantly, experiment with various blends of players.

Arrogant they possibly were, but immune from being dropped they
certainly were not, and out of the side to face Everton at Old Trafford
went Charlton and Morgan. Even with the arrival of Moore who wasn't
included, and the other new addition in Buchan, few of the others looked
apprehensive about their future, even with the transfer deadline a few
hours away and the possibility of further additions to the side.

For United, without a win at home since 5 December and their visitors
not having won away in thirty-two outings, the 0-0 score line was not a
surprise; the performance, however, was.

'A dreary start to United's new era' proclaimed the *Guardian*, with Eric
Todd telling his readers that it was 'a wretched exhibition', while others in
attendance considered it 'a shambling shocker of a goalless game'.

Three days later, Ian Moore entered the fray against Huddersfield Town
and immediately gave the place a lift, making a considerable contribution
to the 3-1 victory. Even George Best was revitalised, scoring his first
League goal since November. But all eyes were on Moore and the new boy

did not disappoint, only deprived of a more memorable debut by a fine display of goalkeeping from David Lawson.

Best had given United the lead and had refused to be overshadowed by the newcomer, perhaps now realizing that here was someone who could nudge him out of the team should he ever decide to stage an impromptu disappearance act. Moore rose to the challenge of proving that he was well worth the huge outlay of cash paid for his services, by scoring United's second with a firm header just after the hour.

The 2-0 victory pushed United up to sixth, but they were still some nine points behind neighbours City, although they did have a game in hand. Pushing for the title was not even a dream, but getting to Wembley certainly was, with Stoke City once again standing between them and progress in a cup competition. Having been knocked out of the League Cup by the Potteries side, vengeance as well as progress into the semi-finals was high on the agenda.

Moore's arrival had certainly rejuvenated George Best, but it was Stoke, playing their twenty-first cup tie of the season, who took the initiative with Jimmy Greenhoff scoring on the hour. This might well have been their second, as just before half-time, James had brought down Dobing inside the box, but the referee waved play on despite numerous appeals.

The advantage was held until the dying minutes, when the wayward Irishman slipped the ball past Banks. Though earlier Charlton thought he had equalized, but was penalised for shouting 'leave it' without adding a name. So, it was yet another 90 minutes, or more, against Stoke and the fifth visit to the Victoria Ground this season.

The game was slow in gaining momentum, compared with the previous instalments, 20 minutes passing before either 'keeper made a save, and it was not until the 71st minute that the packed ground, with some 15,000 locked out, were treated to a goal. Best was once again on the scoresheet, giving United the lead.

Three minutes later, it was 1-1 – Smith forcing home Eastham's corner.

As the game moved into extra-time, United could only blame themselves for being in such a position, as once again they scorned scoring opportunities, failing to translate their superiority into goals, while Banks in the Stoke goal thwarted Kidd and Charlton either side of his team's winner. Conroy making the breakthrough 11 minutes into added time.

United immediately brushed away the disappointment of the cup defeat with a 4-0 victory over Crystal Palace at Old Trafford, and once again the name of Ian Moore was prominent in the headlines, the new signing scoring the third and making the first. Despite the score line, it appeared to flatter United, as once again their overall performance came under review in the national press and was considered to be 'lacking in atmosphere and was rarely exciting', with the game as a whole 'full of dross'. United, having taken a 4th minute lead and failing to capitalise on it, at the root of the comments.

Moore made it three in three, as well as having a hand in the first of the three goals that enabled United to scrape past relegation haunted Coventry City by the odd goal in five. Those highly creditable performances, however, had come against three of the bottom five clubs and the impending visit of Liverpool to Old Trafford would prove to be a more testing 90 minutes for both player and club.

As it materialised, they could just turn it on against the divisions lesser lights, with Bobby Charlton's record-breaking 564th appearance simply going into the record books as a 3-0 defeat. The victory took Liverpool to within one point of leaders Derby County, but clearly illustrated to United that there was still much work to be done if they were to again consider challenging for such a lofty position.

United did enjoy a favourable first 45 minutes, actually playing their best football for some time, but fell apart after the interval with Liverpool scoring twice while fans battled on the terracing, the visitors third coming 5 minutes from time.

That defeat seemed to knock any confidence that hovered around the team at this time and against Sheffield United, who had slipped to tenth from their early season joust with leading the pack, O'Farrell began looking to the future by leaving out Stepney, Gowling and Law and introducing John Connaughton in goal for his debut, back from a loan spell with Torquay, and giving Tony Young his first competitive start in place of Law.

While Moore had stood out in recent fixtures, Buchan had also caught the eye with his confident manner, looking a shrewd investment by O'Farrell. Neither they nor the youngsters could prevent the manager from suffering a 2-0 defeat by Leicester City upon his return to his old stomping ground.

This latest setback was followed by an even more humiliating one in a 3-1 home defeat by title hopefuls, Manchester City. Buchan for once was caught out like a rabbit in a car's headlights, although he was to claim the goal that gave United the lead 15 minutes into the second half. Starting the move in his own half, he continued to move forward, dispatching Gowling's centre past Healey in the City goal with a fine shot.

Moore had seen an earlier effort disallowed for offside, a lead that would have put United in the driving seat, but as it was, City were level in 2 minutes through Lee, going in front 4 minutes later from a Summerbee free-kick before sealing victory in the closing stages through Marsh.

Some self-respect was restored against Southampton, the 3-2 victory could have been accompanied by terrace chants of 'can we play you every week' as this fourth encounter of the season made it thirteen goals scored against the south coast club. Unfortunately, not all opponents were as accommodating as Southampton with the final three games of the season producing only one victory.

Nottingham Forest at the City Ground was a nondescript 90 minutes, while the 3-0 defeat inflicted by Arsenal at Highbury in the penultimate fixture of an often grueling campaign was described as 'the most inept performance that I personally have seen from a United side in the modern era', according to Robert Oxby in the *Daily Telegraph*. He went on, 'had this match been played at the start of the season, one would have forecast them as certainties for relegation.'

With 90 minutes of his first season in charge remaining, Frank O'Farrell stated that he was reasonably satisfied at how things had gone.

> At the beginning a great many critics took a very gloomy view of the prospects at Old Trafford. At least we did better than they expected. To establish a five-point lead in the first Division at the halfway stage is no mean achievement.
>
> I believe we have got something to build on, something from which we can go on to better things next season. After all we have won more points than last year and we progressed in both cup competitions.
>
> At the same time, I am well aware of the shortcomings in the fabric of the club which have to be worked on. We need an improvement on team work. Others have established an advantage over us in this respect.

The season fizzled out with a victory against a team that certainly appeared to be United's opponents every week, Stoke City, as this was the seventh meeting of the season between the two sides. United finally came out on top with a 3-0 win in what was described as possibly the friendliest ever league match played at Old Trafford, due to its lack of tackles. More than likely, the players just wanted the season out of the way and the opportunity to relax on some sun-kissed beach.

One individual was already soaking up the sun on the beach and had been for the past week, although the 'official' line read differently.

Prior to the away fixture at Nottingham Forest on 22 April, Manchester was awash with rumours that George Best had not been seen at the Cliff training ground all week, but manager Frank O'Farrell, when prompted about the player said,

George has had a very heavy cold all week and hasn't been feeling well generally. He has been under the doctor's care and that's the season why he has not been doing any training this week. I wouldn't think he will be playing on Saturday, but that depends on the doctor's report, of course.

Echoes of the Four Top's Motown hit 'The Same Old Song' could be distinctly heard in the background, as it was soon revealed by Mrs Jean Fullaway, whose mother was Best's landlady, that when he had turned up at her mother's home in Chorlton, 'he wasn't showing any signs of a cold and seemed perfectly all right'. She added further to the plot by saying 'he said he had been given a few days off by the club but he didn't say where he was going'.

There had been no hint that anything was actually troubling Best, as he had only a matter of days before, in his regular *Daily Express* column stated that he had already prepared a diary of events facing him once the last ball had been kicked with United. This included a testimonial for the West German forward, Uwe Seeler, in Hamburg on 1 May, and a ten-day business and pleasure trip to the Seychelles starting on 4 May, before returning to Britain for the home international fixtures. With no time to rest, it would be off again to catch up with his United teammates in Greece for the final two games of the close season tour. Once this was over, his intentions were to head off with a couple of mates in the direction of Majorca. All of that, (except for the German date), was now up in the air, as he had bypassed everything else and headed straight for Spain.

His absence continued to create much speculation and, as the home internationals beckoned, the Northern Ireland selectors were prepared to turn their back on him when he failed to turn up for their match against Scotland in Glasgow, despite the team coach waiting for some three hours.

Patience was growing thin everywhere amid new reports that he had left his hideaway in Marbella and was heading for Madrid. Eric Todd of the *Guardian* perhaps summed up everyone's thoughts and feelings perfectly, writing that 'the player had his own set of self-defying rules' before going on to say,

He has been disciplined too leniently by Sir Matt Busby and Frank O'Farrell. Now, surely, for the good of the game and especially in deference to all players who comply with their club rules, Best should be brought finally to heel. No player, not even Best, is indispensable in spite of belief to the contrary. I cannot believe that the rest of the Irish players who were generous enough to ask for his inclusion in the side to meet Scotland, were motivated by anything but lack of confidence in their own ability.

Of course there may be a perfectly valid reason for Best's absence. On the other hand, his booking in at a luxury hotel in Spain to cover the period of the home internationals does not suggest validity, or did Best forget the dates of the internationals?

Todd continued, 'Best has been spoiled all his playing life, and because he is who and what he is, has been pampered and over-publicised. His private life is his own concern – or it should be – but when he clears off when the need takes him, it is tie to call a halt.'

At the end of the season there had been rumours that he had asked United for a transfer, favouring a move to London in order to be closer to his business interests, with the player fuelling speculation when asked if his problems were football-related, his reply was 'they might be'. This gave weight to the suggestions that all was not well, and that there was a possibility that he might be considering quitting the game.

When his actual whereabouts became known, a posse of reporters were soon flying out to Spain in an attempt to capture something exclusive, but they were in vain, as the United player, for the time being at least had already sold his story although counter-bids of £5,000 were still being made.

Across the Mediterranean, Frank O'Farrell, with United in Majorca, when asked about his player simply said, 'If you think I am going to chase George Best all over the Costa del Sol then you've got another think coming. It's Northern Ireland's problem not mine.'

They were soon to become O'Farrell's and United's problems, as on the morning of 21 May the *Sunday Mirror* hit the streets with the front page, world exclusive headline – 'I QUIT by George Best', with the sub-heading at the bottom of the page adding 'WHY: "I am a bloody wreck ... for the last year all I have done is drink"'.

Copies of the newspaper flew off the shelves, everyone wanting to read what the player had to say. Some cared little, as they had lost faith in him a long time ago. Others, continuously mesmerized by his unique talents, offered sympathy. Best had little thought for either, although he was apparently in tears as he told his story in room 645 of the Skol Hotel, a story that filled both the front and back pages of the paper.

Best admitted to being mentally and physically wrecked, with trips to his doctor failing to produce a remedy, and sleeping pills no help as to aiding his comfort in those early hours of a new day. His only comfort was apparently coming from a bottle not prescribed by any doctor.

Strangely, he admitted that he had not informed either Manchester United or Northern Ireland of his decision to quit the game, but it was something that he intended to do over the course of the next few weeks.

A hint of sadness could be detected behind the confessions. Sadness in letting down Sir Matt Busby and Frank O'Farrell, both of whom had been 'patient and helpful', but there seemed to be a hint of friction between Best and his teammates. He admitted that they had always helped him, but mixing socially with them was something that never occurred.

As for the fans, he considered that now was the right time to go, as in his current condition he could offer them little and that he did not want to leave them with tainted memories and that they should remember the 'real George Best'.

Sadly, 'the real George Best' was a thing of the past, a memory of greatness that had been painfully tarnished. The last year or so had seen him in a different guise. Had he remained, or been allowed to remain, simply a footballer, who knows what greatness he would have achieved. United had tried to help him keep on the straight and narrow, but the pitfalls were numerous and deep.

In Majorca, when asked about the player he had introduced to the world, a stony-faced Sir Matt Busby simply replied, 'You must talk to Frank O'Farrell. He is handling the matter.'

The United manager was clearly bemused by the whole state of affairs, stating,

> The situation remains exactly the same. I'm expecting – and obviously hoping – that George will come to me next Sunday in Israel. But if he doesn't show then we will have to take action. We are not going to pressurise him. This is something he has to do for himself.
>
> Can we survive without George? Well Manchester United lost how many brilliant internationals at Munich and I think the record tells us that they survived. I think that speaks for itself.

O'Farrell was also quite hard-hitting, and showed himself to be a man who would not takes matter lightly.

> Frankly, George Best has not played well all season. He has had his moments, but his form has not been consistent. Since Christmas he has not done anything for us. It is true that when we signed Ian Moore, he showed some flashes – but let's face it, it didn't amount to much.
>
> I am taking nothing as final until I have spoken to George, although I admit he sounds fairly emphatic. Obviously we do not want to lose George. I don't think football as a whole can afford to. Let's face it, football is sometimes so negative, so defensive, that we all love to see a George Best performing out there.
>
> He should know that both myself and Sir Matt Busby are eager to help

him. But I have to admit that this seems a problem that George has to sort out for himself.

We will not take action against George about his failure to report to the Irish team and we will not take action ourselves unless George does not report to us in Tel Aviv next week.

His teammates were asked to restrain their reactions to his walk out, with only Ian Moore commenting, 'I cannot believe that George has been on a bottle of whisky a day. I don't even believe he takes the stuff. And as for hanging around for the pubs to open, this is daft. If you want a drink you can always have it in the house.'

Best had no intention of turning up in Tel Aviv and to O'Farrell's despair, didn't. He had continued to pour his heart out while most probably pouring copious amounts of alcohol into glasses. But within his 'world exclusive' confession, was a portrait of a misguided and lonely soul. Someone who had everything, yet had nothing. Someone who simply wanted a friend, a real friend, who would put an arm around his shoulder, keep him away from the glare of the spotlight and help give him a few hours as a natural human being.

Because that special friend had never been found, Best had to make his own decisions, taking the path he thought was the right one in the maze of life, only to discover it was the wrong one – he had walked into a brick wall.

When the sun set in the Mediterranean and any alcohol that had been consumed had worn off, it suddenly occurred to Best that he had been wrong. He had made a mistake. Getting certain matters off his chest had helped exorcise the demons, for the time being at least, and he reached the conclusion that he still wanted to play for Manchester United. To be part of an inner circle that gave him contentment for a couple of hours a day. He wanted to come back and be forgiven. But would the club and its supporters be prepared to do so?

If they had not already made up their minds, then they had to do so on 9 June, when it was officially announced that Best, who had in the meantime returned to Manchester, had made a complete turnaround and now wanted to stay at Old Trafford. There had been rumours the previous week that he had hinted that he was having second thoughts, but now it was all out in the open.

There was little in the way of an indication on how the club felt, all Frank O'Farrell would say was 'George Best will be informed of the action we propose to take when he reports back for pre-season training.'

From a prepared statement the manager read:

I wish to confirm that George Best has approached me personally to tell me he wants to play for Manchester United – despite what has appeared in the newspapers. The board and I will discuss his request and also his breach of contract in due course for not reporting in Tel Aviv. The newspaper article was also in breach of contract as he did not submit the article to the club for approval before publication.

Although Best had incurred the wrath of both United and the *Express* newspaper group by speaking to the *Mirror*, he continued to speak with the latter publication, telling their Manchester correspondent Bob Russell,

I realise what I'd have been losing. But at the time I was in a hell of a state. I couldn't think clearly, what with all the drinking and the disenchantment of last season. But it's incredible what a few weeks with the sun on your back can do. It's amazing really the way it has all changed. Nobody influenced me. I saw the boss Frank O'Farrell while I was back in Manchester, but my mind was already made up that I wanted to play again. He seemed to understand what had been eating into me. What happened now I don't know. It's up to the club to decide what action to take. All I want to do is play again.

Through it all, Sir Matt Busby had retained his silence on the player. When well away from the furor in Kingston, Jamaica, he finally spoke. 'One thing we have to understand, George Best is a genius. But we are no longer prepared to tolerate his wayward behaviour. His re-entry into soccer will be subject to certain reservations.'

A brief statement, but it was one that got the former manager into hot water, causing further friction at the club, with chairman Louis Edwards saying,

Sir Matt had no right to say anything. It was agreed we would keep quiet until our next meeting. If Sir Matt is laying down conditions, it is a lot of tripe and nonsense.

We have nothing to say until our next meeting when the George Best position will be discussed, because there is nothing to be said.

It was a season that had begun eleven months previously, and was clearly going to overlap with the next as the George Best saga rumbled on. Everything between now and the start of pre-season training would be nothing more than rumours, idle gossip, with life at Manchester United never standing still.

5

A SEASON OF DISARRAY

The new season was eagerly looked forward to by players and supporters alike, hopeful that the new campaign would see the club banish the dismal performances of the previous few months into the history books and start afresh, laying down the foundations of a new and exciting era. Those who paid their hard-earned cash at the turnstiles were also more than eager to find out what the club had in store for one certain individual. Whether or not George Best would indeed return to the fold and find his name on the team sheet in the immediate future.

Surprising to many, Best did make a reappearance, reporting back for training three days early, but whether or not he was keen to learn of his imminent punishment and indeed future, or simply wanted to show enthusiasm in the hope of a leaner backlash from the United board was open to debate.

He had, however, to wait until Thursday 20 July to learn of the club decision, and it would have come with a long sigh of relief when it was announced that he was simply suspended for a fortnight and ordered to live with Pat Crerand, who now held a coaching position at youth team level. Crerand, it was added, had volunteered to accept Best into his home and there was no timescale set for his stay with his former teammate. Best's home in Bramhall was now up for sale for £40,000.

For a player who had walked out on his club and professed that he never wanted to play for them again, the punishment was extremely lenient. Other than put him on the transfer list, there was little else that United could do due to Football League regulations. Undoubtedly, there would have been other unwritten rules for Best to observe, but the punishment certainly did not go down well with a number of the more influential supporters, who had been so incensed by his actions that they were of the opinion that he should have been given a free transfer in order to maintain the club's dignity and standing within the game.

The new season had not even begun, and already there were black clouds over Old Trafford.

Pushing all thoughts of George Best to the side as the open fixtures edged closer, Frank O'Farrell outlined some of his plans and ideas for the coming campaign.

One does not want to turn the players into robots, but the fact is that in recent years, footballers have become more athletic, with their running capacity much increased. We have probably been a little weak in this aspect compared to other clubs. If you have good running, it means that when games are even, and individual skill hasn't won it for you, then pressure can sometimes turn it your way. This can only be done if your team has the capacity for it. I don't want United to lose their special flair, but we are trying to blend it with more team work and running.

The United manager also added that he was still looking to strengthen his team, but continued to talk as if he was preparing for the Olympics rather than the first Division by saying 'I also hope this time, after proving good at the half mile, we shall go the full distance and cover the whole mile with distinction.'

There had been numerous important seasons strewn across United's history, but the forthcoming campaign of 1972/73 would be like no other as it was a pivotal moment with the club's long term future very much in the balance.

The great decade of the sixties had unsteadily merged into that of the seventies, with the wrongful appointment of Wilf McGuinness as coach and then manager. A decision that was wrong for the man and also wrong for the club. Into the breach came Frank O'Farrell, a more experienced individual at managerial level, but who had inherited the same problems as his predecessor. Problems that needed to be solved sooner rather than later.

From the aristocrats in the top flight in English football and a force in Europe, to the ageing beauty who was still capable of turning the odd head, but no longer had the allure to make a whole room sit up and take notice; this was the Manchester United of today.

Prior to the big kick-off, David Meek wrote in the *Manchester Evening News*,

Manchester United bid once again for success in-keeping with their distinguished post-war history of glory and honours. But things may get worse before they get better. Manager Frank O'Farrell has a great many problems to sort out before Old Trafford can be said to be ready for a real challenge at the top. It's a time of change, an era of rebuilding that will take much longer than the twelve months manager Frank O'Farrell has had in the hot seat ... it would be a testing time, for Manchester United have more prima donnas than simply George Best.

The experienced men remember only too vividly those great days of sunshine and roses, with winning the European Cup the pinnacle of achievement. But that was five seasons ago and they have won nothing since. Those warm cosy days with Sir Matt Busby, when all the maestro had to do was to tell them to go out and enjoy themselves, have gone.

It's a different world at Old Trafford these days. They are no longer a great side, some would say not even a good one. Football is a harsh, demanding business and United's senior players must recognise that yesterday's achievements are of little help towards tomorrow's ambitions.

United's senior players were responsible to a certain extent for the failure of Wilf McGuinness as manager at Old Trafford. 'He failed to win their support' said Sir Matt at the time. It could be that some players are not prepared to support any manager. There is a distressing lack of team spirit in some areas at Old Trafford these days.

The most heartening thing for Manchester United is that I don't think the manager will be swayed from sticking to his policies and making the right decisions for the future of the club.

If the players make him do it the hard way, the rebuilding will be a great deal more painful … and that would be a pity for Manchester United.

Pre-season friendlies are little more than fitness gaining fixtures, with more concern placed on overall and individual performances, rather than the actual score itself. But for Frank O'Farrell, the outcome of the quartet of friendlies on United's itinerary must have caused him some concern; a goalless encounter at his old club Torquay followed by a 3-1 defeat at nearby Bournemouth. Then the solitary victory against the amateurs of the Danish Olympic X1, before rounding things off with a 2-2 draw at West Berlin. All adding to the concerns of the United manager even before the League programme had got underway.

Ipswich Town travelled to Old Trafford for that openingday First Division fixture and left with both points following their 2-1 win. Many missed Law's goal 4 minutes from time, as they were either in the nearest pub or on the bus journey home, following the visitor's second goal 2 minutes earlier. The empty red seats glistening in the late afternoon sunshine and the gaps on the terracing containing litter where spectators once stood, were a painful backdrop.

There were also boos echoing around the ground, but they were aimed more at the manager than the players, due to his substitution of Bobby Charlton. Although a number of individuals were playing badly, O'Farrell, knowing that his side had little hope in salvaging any crumbs from the remaining minutes, was proving a point to the others that no one was immune from being dropped or substituted.

George Best, who had missed the pre-season fixtures, returned to the starting eleven, which showed only one change to the team that had played against Stoke in the final game of the previous campaign, with Morgan replacing the injured Law. The Irishman displayed odd flashes of individuality, but clearly lacked fitness and had the discomfort of a broken bone in his hand. The other nine outfield players were completely out of sorts, with Peter Fitton of the *Sun* writing 'this United side is going only one way … to the breaker's yard'.

So, a disappointing start for O'Farrell – and it didn't get any better. Two trips to Merseyside over a four-day period produced even more dismay, with 2-0 defeats at both Anfield and Goodison.

Against Liverpool, the overall performance showed a slight improvement on the Ipswich debacle, while across at Stanley Park, even the home crowd were stunned to hear that Bobby Charlton had been dropped, with the 90 minutes that followed yielding yet another inept performance, with Best again struggling to produce anything remotely like his form of old. There was little co-ordination between midfield, where Buchan found himself in an unfamiliar role and the forward line and even the graft and guile of Messrs Best, Morgan and Moore failed to make any great impact on the proceedings.

Three games, three defeats and only one goal scored. United were already propping up the First Division table. The problems of the past two seasons had intensified and all was not well at Old Trafford.

Ron Crowther wrote in *Daily Mail*:

It's going to take £1 million and a lot of patience to make once-mighty Manchester United again.

That's the price this proud club must now be prepared to pay for four years of neglect and decay. It has already cost close on a million to turn their Old Trafford ground into a soccer showplace worthy of a famous team. But now, for the first time in a quarter of a century, they no longer have such a team.

Even after three defeats in the first week of the season, which has left United floundering at the foot of Division One, it is too early for anybody to panic about the situation.

But after two years of warnings from me about the creaking machinery at Old Trafford, it now seems quite fatuous when fans ask what is wrong with United.

They have problems in defence, midfield and attack. They have ageing players who must be replaced. They have too many players of dubious ability with which to replace them. And they have too many people associated with the club – spectators included – for whom time stood still since that night of glory when they won the European Cup.

Harsh words from the *Mail's* respected writer, but he wasn't finished. Far from it. He continued his assessment.

> Twenty years ago … fifteen years ago … or ten years ago United could, and did, tear great teams apart and replace them from the ranks of those rousing Busby Babes.
>
> But where are the Busby Babes? Where are the budding Bobby Charlton's, Roger Byrne's and Dennis Viollet's?
>
> And what happened to those once prolific production lines after George Best stepped off them eight years ago as the last of the truly great discoveries. It is in this perspective that one must now look at the problems of Frank O'Farrell.

A rare sliver of light appeared through the gloom with a 1-1 draw against Leicester City at Old Trafford, while another point was salvaged when Arsenal travelled north, although the blank score line did little to appease the fans. Neither did the club's inability, or perhaps the lack of inclination to venture into the transfer market, especially when players of quality had been available and their team was crying out for new blood to be injected.

David Nish, a player O'Farrell was more than familiar with, had joined Derby County from Leicester City for £225,000, Mike Bernard; a forceful defender/midfield player, cost Everton £140,000 from Stoke City; another defender, Trevor Cherry moved across Yorkshire from Huddersfield Town to Leeds United for £100,000 and the charismatic and highly skilful Frank Worthington, a player ideally suited to the Old Trafford stage, also left Huddersfield, joining Leicester City for a meagre £80,000. Many were of the opinion that those four individuals would have given United a strong backbone, a quartet they could have purchased in a series of deals without having sleepless nights studying the bank statement that followed. They were wrong, as it was revealed that to do so the club would have to plunge into the red, and the bank manager couldn't be sweet-talked into releasing such transfer funds due to last season's loss of around £250,000.

The bottom line was that the bank statement read a paltry £400,000, with chairman Louis Edwards revealing that the main reason for the loss were the transfer fees paid out for Moore and Buchan. But if the club were going to lift themselves up out of the gutter and appease their supporters, who were already demanding reinforcements to the squad, then they were going to have to plunge deep into the red.

There were other players who had recently moved for what could be considered 'big' fees, who United could have attempted to lure to Manchester – the likes of Alan Mullery, Bobby Hope, Peter Cormack, Geoff Hurst and Jimmy Robertson. All would have helped the needy cause.

The club line was 'the players we are interested in are not available'. Who knows who they were, but even if they weren't available then those previously listed were. It is little wonder that the supporters were frustrated.

Against Arsenal, there was once again no place in the team for Bobby Charlton. Now in his testimonial year, the thirty-five-year-old was perhaps entering the twilight zone of his career, but with United struggling, his influence could have been vital in grasping that lifeline required to haul the club to safety from the depths of the First Division. But while Tony Young and Sammy McIlroy took the number eight and nine shirts against the Gunners, with Eric Young occupying a place on the bench, Charlton was playing reserve team football for the first time in twelve years at Gigg Lane Bury.

Although Charlton had personally asked to play for the Central League side when he learned there was no place for him in the first eleven, there were clubs who were more than interested in acquiring his services if United had longer any need for him. 'We had an enquiry' said O'Farrell, 'but I told the club concerned that Bobby is not available. I will say the same thing to any other manager who comes on about him.' The name of the club in question was never revealed or indeed noted. Whether Charlton would have considered moving on is also up for debate, along with the countless others unasked and certainly unanswered questions of late.

Charlton did make the bench against Chelsea, grabbing 18 minutes of action after replacing Ian Moore, but still United sought their first victory of the campaign, once again firing blanks in the 0-0 draw. Some thought the corner had been turned when they heard that United had actually managed to double their 'goals for' column, scoring twice against West Ham United at Upton Park, but once again the points were shared in a 2-2 draw. A more general view was that United were lucky, and had they been playing a more formidable opponent, they would have conceded at least four.

It was a mystery to some; how had George Best remained in side while not playing overly well and Bobby Charlton had to observe the club's decline from the sidelines? There was even more head scratching when it was announced that Best had been awarded a new six-year contract that would keep him at the club until 1978, when he would be thirty-two, along with casual hints dropped that there was also the possibility of him becoming club captain in the not too distant future. Not bad for someone who, not too long ago, had walked out of Old Trafford and packed the game in.

'I'm enjoying my football more now than at any time' Best said. 'If four months ago anyone had asked me if I would be happy about this situation with United struggling and me doing well, I would have laughed. But right now, all I want to do is play my part at Old Trafford. It's a new challenge for me.'

Even Denis Law was singing his teammates' praises.

Nobody has ever questioned George's talent – he remains one of the world's great players – a position he has held for several years, but in the first difficult weeks of the season he has proved himself as a man, not just a player. Whatever our problems at Old Trafford, George cannot be held responsible. He has accepted a more demanding midfield role in the side which means he does not get the opportunity to grab the headlines with brilliant goals. He has done it with a dedication and resolve, which reflects great credit on him.

The League Cup offered some slight relief away from the hustle and bustle of the First Division dogfight, but in effect, it set United up for a bigger fall from grace and the hands of one of the game's lesser lights; Oxford United being given the opportunity to cause something of an upset.

On what was their first visit to Manor Ground, United were within 4 minutes of going out of the competition at the first hurdle, but the Second Division side were stunned by a Bobby Charlton blockbuster; their goalkeeper not moving until the ball had rebounded back into play.

Six days later, in the Old Trafford replay, two George Best goals and another from Ian Moore gave United a safe 3-1 passage into the next round and a hint of respectability. Something that was more than welcome following yet another League defeat, 1-0 at home to Coventry City. An elusive first League victory was still as far away as ever.

Even further away was the possibility of big-name signings to help the club off the bottom rung of the First Division table. Despite the fear of going into the red at the bank, these were steps that should have been taken, as gate numbers were falling rapidly, with only 21,486 inside Old Trafford for the visit of Oxford United – the smallest attendance for eleven years. If the current slump continued, then more would desert the sinking ship and turning things around would prove to be even more difficult for the manager.

Across Manchester, neighbours City were also experiencing problems and were only a couple of points better off than United. Though as late, they had managed to haul themselves away from keeping United company at the foot of the table. So it came as something of a surprise to both sets of supporters when United, despite their lack of funds, eventually lunged into the transfer market, agreeing to pay the Maine Road side £70,000 for Welsh international Wyn Davies. A move that left many shaking their heads in disbelief.

The thirty-year-old decided to make the 2 mile cross-city journey, having fallen down the pecking order within City. Whether or not he was the type of player United required, or perhaps more to the point, could he fit into the United team would remain to be seen.

Frank O'Farrell was in no doubt that he would indeed fit in when he commented on his new acquisition. 'I think Davies will be a big help to us. He will provide us with additional power up front. He is a brave player and I'm confident that he will do a good job for us.' Davies, who had only moved to Maine Road thirteen months previously, said,

I will do my utmost for United. The main thing will be for me to take some of the weight off the other forwards, going up and challenging all the time. It's something I have been doing all my career. The move was a bolt out of the blue. I was down for light training at Maine Road and was about to leave the ground for lunch when Malcolm Allison called me into his office. I thought he was going to ask me how my broken nose was and if I would be fit for Saturday, but to my surprise he told me that there was not a first team spot at Maine Road for me anymore, but then stunned me by saying, 'but there is a chance for you to sign for Manchester United and I think you should take it'.

If the signing was a surprise, the added comment by Davies that 'at the moment I'm not fully fit, but I'm really excited about my first match, though I don't know when that will be' would really have stunned those of the red persuasion.

So, United have not exactly got money to burn, but they go out and spend £60,000 to £70,000 or whatever on a player who might, or might not fit into the swing of things and who isn't, by his own admission, fully fit. It was little wonder that the club were in the position that they were.

The fall from grace was accelerated even more with a 2-0 defeat at Wolverhampton, 90 minutes of total malfunction with the defence continuing to falter and the forwards, without the recently signed but unfit Wyn Davies, apparently requiring a map to find their way to goal.

Coventry City had attracted a slightly better attendance to Old Trafford than Oxford United, with 37,073 clicking through the turnstiles. Those same turnstiles went into overdrive on 18 September when 60,538 (a British record for such a fixture) were present to pay homage to Bobby Charlton, now reinstated into the side, on his testimonial night with Celtic the opposition.

Arguably, the crowd was augmented by countless green and white clad followers, but such numbers were once commonplace at this ground. Although United stepped up their game a little, they still failed to score and display anything that suggested improvement even although it was little more than a friendly.

George Best soon found himself dragged in to more controversy when it was suggested that he had deliberately missed his teammate's testimonial match, due to the pair not being the best of friends. It was a suggestion that was never proven as being true, with Best himself saying,

> The open secret that Bobby and I do not always see eye to eye must have given rise to this latest bit of sensational speculation. The answers are simply these. I was not fit, therefore I did not play. I do not like watching football, therefore I did not stay. I wanted as much as any of the lads to help pay tribute to a well-respected and great sportsman, but it would have been foolish to risk further damage to my injured ankle.

The press however, were quick to pick up on the non-appearance of the Irishman, while there was also talk of the after-match celebrations. A token 5 or 10 minute cameo appearance would not have gone amiss and would have squashed any such rumours, but totally ignoring Charlton's big night only added fuel to the fire. More so when instead of staying at home and resting his 'injured ankle', he was out on the town.

It also, in many cases, added to already well-worn suggestions that all was not well within the Old Trafford ranks. The pinprick sized problems of four or five years ago had grown, with individuals blaming each other for the club's current plight as it hurled along like an out-of-control train.

Along with the feeling of mutual dislike among some of the players being a minor reason behind the decline of the former European champions, the main reason could be analysed as being simply down to tactics or, more to the point, the failure of individual talents to adjust to a different style of play.

Throughout the Busby era United, although thriving to success after success through teamwork, relied more upon individual brilliance to carry them through. Now, with those once brilliant individuals pushing towards retirement rather than a route to goal, they were finding it difficult to become more tactically aware, in adapting a new style of play as the game itself developed. They were not prepared to adjust to change.

Previously, the defence would break down the opposition's attack, push the ball forward via the half-backs then allow the forwards to complete the job. Today however, more running off the ball was required, more support work needing to be done, with O'Farrell quick to admit to the failing. 'The League table shows that there are twenty-one teams in the First Division who are better than us at supporting the man with the ball.' His assistant, Malcolm Musgrave, added,

> We can't complain about their [the United players'] attitude or their effort, they are all giving everything. They'll run with the ball, or after the ball, but teaching them to run just to make things easier for someone else … well, they've never had to do this before. It's hard getting this across.

Fingers had been pointed, quite rightly so, at the defence, which had been compared to 'a moth-eaten umbrella', but it was to stand secure against Derby County at Old Trafford on 23 September, where the team and debut-making Wyn Davies came under the microscope for even closer scrutiny.

'All we needed was confidence, and this excellent win (3-0) over Derby will give it to us' said assistant manager Malcom Musgrove, accompanied with a huge sigh of relief. Perhaps Frank O'Farrell should have stayed away more often, as his assistant was in charge of things as the manager went elsewhere on a scouting mission.

Davies rose to the occasion, scoring United's second, while causing Derby numerous problems throughout, his cut head and mudded shirt testimony to that, with Moore and Morgan netting the other two as the beleaguered support celebrated the first victory of the season.

O'Farrell took his spending to half a million in the past seven months when he paid Bournemouth £220,000 for noted goalscorer Ted MacDougall, a player who had made his mark in the record books after scoring nine in Bournemouth's 11-0 1971 FA Cup victory over Margate. It was a transfer that made a mockery of United's dwindling cash fund, although it did raise the speculation that the United manager would now consider offloading one or two players to help balance the books. Derby were still keen on the man they had lost out on, Ian Moore, while MacDougall's arrival could make Brian Kidd surplus to requirements.

MacDougall, Widnes-born and who professed to having watched United from the Stretford End as a youngster before joining arch-rivals Liverpool, had apparently been in O'Farrell's sights for three years. On Wednesday 27 September, he finally got his man, prising the Third Division striker away from his former West Ham teammate John Bond at Bournemouth, announcing after the deal was concluded:

> I have wanted Ted for a long time. When I heard that offers would be received, I was interested at once. This sort of player doesn't become available every day. I am sure he will make a great impact on Manchester United's plans and First Division football in general.

Manchester United have this tradition for scoring goals and it is something that must be kept alive. We may have weaknesses in one or two other positions but I am anxious that we should fulfil the tradition of the club and play the kind of attractive football that has made the so popular in the past.

It is not often that a proved goalscorer becomes available. It might not happen again for a long time, and this was something I had to bear in mind when assessing the fee that we should offer.

If a corner had been turned against Derby, a little of that missing confidence restored, then referee Norman Paget clearly did not want Manchester United to begin a run of success that we see them move away from the foot of the table, as his handling of the away match against Sheffield United was described as 'absolutely atrocious' by Frank O'Farrell, who went on to say that the official 'made many bad decisions for both sides and I'm sure Sheffield United were as far from happy about his handling of the game as we were.' The main gripe of the United manager being the dubious penalty awarded the home side 3 minutes from time, Woodward converting the spot kick for the only goal of the game.

Perhaps the referee was simply making amends with his decision to award the kick, as he had turned down a more blatant shout for a penalty 10 minutes earlier when Buchan tripped Woodward inside the area, and it was nothing more than sour grapes from the United manager as general opinion was that the home side deserved to win.

Scoring goals was indeed a problem for United, with only seven in the eleven League games to date, although just as much emphasis had been focused on their defensive failings. But it was the forward line that O'Farrell had his sights on improving, while others would have shored up the back line and then worked forward; he at least displayed that he remained true to United's attacking ethics.

Impatience was growing and the 1-1 draw at Bristol City in the League Cup did little to relieve the tension surrounding the club. The Old Trafford replay pushed that patience further, piling even more anguish onto an already shambolic season, the Third Division side notching a 2-1 success. George Best's penalty miss not helping matters.

Much was now resting on the shoulders of Ted MacDougall with the new signing handed the number eight shirt for his United debut at West Bromwich, his presence taking on the form of a pick-me-up tonic, with his new team looking slightly more competitive, snatching a point in a 2-2 draw. The new signing came close to starting his United career with a goal, but that had to wait until his home debut against Birmingham City the following Saturday. This solitary strike being enough to give United victory.

Obviously overjoyed with the goal, MacDougall confessed,

> It was a tremendous feeling to score on my home debut, but I honestly
> felt mentally shattered during the match. I suppose it was due to the
> mental pressure that built up before the game. It was a much greater
> ordeal than my first game because I wanted to prove myself to the fans
> and the team. Quite frankly, I didn't feel at all sharp and feel I can do a
> lot better now after settling in. But that goal certainly gave me a bit of
> a lift. I knew it was on after Wyn Davies made a great run to draw their
> defenders. I desperately wanted to score and when I saw my header cross
> the line I could have jumped over the stands.

Immediately, it was back down to earth with a bump. Newcastle snatched
victory with the odd goal in three and then Tottenham travelled north and
tore United to shreds in a 4-1 demolition job. By the time Martin Peters,
scorer of all the visitor's goals had notched his fourth in the 79th minute,
many had once again left early.

In his match summary for the *Sunday Times,* Brian Glanville wrote 'for
the sake of this great club, one must hope United won't be doomed to
shuttle between the First and the Second Divisions. A crowd of 52,497
showed remarkable loyalty – or optimism – of their support.' Glanville
added that the back four had all the solidity of a wet paper bag, and the
expensive spearheads looked as if they still had to be introduced.

Following the defeat, O'Farrell said that he had no intention of resigning,
but if what was termed as a 'crisis' continued, he would find himself under
even more pressure and was later to talk of indirect interference from Busby.

> He was always about somewhere where the players could find him.
> After one game, he told me I shouldn't have dropped Bobby Charlton.
> Obviously he said the same to Charlton, because the player was moping
> round the place. Another time he told me Martin Buchan was responsible
> for letting in all these goals, when it clearly wasn't his fault. He was
> interfering.

O'Farrell found some much-needed support in the *Manchester Evening
News* journalist David Meek, who called for 'dynamic leadership from
the board to counter hypothetical questions about O'Farrell's future'.
Meek, having followed the club's fortunes for the local paper since 1958,
was as concerned as any supporter and was merely unhappy that some
of the players were blaming the manager for recent events, rather than
themselves, and felt that the manager deserved more obvious support
from the board.

Les Olive, the club secretary, thanked Meek for his article and support, but hours later, a letter signed by Olive arrived at the *Evening News* offices stating that the club had forthwith withdrew Meek's privilege of travelling with the team to away games and he was no longer welcome on the coach or train.

O'Farrell's future was obviously a touchy subject within the close confines of Old Trafford.

A 2-2 draw at Leicester City produced a chink of sunlight, then it was an all-singing, all-dancing afternoon down by the Ship Canal when arch-rivals Liverpool were beaten 2-0, MacDougall and Davies having finally been introduced, notching the goals. Liverpool's cries of deliberate handball by the former and moans of a denied penalty failing to cast a shadow on the afternoon.

Having defeated Liverpool, next up were an even bigger foe in the shape of Manchester City. Football took something of a backseat during the 90 minutes, which James Mossop of the *Sunday Express* considered the game little more than 'a muck-raking shambles and a disgrace to two famous clubs'. United perhaps found themselves distracted, the players getting involved in petty feuds, allowing Colin Bell to snatch a hat-trick amid a back dropped of snarling supporters.

Against Southampton at Old Trafford, a 2-1 win for United, George Best was indifferent in the victory, with one correspondent penning that the victory was 'in no way due to George Best, for he spent most of yesterday's rainy afternoon closer to the main stand and the changing rooms than the action. He seemed to shrink back from following the attack and was removed and remote from it all.'

The following week, Best was back to his old self, missing training. When he did eventually turn up, two days before the home match against Norwich City, he only stayed for half an hour, long enough to be told that he would not be playing that Saturday. He was also informed that he would be summoned to appear before the board of directors in order to explain his recent actions, as well as being fined, ordered to stay away from night clubs and to put in extra training sessions.

David Meek, who had stood by Frank O'Farrell, did not show the same loyalty to George Best, writing that United would be better off without him and that the player was now making a mockery of the club. The player, due to face the board, had once again took to his heels and headed for London, something that did not surprise his manager, who said 'it is normal form for George when he has to face anything slightly unpleasant. It's strange really. He is so brave on the field, but can't face things off it.'

The arranged board meeting went ahead at Old Trafford without the accused, the verdict coming as nothing of a surprise. George Best was put up for sale and suspended for fourteen days. A fee of £400,000 was put on his head, or perhaps better to say his feet, but few expected United ever to bank that amount, as they felt that the player would simply ride off into the sunset and once again announce 'I quit'.

Despite his now frequent Houdini acts, there was immediate interest in attempting to secure his signature. Brian Clough's Derby County, were one of the forerunners, while Ladbrokes even opened a book on where the player might go, offering 6-4 Chelsea, 3-1 Tottenham, 4-1 on a European side, 8-1 Crystal Palace and Derby County and 12-1 Everton. Bournemouth manager, John Bond, also admitted a serious interest, but stated that he would be prepared to pay no more than £250,000.

Just over a week later came the stunning news that Best was back at United, once again going through his paces at the Cliff training ground, making a bigger mockery of the whole situation.

In a club statement, chairman Louis Edwards said 'I have seen George Best today and discussed recent happenings with him. He only wants to play for Manchester United. I've spoken to directors and our manager Mr O'Farrell. Best will start training as soon as possible and I believe he has been training tonight'. When asked if that meant he was off the transfer list, Edwards replied 'I suppose it does. I don't want to say any more until we have had a full board meeting to discuss the situation.'

All was not well at the ailing club, few had a good word to say about them and rather ironically, the lights really did go out on United when an electricity failure during the half-time interval of their 2-0 defeat at Stoke delayed the second half by 12 minutes; a result that pushed United within two points of bottom club Crystal Palace.

By a strange quirk of fate, United travelled to south London to face Palace the following Saturday, 16 December, a game that could lift the dark cloud that hung over Old Trafford, if only momentarily, and create a bit of breathing space between them and the bottom club.

Best was still suspended, Charlton was missing with flu, both could arguably put up a better performance than some of the eleven at Selhurst Park that afternoon. Palace didn't simply beat United, they destroyed them, the 5-0 score line not emphasising that the home side were in a false position, but emphatically demonstrating that United had huge, perhaps unsolvable problems.

'Oh my God' uttered O'Farrell at full-time, while an unnamed United forward mumbled 'we had no bloody defence' to which an equally frustrated teammate replied 'what chance have you got with forwards who want to do it all on their own?' Things were obviously not well.

The reinstating of Best, coupled with the latest inept performance, once again allowed others to poke fun at the club and its rather brittle-backed directors. Two days after the 5-0 lacklustre performance, Eric Todd of the *Guardian* spoke for every United supporter and indeed lovers of football everywhere, when he wrote in an article headed 'United Must Now Clear the Air':

Sometime this week, with a bit of luck, we shall learn how wrong we were to attach any credence, let alone importance to these utterances (Sir Matt saying he would have far less to do with the playing side and Frank O'Farrell saying he would have full control) or to what extent Sir Matt Busby be he team manager, general manager, director or anything else, controls the destiny of Manchester United. And whether O'Farrell, like McGuinness was before him, is a mere figurehead after all.

The monotonous saga of George Best, having come once more to a head, United for the last time must make it clear (a) why Best has been accepted back into membership and (b) who was responsible for this astonishing volte-face and why.

There must be no more talk of O'Farrell's authority being undermined, for the simple reason that he has none to undermine, at least in the instance of Best.

O'Farrell, quite understandably, found it impossible any longer to cope with that player and equally understandably, left it to the board to see if they could fare any better.

With or without the approval of the manager, they put Best on the transfer list and suspended him for fourteen days. With or without the approval and the knowledge of O'Farrell – I suggest without – they changed their minds and paved the way for Best's rehabilitation. O'Farrell can therefore have no justifiable quarrel with his employer's actions, having himself opted out of the wretched business.

It would seem that United can have Best or O'Farrell, but not both. It would seem that they would rather have the player than the manager.

On the face of it, O'Farrell has no option except to resign. United might also feel justified in sacking him because he has not been able to bring Best to heel or because he has not achieved the results they expected – presupposing it were possible to do both. Obviously there is a lot still wrong at Old Trafford, and until somebody has the courage to reveal the true facts instead of making nebulous, misleading statements and holding secret meetings, United must not cavil if conjecture runs berserk. Above all, it is time that it was made clear who is running Manchester United, time that the manager, whoever he may be, now or in the future, knows his terms of reference.

One more thing. As George best sits quietly in the corner of his favourite pub, I hope that it will dawn on him eventually just what misery and unrest he has generated in a once-famous and respected club.

Eric Todd was not alone in his thoughts, with Derek Potter of the *Express* stating that same day that 'O'Farrell would resign this week, with his contract terminated by mutual agreement', his fellow columnist Alan Thompson equally forthright, adding, 'With all the rumour and speculation that Frank O'Farrell will either resign or be asked to at tomorrow's board meeting.' Thompson was also quick to point the finger at the directors, blaming them for the problems that now beset the team and club.

So, Tuesday 19 December was going to be a pivotal day in the history of Manchester United, and one that would surely put to an end any speculation as to the future of Frank O'Farrell.

David Meek was certain that O'Farrell would not resign, nor would he be sacked, suggesting, 'but sacking the manager after only eighteen months of a substantial contract would only aggravate the problems.' He also stated that one of the current problems was the Best situation, and the way round that was to leaving the Irishman on the transfer list and give the manager the control of the situation. He added 'the alternative would be to sack O'Farrell and virtually make Best manager ... and that is too ridiculous for comment.'

On the morning of the board meeting, it was revealed that there was a new twist in the tale when Louis Edwards said that O'Farrell had rejected an invitation to attend a 'clear the air' press conference. The chairman said 'this morning I mentioned to Mr O'Farrell that I was going to meet the press and make a statement, and I invited him to come along. He said he had a lot of things to do and would rather not come.' When asked about his non-appearance, the manager replied 'I was not invited to any press conference. I do not know what you are talking about.'

At the press conference, Edwards outlined the details behind the Best situation, stating that O'Farrell had been constantly kept in the picture. No matter what, there was clearly a rift between chairman and manager, which was not the ideal situation with such an important board meeting only hours away.

Midday would have been a better time for the meeting – 'high noon at Old Trafford' – with Edwards and his posse packing their six-shooters, waiting for O'Farrell to ride down from Warwick Road towards the (not) OK corral along the side of the railway. But it was held at 11.00 a.m. in the Collyhurst offices of Louis Edwards, with a second meeting due to take place at the ground later in the day.

As O'Farrell approached Old Trafford that cold, sunny late afternoon, he turned to his driver, chief scout John Aston, a member of Busby's first great United side, and said, 'What a lovely day John, just the sort of day for an execution.'

The sky soon darkened over Old Trafford, and not simply due to the time of day, the waiting reporters and supporters shrugging off the evening chill beside the large wooden doors that allowed the chosen few entry into the inner sanctums of the stadium. Just after 5 p.m., those doors creaked open and club secretary Les Olive, himself a former player, stepped forward to confront the throng before him.

As the scuffling and the rustling of paper subsided, Olive, reading from a sheet of club notepaper read,

> In view of the poor position of the club in the League, it was unanimously decided that Mr O'Farrell, Malcolm Musgrove and Mr John Aston be relieved of their duties forthwith. Furthermore, George Best will remain on the transfer list and will not be again selected for Manchester United as it is felt it is the best interest of the club and the player that he leaves Old Trafford. In the meantime, the board will assume responsibility for team selection and the position of manager will be advertised.

But that wasn't all. There was a postscript still to come which said that prior to the meeting, a letter had been received from George Best that indicated that he did not want to play football again. Olive stated that the letter had not been opened prior to the decisions mentioned in the above statement.

Few, if any, supported the United board. When they left the ground later that night, they had to step through a pile of discarded, torn up team pictures, rosettes and a scarf, left at the office door by a disgruntled fan. They were fortunate that they were not faced by a full-blown protest, but many had simply lost heart and couldn't be bothered, as they felt that any complaints or whatever would simply fall on deaf ears.

The two men at the heart of the manager's dismissal, Louis Edwards and Sir Matt Busby, both spoke of the drastic League position being the overall reason for the sackings. The latter adding 'the situation reached the stage where we wanted to clear the air completely. We had to sweep the board clear.' Busby was also quick to confirm that he would have nothing to do with team matters once the new manager was in place, and that he could 'not understand the accusation that I have interfered. I have always given full co-operation since Frank O'Farrell came here. He had a completely free hand to do as he wished.'

Alan Thompson of the *Express* wrote that the reason behind the sacking was,

A sad, sorry, squalid and pathetic excuse to serve upon two men because they could not overnight save a long-ailing giant. John Aston was sacked for the same reason, a man who has known no other club and who has never wanted one. What a pathetic reward that is for loyalty and devotion.

Others thought differently, suggesting that O'Farrell had been destroyed by the players' mafia, with one player admitting that 'some people actively worked for his downfall from the day he arrived and that Denis, Bobby and George were totally closed to new ideas and new tactical developments.' Another was 'hostile' to the attempt to replace the flair with strength and running.

John Aston received a year's wages as a 'reward' for his services. Musgrove was not so fortunate, as he was working without a contract and would only get three months' salary. As for the deposed manager, he would receive somewhere between £35,000 and £42,000. It was little in the way of compensation for not being allowed to finish a job he thought he was capable of doing.

Alex Stepney sympathised with his former manager.

Before Frank, we had Wilf, who wasn't very good at handling players at training. It wasn't all his fault perhaps, but he lacked experience and couldn't get the response he wanted, but with Frank, we thought at first it was a great appointment and we went like a bomb for a time. But he didn't buy any new players in the beginning and you need new players sometimes to give you that extra boost. Otherwise there's not enough competition for places and some players tend to get complacent.

When we started losing, the pressure was on us and eventually Frank went into the transfer market, but it was too late. Somehow or other, Frank seemed to go against the experienced players and some of them lost their respect for him especially when he started treating them like children instead of grown men.

O'Farrell himself was stunned by the decision.

I'll never forget it. The secretary had a scrap of paper in front of him and he mumbled', 'We've terminated your contract'. Matt Busby, who had admitted that he'd let things go, in terms of not bringing in new blood and giving me a five-year deal, and telling me that I'd got three years to sort it out, was sat at the head of the table and he didn't utter a word.

I thought 'I'm not going out of here without him telling me why', so I asked Busby. He looked straight ahead and said, 'No reason.' My time at

Manchester United was over and a week later I was signing on the dole at Chorlton Labour Exchange.

The misery however, was not over for O'Farrell, as a dispute arose with the club over his contract. 'United should've said, "Thank you, it's not worked out, here's your money", but they didn't do that. I had to sue them for my contract.' The £70,000 he was looking for never materialized, and he had to be content with £40,000 in an out of court settlement.

Frank McGhee of the *Daily Mirror* hoped that Best's latest announcement that he was to give up the game would be his last and accused the player of taking some good men down with him. But the reporter also gave his thoughts on why O'Farrell had failed, adding that his ability in the transfer market was one doubt, that although having signed the likes of Moore, MacDougall, Buchan and Davies, he did not sign the much-required midfield player and a centre half. McGhee also questioned his somewhat remoteness from the training ground, when he had been expected to be more prominent and visual in a tracksuit, while adding that his appointment should have 'brought some discipline and harmony to the dressing room, but to be fair, no neutral now believes anyone could have succeeded here.'

In the *Sun*, Peter Batt wrote, 'single-handed, George Best has inflicted upon United a tragedy that is second only to the horrific Munich disaster.' While McGhee's stable mate, Derek Wallis penned, 'the directors have made two attempts to replace Sir Matt Busby while the team has collided head on with crisis and controversy, to the point where it is virtually a First Division write off. Is the job now beyond any man?'

Bobby Charlton was more forthright as regards to his former teammate.

My attitude to George Best is very simple. As captain of the club, I could not and never would, approve of the situation where the players were running 5 or 10 miles a day in training, sweating their guts out for the club, while Best was away missing. Then he would come back as though nothing had happened.

I am not sorry to see the end of George Best.

Alan Gowling countered,

I wouldn't blame George for anything. He pulled out some match-winning performances and in my early days, I could see how much he contributed, not just by sheer genius, but by his readiness to chase back and help out in defence. Like with Wilf, there were changes being made that did not go down well with certain players.

Things began to fall apart at the seams just after we played St Ouens in Jersey. When you are winning, you can paper over many cracks that are in the façade, but when the results start going wrong, those cracks begin to appear again, in no uncertain manner. And that was how it was with Manchester United.

Initially, Frank O'Farrell's appointment was successful, but things changed when he started bringing in new blood.

Manchester United were now in a bigger mess than ever and, as Derek Wallis asked, was the job of managing the club beyond the capabilities of any man? Some might be wary of taking on the job, given the situation with both McGuinness and O'Farrell, but no sooner was the latter's sacking announced than the media were in full flow as to who would be the next manager at Old Trafford.

As the media speculated, and although Louis Edwards had said, 'in the meantime, the board will assume responsibility for team selection and the position of manager will be advertised,' the new man had more or less been decided upon and was possibly even waiting slightly off-stage ready to be called into the spotlight.

The story goes that Scotland manager Tommy Docherty had travelled to Selhurst Park at the request of Crystal Palace manager Bert Head, to run the rule over Glaswegian defender Tony Taylor with a view of perhaps including him in a future international squad. Having witnessed United's humiliating 5-0 defeat, Docherty was in the boardroom when Busby approached and, after exchanging pleasantries, the United director said 'there's a lot of trouble in the camp, do you fancy a job?' Taken slightly aback, Docherty simply replied, 'You've got a manager.' 'We won't have by Wednesday. Think about it', came the shocked response.

So going by that account, an unofficial approach had been made to replace Frank O'Farrell, whose position at the club must have been under scrutiny for some time as the newspapers went from the 'O'Farrell Sacked' headings of Wednesday 20 December's editions to 'Docherty Takes Over at Old Trafford' on those of Saturday 23 December. Three days to make such an important decision, more so after the two previous 'failures', does not ring true. But no matter what had been said at Selhurst Park and in telephone conversations following the fixture, Tommy Docherty (a former Preston North End teammate of Frank O'Farrell) was now manager of Manchester United, having flown from Glasgow to Manchester to meet Louis Edwards and Les Olive and 'officially' agree terms at the airport in the back of a car, before being taken to a Cheshire hotel to meet the players who were staying the night there in preparation for their game against Leeds.

The outspoken forty-five-year-old Docherty was no stranger to controversy since he hung up his boots as a no-nonsense half-back with Celtic, Preston, Arsenal and Chelsea before stepping into coaching and management with Chelsea, Rotherham United, Queens Park Rangers, Aston Villa, Oporto, Hull City and Scotland. As one heading said, 'Tommy Docherty – Some like him. Some loathe him. But no-one can ignore him!' But what would he bring to a disenchanted United?

Having restored faith to a flagging Scottish national side during his fourteen-month spell in charge, taking on the United job, earning £16,000 a year – £7,000 more than his salary with Scotland, but no more than Frank O'Farrell – Docherty would certainly have his work cut out. 'I am delighted about the way things have turned out. I was overwhelmed with the offer and could not refuse it. It seems a question of restoring their confidence. But I must wait until have seen them in action. Then I can take stock,' he said, after agreeing to the deal. If anything, he had the personality and presence not to be made a fool of by any of his inherited players. Those individuals would soon be well aware of where they stood.

Docherty was certainly well aware as to what the job at hand entailed, and pleaded with the often frustrated support to give him time, while also assuring the players that he had inherited that they would be given the opportunity to show what they could do. He hoped that by showing confidence in them, they could produce the form and results that would see the current league position improve.

Although desperate to get on with the job, the new manager made no immediate move to install a number two alongside. Pat Crerand, currently coaching at youth level, was widely tipped to step up and become Docherty's assistant. Others like John Mortimer, who worked with the new manager at Chelsea and Arthur Cox of Preston, were also hinted as being under consideration.

Prior to the match against Leeds, Docherty was introduced to the Old Trafford crowd for the first time. The 46,382, though 5,000 more than had watched the previous home match against Stoke, was still 9,000 less than had watched the 2-0 defeat of Liverpool the month before. Was it simply a case of it being the usual drop in attendance on that last Saturday before Christmas, or was it more a case of many deserting a sinking ship?

The point in the 1-1 draw against Leeds was not perhaps the ideal start the new manager wanted, but it did mean that United, depending on how the other clubs at the foot of the table fared, would require twenty points from their remaining nineteen fixtures to ensure First Division survival.

Docherty moved Law into a midfield role, while Charlton was fit to return, but other than that, those who had stuttered along in recent weeks kept their places. There was in any case, little else to replace them with.

Morgan recaptured a lost zest in his play, while Buchan rose to the occasion, perhaps the one bright spot in O'Farrell's dull reign. Law showed flashes of his old self and Moore and MacDougall showed their new manager that they were worthy of a place within the new regime. Some fourteen points separated the two clubs, but Docherty enthused, 'There is little difference between top and bottom.' Old Trafford regulars might have told him different.

The 3-1 Boxing Day defeat at Derby County, however, opened Docherty's eyes to the gulf between those at different ends of the table. The glitter and all the sparkle associated with Christmas was suddenly torn away to display the shoddy goods and the grime and cobwebs underneath. The 'Doc' was now aware that his ailing patient needed much more than a couple of pills if it was to make a quick, steady recovery. Derby's mud-heap of a ground did little to help United's game, but it could in no way be used as an excuse for the faults of recent weeks being well to the fore once again.

There were only four days of the year left, a dismal twelve months in the history of Manchester United, but Hogmanay celebrations were far from Tommy Docherty's mind, as he set about rebuilding, caring little for the ultimate cost, reputations or whatever. He was the manager and things would be done his way. Time was certainly not something that was on his side.

Within 24 hours of the Boxing Day defeat that had, once again, pushed United to the foot of the First Division, Docherty found the often hidden United cheque book and swooped on one of his former clubs, paying Arsenal £120,000 for midfielder George Graham.

United had lacked such a creative influential since Pat Crerand had pulled the strings; the Glaswegian, now a youth team coach, had been instrumental in United's success-strewn sixties, but the need for someone to dictate play and force the play of the game had been wanting for so long. If anyone could fill the void, then it was the transfer-listed twenty-eight-year-old Gunner.

His being available was more than a plus point, as was his presence in Docherty's Scotland side and his role in their revitalized performances. Both men also held a mutual respect for one another. Graham oozed class, with a hint of arrogance and if ever there was a stage for his undoubted talent, then it was Old Trafford.

Docherty enthused on the decision.

He has always played well for me. He was one of my best bargains at Chelsea when I signed him from Aston Villa for £6,000.

I didn't want to sell him to Arsenal for the £75,000 they paid, but circumstances at the time forced me to do the deal.

When I became Scotland team manager, I had no hesitation in picking him for my World Cup squad. Again he did a marvelous job. I am confident he will do a vital job for us.

Graham, who had been on the verge of joining Everton, but had held back on putting pen to paper when it was revealed that Docherty was interested in signing him, was quick to let his new teammates know what life with the Doc would be like.

> He doesn't hold any grudges. He is essentially an honest man. He's blunt, outspoken and he says what he thinks, sometimes irrespective of the cost. If you are playing well, there is no one like him in the game to build you up and fill you with confidence.
>
> But if you're playing badly watch out – he'll drop you as quickly as look at you. But at least you know where you stand with him. Once he makes his mind up on a course of action that's it.
>
> Obviously every decision he makes is not going to be right, but at least there are no half measures with the man.

Barely had the ink dried on the cheque that brought Graham north, than Docherty was again fumbling for the pen in his pocket to write another, turning once again to a member of his former Scotland squad and paying Partick Thistle £100,000 for their twenty-year-old attacking full-back Alex Forsyth.

Forsyth had sprung to prominence as a member of the Thistle team, which had surprisingly defeated Celtic 4-1 in the 1971 Scottish League Cup Final. Despite his relative inexperience, he was another player who Docherty felt could be an asset to United. The actual transfer only took minutes and few words. Following the initial pleasantries, terms were mentioned, the United manager said ,'Well son?' to which the player replied 'yes', and that was that. 'He's an ambitious lad,' exclaimed Docherty, 'We did not need to talk long to close the deal. He is a great full-back, on the right or the left side. In fact, we've got three players for the price of one.'

'It has always been my ambition to join a top English club,' said the thrice-capped Forsyth, 'and I am delighted that Manchester United have given me the chance. I have enjoyed working with Mr Docherty with Scotland, and am looking forward to this challenge.'

Both Forsyth and Graham were due to make their United debuts at Old Trafford against Everton on 30 December, but a severe country-wide bout of influenza, which had threatened to play havoc with the entire fixture list, saw Everton, their scheduled opponents, have ten senior players on the 'sick list' that forced a postponement of the game. Another fixture to fall foul of the epidemic was Nottingham Forest *v.* Hull City, with the former suffering like the Merseyside club. Upon hearing the postponement of this particular game, Docherty was immediately on the telephone to fix up an Old Trafford friendly with his former club, giving the supporters and the manager himself an early opportunity to cast their eyes over the new additions to the squad.

So it was a new look United who emerged from the Old Trafford tunnel that cold December afternoon, Docherty making four changes to the team who had played against Derby County four days previously. Out went Tony Dunne, Tommy O'Neil, Ted MacDougall and Wyn Davies, and in came Tony Young, Alex Forsyth, George Graham and Denis Law. The Scots were taking over.

Well the majority of them were. One was about to find that just because you qualified to wear the tartan, you did not have exclusive rights to wear the red of United.

Being dropped from the team to face Hull City did not go down too well with the recently signed Ted MacDougall, who was quick, perhaps too quick, to comment on the manager's decision. 'It does not seem that I fit into his plans,' said the disappointed MacDougall.

It has led to some conjecture this weekend and there is no smoke without fire. I wouldn't want to leave under normal circumstances, and there is no question of me asking for a transfer. But Mr Doherty is now the manager and does as he thinks fit.

"Since Tommy Docherty was appointed manager, I felt my face would not fit. With some managers you know you are not going to be wanted.

All the manager would add was, 'I picked what I thought was my best team. MacDougall wasn't selected.'

Wyn Davies, another missing from the 2-1 victory over Hull, a game that meant little at least, brought a little bit of self-belief to the beleaguered side, and was also considering his future. As in the case of MacDougall, numerous clubs were alerted to the possibility of the player being available for transfer. Sunderland, for one, sat poised to make a £60,000 offer should the Welshman become available.

While all eyes were on movement in the transfer market, there was also talk of changes within the confines of the boardroom. John Thomson, a retired textile merchant, whose father had been involved in saving the club from bankruptcy in the 1930s, had stepped forward as the leader of a five-man consortium who were attempting to wrestle control of the club from Louis Edwards.

Thomson had apparently written to the United chairman requesting a meeting, which would lead to his immediate resignation, while also outlining their dissatisfaction at the recent events surrounding the club. Along with a QC, a doctor and three industrialists, all of whom wished to remain anonymous, planned to purchase the complete shareholding of the club, at an agreeable price, and if they were to be successful in their takeover, would reinstall Frank O'Farrell as manager and dismiss Tommy Docherty.

Edwards treated the matter 'as a joke, which I and the club in general are thoroughly enjoying. I have not received any such letter yet, but I cannot see what they hope to achieve, even if they in fact do exist. It is all rather pathetic.'

The matter, unlike the problem between Docherty and MacDougall, soon disappeared.

There was clearly an issue between the player, who had scored thirty-four goals in eighty-four games for York City and 103 in 146 outings for Bournemouth, and the manager. His goals were obviously scored at a lower level within the game, but he was still a player who could prove beneficial in United's fight against relegation and one in which a number of clubs began to show interest in as soon as the rumours began to surface that he could be available for transfer.

MacDougall was an unused substitute in the 3-1 defeat at Arsenal, and was nowhere to be seen in the 1-0 FA Cup defeat at Wolverhampton. Had it not been for Docherty's hard-lined stand, could the results have been any different? Perhaps, as MacDougall's name was back on the team sheet when West Ham United visited Old Trafford on 20 January, the manager perhaps giving him one final opportunity to convince him that he should remain on the United payroll.

'Super Mac' did indeed claim the headlines in the match reports that followed the 2-2 draw, but it was not MacDougall, although he did manage to remain on the pitch for the whole 90 minutes. It was actually Lou Macari, one of the latest duo of tartan clad individuals to arrive at the club.

Prior to Macari's £200,000 signing from Celtic, Docherty had secured the signature of former West Bromwich Albion reject Jim Holton, paying Shrewsbury Town £80,000 for the unknown Scottish under-23 international, as well as paying out £10,000 and £25,000 for the equally unknown Trevor Anderson from Portadown, and Mick Martin from Bohemians.

Holton had also been on Celtic's books, but had been unable to secure a contract. It was only when a letter arrived, at the Scottish Football Association headquarters at Park Gardens in Glasgow, which recommended the rugged young centre half as a possible candidate for the under-23 side that he had come to the Docherty's attention. The Scotland manager travelled south to cast his eyes over the player and liked what he saw, penciling his name into his notebook for future reference.

It was former United goalkeeper Harry Gregg who had taken Holton from West Bromwich to Shrewsbury eighteen months ago, playing an enormous part in his rapid spiral to the top, but he was quick to stress that despite being 'a big strapping lad and particularly good in the air', he also had 'certain limitations in his ground play, but no more than any other developing centre half in England.'

Perhaps somewhat strangely, in the week prior to his move, Holton had been made available for sale by Shrewsbury. United had been tipped to sign centre half Stephen Deere from Scunthrope, with a £50,000 deal all but agreed, but attention soon swung to Holton and the transfer quickly completed. Despite his inexperience, the twenty-one-year-old from Lesmahagow was immediately thrown into the relegation fray by United and his uncompromising style and never say die attitude was soon to endear him to vast Old Trafford support.

Lou Macari had been unsettled at Celtic, and was tipped to join United after Celtic finally agreed to listen to offers for the player. Though Docherty knew he would have to dig deep to secure his signature and pay what would be a record fee, beating the £180,000 paid by Everton for Aberdeen's Joe Harper.

Negotiations were expected to start following United's defeat at Arsenal, but for some reason they failed to materialise. Thinking no interest was forthcoming, Macari travelled to Merseyside for talks with Liverpool. A chance meeting between Pat Crerand, now Docherty's assistant at Old Trafford, and Macari at Anfield during Liverpool's FA cup replay with Burnley, altered United to the possibility of signing the player.

Crerand, unaware of the impending move between Macari and Liverpool, enquired as to what the player was doing at Anfield and was surprised to hear the story. He immediately asked his fellow Scot if he would be interested in joining United. With a positive reply, he told Macari not to sign for Liverpool but to wait for Docherty to get in touch.

Macari returned to Glasgow, and the following day Docherty and Crerand were in their native city, close to where both had in fact grown up, to sign the player. Jock Stein wasn't entirely happy with the player going to United, due to his close friendship with Bill Shankly, but he wasn't too concerned about losing him. It was however, a transfer that almost had fatal consequences and one that would have plunged Manchester United into further disarray and turmoil.

'Manchester appealed to me more than Liverpool' said Macari after signing. 'I felt I would settle down earlier here, because several members of the Scottish international team are with the club.'

Having finalised the transfer, the trio headed south for Manchester. On approaching the Scotland/England border at Gretna, Docherty's three-day-old £5,000 Mercedes was struck from the rear by a lorry in foggy conditions, which then ploughed along its side, ending in a multi-vehicle pile-up. Fortunately no one was hurt, but a rather shaken Docherty said,

> We were very lucky. It could have been a really nasty one, particularly for Lou in the back. There was fog about and this lorry following us had evidently been hit from behind. It thumped into the boot and kept coming, ripping the side of the car.
>
> Lou got quite a jolt. He's ok. He'll pass the medical in the morning, but I shudder to think what could have happened.

The narrow escape was echoed by Crerand, who added 'it's fortunate we were using this car. The one Tommy had been using was much lighter and I don't think it could have taken that kind of impact.'

So it was £1,155,000 spent in the past eleven months – 'The Million Pound Panic' was how the *Daily Mirror* described it, a figure that would have concerned the money-fixated board, as the previous September the club had announced a £245,958 loss, the biggest in the club's history. A figure not helped by the wages and bonuses paid out. £150,000 had been recouped in the past year through the sales of Alan Gowling to Huddersfield (£80,000), Francis Burns to Southampton (£40,000) and John Aston to Luton (£30,000). The manager would now surely have to balance the books and release his apparent firm grip on the United cheque book.

Strangely, following the signing, Docherty said 'I think Macari and MacDougall will form a very good spearhead', and it was a partnership that MacDougall looked forward to building on, even though he confessed that the new signing was a threat to his place in the side.

United had shown spirit against Arsenal, a smattering of style along with a hint of a different tactical game plan, but they were still comprehensively beaten by the Londoners, perhaps due to the deployment of a less than attacking attitude. With time not exactly something United were blessed with, the 3-1 defeat firmly cemented them at the foot of the table, their options, despite the influx of new players, were clearly limited and the FA Cup defeat at Wolverhampton, actually being a blessing in disguise, displayed an even bleaker side to United's perilous position.

Spending vast amounts of money on players, who in general were untried on the First Division stage, was a gamble and was certainly no guarantee against avoiding the drop. If the sure-footed approach by McGuinness and O'Farrell had been proved a failure, then Tommy Docherty was certainly going to cast fate to the wind and gamble if need be against his team's drop to Second Division status.

The support had certainly not deserted the cause, and it could be said that they were invigorated by the arrival of the new manager and his collection of new signings, with 50,878 turning up for the visit of West Ham United on 20 January and 58,970 for that of Everton four days later. The attendance for the visit of the 'Hammers' was perhaps rather surprising, due to the team's performance in the previous two fixtures and the dismal weather on the afternoon, saw numerous supporters wearing tartan 'tammies', the Scottish lion rampant flag appearing on the Stretford End and a pipe band version of 'Amazing Grace' echoing out of the loud speaker system. The eight Scots in the United line-up would certainly have felt at home.

The afternoon, however, would belong to only one of that octet from north of the border, with Lou Macari immediately ingraining himself to the United followers by scoring an 80th minute equalizer, giving United a well-earned point from a 2-2 draw, fighting back from being 2-0 down.

Another point was won in the fight against relegation with the 0-0 draw against Everton, but it was the game that produced further conflict between Docherty and MacDougall. After 56 minutes, Kidd replaced the Scot, a decision which the crowd did not take too kindly too. MacDougall also left the ground as quick as it took to have a shower and get changed, much to his manager's annoyance. His actions played right into Docherty's hands, supplying sufficient ammunition to warrant a place on the transfer list and his eventual sale. Rather surprisingly, a chat between the pair ended amicably and the early departure from Old Trafford was forgotten.

Despite the influx of new players that the cheque book had brought to Old Trafford, Manchester United still had their problems. The injection of Scottish blood failed to give Docherty's side a solid backbone, a clannish solidarity that would fight to the death for the cause at hand.

The fight was certainly there, with another vital point salvaged against Coventry City, but it was immersed in a series of petty and retaliatory fouls which Highfield Road's biggest crowd of the season did not take kindly to, booing the visitors off the pitch at full-time. Even Docherty's replacement as Scotland manager, Willie Ormond, was not impressed. 'I thought United were a poor side', he was to comment. 'But I liked Jim Holton, the lad who scored their goal. He's a bit crude at the moment, but once they get rid of the rough edges, I reckon he'll develop into a really fine centre half.'

Two Bobby Charlton goals against Wolves at Old Trafford gave Docherty his first win as United's manager, making it six points from seven games, certainly not trophy-winning statistics, but enough to take United from propping up the table to fifth bottom, three points clear of West Bromwich Albion.

A 4-1 defeat at Ipswich, however, knocked the wind out of their sails, but suddenly it was like bygone days at Old Trafford, European football was back on the agenda. Well, European football of a sort and one that the support was certainly not enthused about, with a meagre 23,951 clicking through the turnstiles for the visit of Fiorentina in the Anglo Italian Cup. By the time the final whistle blew, many were long gone, such was United's performance. If a cup tie could not revitalise the ailing club what could?

Bournemouth were due a bonus of £20,000 if Ted MacDougall was to score twenty-five goals in a red shirt. Had they known a change of managers would take place not long after selling their prize asset, then they might have rewritten the 'add-on' part of the contract to 'playing twenty-five games', rather than waiting on the player to score twenty-five goals. Even then they would have lost out.

In reality, United would have been more than happy to pay out the £20,000 (they had to a number of years later when Bournemouth successfully took them to court over the contract clause, stating that the player never had the opportunity to score twenty-five goals), but instead they recouped £150,000, by selling MacDougall to West Ham United, after putting the player on the transfer list. Docherty claimed that MacDougall had told him he was unhappy with his current form, and that a move would be in his best interests, adding that the player's wife had failed to settle in Manchester and wanted to return south, with the family home already on the market.

MacDougall would later speak of a far from settled and harmonious club, with a dressing room that was anything but happy, and one that contained something of a split, with a 'them' and 'us' mentality between the older heads and the new signings, adding that some of the latter had to get changed in the reserve dressing room prior to training. He was also to say that Sir Matt Busby never spoke to him once during his five months at the club.

A move certainly suited MacDougall, as he was glad to get away from Docherty more than anything and with a straight choice between Tottenham and West Ham, he chose the latter. Strangely, Docherty tried to sign MacDougall a number of years later when he was a manager in Australia.

Training under the new regime was a far from leisurely affair, more so since the arrival of Tommy Cavanagh from Hull City, who was responsible for much more than running onto the field with a sponge bag if a player was injured.

Cavanagh was old school, a rigid regimental individual, who bullied his charges until they were virtually on their knees. No one was spared and Ian Moore, who had experienced the gruelling sessions under the new trainer while at Nottingham Forest said, 'I don't think any of the other lads had ever been through a training session like it before.' Despite the intensified hours out on the training pitch, no amount of hard work could guarantee results, as a 2-1 victory was typically followed by a 3-1 reversal at Birmingham City. United simply could not generate a winning run and accumulate the points that would lift them clear of relegation zone. They were one of three clubs on twenty-four points, with only West Bromwich Albion below them, two points worse off.

At times, physical strength more than skillful football could earn you the rewards that were on offer. While the post-war Manchester United were noted for their attacking flair, there was always the odd individual who was not afraid to take the knocks that went part and parcel with top flight football. They were not, however, a team that you would associate with the rougher side of the game. At least not until now when the chips were down, and if you were going to have to scrap to grasp any morsel that would ensure your First Division safety, then so be it.

This was something of a new era in the club's history, moving from one age to another. Docherty's men had not dropped as far as the Stone Age, becoming Neanderthals, but reports following their 2-1 victory over Newcastle United spoke of 'having entered the Iron Age in their craving for survival', and 'a game which was always hard and tough without being ugly'.

'It's a shame that Manchester United have to go down in the world to stay up in the League', wrote the *Sun's* Tony Carter, while the *Mirror's* Ted Macauley penned, 'like cornered men, they are fighting fiercely for every chance of escape and inevitably somebody, something is going to get hurt. I feel it will be United's reputation. All that is dangerous in ramming steel into your tactics exploded in a shameful finish.'

United already had a reputation for thuggery and premeditated violence off the pitch, and no-one wanted to see the club stoop to underhand motives during the duration of a game on the opposite side of the touch line, dragging its good name through the mire in an effort to secure its First Division safety.

Newcastle arrived at Old Trafford in fifth place, with the championship crown out of reach and would have been content, as the opening 44 minutes showed, to simply see out the game and return home with a point. United looked likewise simply content to go through the motions, and grasp another point in the hope that it would aid their survival.

But with 1 minute remaining before the interval, Charlton took a corner on the left, the ball was only partly cleared as far as Holton, who volley home from 20 yards out. The goal, plus the half-time team talk, installed a form of belief into the side that had been missing before the break and they approached the second half with a completely different mentality.

From the offset, they pushed forward seeking that second goal and it came, as expected, when Martin drove home from 25 yards in the 53rd minute. They were once again driven to the edge of uncertainty 4 minutes later, when Nattrass slipped through to reduce the leeway. The goal installed a little bit of belief into the visitors and anxiety into United, but through grit and determination the points were secured, despite a nail-biting and all-action finish.

With a matter of minutes remaining, MacDonald and Holton rose to challenge for a high ball, the Newcastle player falling to the ground clutching the back of his head, caught from behind by the United number five. As MacDonald lay apparently unconscious, many thought he was simply making the most of it, including Macari, who attempted to drag him to his feet. Surprisingly, the referee sent Holton off and suddenly the scene was a melee of players.

Smith, who had been earlier substituted, dashed onto the pitch to pull Macari from his teammate, Morgan and Clarke became involved, as Tommy Cavanagh screamed abuse at his opposite number on the Newcastle bench. The referee, for his troubles, was pelted with cushions from the stand as he left the field at the end.

MacDonald, even through the mists of time, clearly remembered the incident.

Frank Clark, our left-back, looked up the line ready to distribute a long ball up to his forwards and I came diagonally towards the sideline, near to the dug-outs. Frank duly knocked the ball beyond the midfield as I timed my run, so that the ball bounced yards in front of me. But as it was then coming upward toward my chest, I duly slowed and shaped myself to cushion and smother the ball with my body.

Jim Holton came running up behind me, as I had the ball nicely nestled on my chest, and 'nutted me in the back of my head, full force, nothing subtle about it, it was a full-blown 'Glasgow Kiss'.

Down I went with stars racing round my head, and then I became aware of a voice screaming all sorts of invective in a heavy Scottish brogue.

'Get up yer cheatin' bastard yer. He nevva touched yer, yer f***ing, cheating bastard'. And so the gentlemanly exchange continued as I was shocked back to full consciousness more by the physiotherapist's cold sponge than spittle-ridden name calling. There was no blood, but a large swelling, no matter, my vision wasn't double, so I was ok to continue the match.

'Yer see ref, there's nuthn' wrang with 'im, he's fakin' it all!'

The referee quite rightly sent Jim Holton off, who knew full well what he was doing as he did it. But it took the United manager Tommy

Docherty all of an hour to forgive me, and was gentlemanly enough to shake my hand at the end of the match, with a sly, 'yer still a cheatin' bastard', out of the corner of his mouth.

The win eased United's relegation fears, momentarily at least, allowing them to secure a more favourable place in the table, but safety was still far from guaranteed.

Holton was no shrinking violet, and despite his inexperience at this level of the game, he was unfazed by reputations and occasions, and was seen by many as raw, uncouth and brawn without brain. For United though, he was their Robert the Bruce and William Wallace rolled into one, taking on all comers in the search for greater glory to the cause.

The Scot had already fallen foul of officials during a friendly against one of Docherty's old clubs, Oporto, when he was sent off following a flare-up in the 0-0 draw and had just returned from a two-match suspension for picking up too many bookings. He was in danger of becoming a marked man, although his performances brought nothing but praise from his teammates. The man directly behind him in the heart of the United defence, Alex Stepney, said, 'Jim's certainly made life easier for me. He plays with great determination. In my opinion, he's the best number five we've had since Bill Foulkes.'

Foulkes himself was also quick to add, 'he is a real hard diamond. The sort of player you can build around. He's extremely mobile and for a big man, he is exceptionally good with his feet.'

If the Newcastle game blotted United's copybook due to the often unsavory play, then the following fixture, another Anglo Italian Cup tie, this time in Rome against Lazio, took on the mantle of the title fight following the warm-up bout.

Somewhat strangely, the competition's fixtures saw English referees in charge in Italy and their Italian counterparts in charge in England. Against Lazio, referee Gordon Hill certainly had his work cut out as he attempted to control a match that continuously looked like bubbling over. Hill, wary of inflaming the volatile crowd, had been tempted to send off one or two of the home players, but decided against it. Though one of the Italian newspapers hinted that had it been a domestic championship encounter, then four Lazio players would have been dismissed and suspended for three games. Their general manager had also been so incensed by the display of his captain that he had wanted to strip him of the position.

The referee was also to injure a hand as he tried to keep warring players apart after Facco broke his jaw in a collision with Kidd with the ball 20 yards away. Littered with petty, as well as retaliatory fouls, it was of little surprise that the game finished goalless.

While in Rome, United could well have been charged for bringing the game into disrepute, with their private audience with the Pope being seen as seeking some divine intervention in their fight against relegation. Ten minutes with his holiness was all that they had, but it could have been enough.

'Never cease to be conscious of the influence for good that you can exercise. Always seek to live up to the finest ideals both of sport and of right living' the Pope told his guests. Perhaps he had witnessed United's previous two fixtures.

The pontiff's words seemed to fall on deaf ears, while his actual blessing seemed to have a more positive effect, with United hitting an unprecedented run, certainly of late, going unbeaten over the course of the next seven games as the season drew towards its conclusion.

Against Tottenham at White Hart Lane, United's reputation continued to be tarnished, the once gifted side now no longer able to depend on silky skills to secure victory, or indeed a point, now relied on whatever means possible to avoid defeat. Had the result hinged on fouls, then the visitors were outright winners, twenty-four to thirteen, although had the referee been more vigilant, or more of an authoritarian then that gap would have been wider, as many of United's more palpable fouls went unnoticed and unpunished.

Had United taken the opportunities that fell to them, both points would have been theirs, but having kept Tottenham at bay following Graham's 5th minute goal, his first for the club, a Jennings save from Charlton and a wasted chance by James, amongst others, proved fatal when Chivers equalized 5 minutes from the end.

The 2-0 victory at Southampton, as March came to an end, was looked upon by many as an act of generosity, extending the hand of friendship when others were quick to castigate, practically gifting United both points and a First Division lifeline.

Unbeaten at the Dell since September, Southampton looked uninterested, while United, for once played a more open game, devoid of the tardiness of recent weeks. Following their goals from Charlton in the 17th minute and Holton 6 minutes into the second half, they displayed, certainly later in the game, a touch of class in midfield, while the defensive pairing of Holton and Buchan enjoyed a comparatively easy afternoon for a change.

United could have now done without their Anglo Italian Cup fixtures, which were by now simply an interference to more important matters. Not surprisingly, Tommy Docherty shuffled his line up slightly, having introduced Peter Fletcher and Paul Jones against Fiorentina, Trevor Anderson against Lazio with Jim McDonagh on the bench. Another youngster, Frank McGivern, was to see action in the 3-1 home victory over Bari, a game devoid of the bitterness previous encountered in those fixtures, as well as the throbbing backdrop from the terraces, a mere 15,000 inside the ground.

Life was still precarious at the foot of the First Division, and the visit of fellow strugglers Norwich to Old Trafford, followed four days later by that of Crystal Palace, arguably the two most vital 90 minutes of the season, would go a long way in ensuring either safety or the prospect of relegation.

On the morning of 7 April, the table read

17	Everton	played 34 points 30
18	Stoke City	played 36 points 29
19	United	played 35 points 29
20	Crystal Palace	played 35 points 27
21	Norwich	played 35 points 25
22	West Brom	played 36 points 24

Norwich offered little in the way of resistance, a club already accepting the fate staring them in the face, while United were equally subdued, unwilling to take risks; there was too much to lose. The first half was bland, while the second, almost equally so before coming to life late in the game, stirred into action by Mick Martin's 81st minute header which secured victory.

As per normal, many had departed before the former Bohemians player had nodded the ball past Keelan, but had they enjoyed the benefit of hindsight, then they would have remained in their places until after the final blast of the referee's whistle, before departing with a tear in their eye.

Having returned from injury against Bari, Denis Law – out of action for some three months – marked the occasion with a goal, ordinary by his standards, but his last in a red shirt. None were aware however, that the sight of the red number ten shirt disappearing down the Old Trafford tunnel at the end of the Norwich City game was a moment of historic significance – an 'I was there moment'. 'The King' had played his last game for Manchester United.

The mane of blonde hair, the cuff of his shirt gripped firmly, arm straightened with a finger pointing skywards, heralding yet another goal, perhaps a trademark bicycle kick, the brushes with authority. They were all part of the Denis Law make-up.

An individual of extreme talent, tailor-made for Manchester United and its Old Trafford stadium. Had the one-time European Footballer of the Year been able to withstand the rigours of the modern game and in recent times retained a more positive level of fitness, then perhaps Tommy Docherty's team would not have found themselves in their current position.

Law was gone. United were much poorer without him.

Crystal Palace arrived in Manchester four points adrift of United, and only one above the two sides below them West Bromwich Albion and Norwich City. When the two sides had met at Selhurst Park back in December, now seeming like a lifetime ago, Palace hammered United 5-0, resulting in Frank O'Farrell's departure. The current United side was a mixture of the old and the new, but few cared about revenge, the sought-after victory was for First Division safety, not re-righting any wrongs. There was however, something in the way of an added pleasure should a victory transpire, as Malcolm Allison, former City assistant manager, was now in charge of the London side. As an often vocal criticiser of United, the opportunity to silence him would be more than welcome.

Don Rogers, who had wreaked havoc on the United defence in south London was fortunately injured, so it was left to Whittle to pose a threat. Having missed an early opportunity, a couple of robust challenges from Tony Young reduced his contribution to the game, with United soon in control.

Although nothing like the United of old, the 2-0 victory was still convincing and all but guaranteed First Division for another season, but it still lacked the polish and the finesse associated with the club. Both were perhaps part of the ideal world, but in the grim fight for survival at the foot of the table points were the staple requirement, and securing them by any manner of means was the main objective.

George Best had not only been missing from the United team sheet of late, but he had also managed to escape the attention of the front and back pages of the national press over that same period of time. What he was up to during his time in self-exile is anyone's guess, but he was certainly keeping something of a low profile. Interest from other clubs, looking more towards next season than the final few games of the current one, had begun to surface, but Docherty said that the player would have to return to Old Trafford and training before anything could be discussed. If anyone was to make an offer for the wayward Irishman, then there was a strong possibility that the board would agree and there would be no need for Best to return to United.

Malcolm Allison, who had hinted at signing the player when he was at Maine Road, expressed an interest in signing him for Crystal Palace, but Best surfaced long enough to say that he had an open mind about such a move, but was not entirely sure if he actually wanted to return to playing.

A few ears suddenly began twitching with the mention of Best's name, with Aston Villa and Queens Park Rangers dropping casual hints that they might also be interested in signing the player as long as terms and conditions were suitable.

With the weight of relegation removed from their shoulders, many expected a more carefree approach to the remaining fixtures. There was no such luck, and Bobby Charlton's 600th League appearance against Stoke City at the Victoria Ground was as grim as any of its predecessors.

'United's football remains sadly mediocre'. 'An afternoon I thought would sing with skills no longer harnessed by the tension was mostly disappointing. As entertainment it was straight from the League of Rubbish'. 'This game slumbered like an extinct volcano' were just a few of the words written about the 2-2 draw, two own goals or one and a deflected Macari shot were the sum total of United's afternoon. Nothing seemed to change.

But there would be change, perhaps not in the final month of the campaign, but certainly next season, when the inclusion of Bobby Charlton on the United team sheet would be no more, as the thirty-five-year-old decided to call it a day and vacate his peg in the Old Trafford changing room.

'I've decided to finish playing at the end of the season. It's a simple statement, but the decision has been reached in the best possible circumstances' announced Charlton to a hushed, packed press conference at Old Trafford on Monday 16 April.

He continued.

I would have hated to leave under worse circumstances, but everything in the garden is rosier at Old Trafford these days. I leave United in the perfectly good and capable hands of Tommy Docherty and there are also a lot of young players on the way up who can take my place.

I am very interested in management, but have no plans. I am taking a PFA course in management this summer. I have been thinking about my retirement for a few weeks now. It would be a clean break at United at the end of this season. When I talk about going into management, I have no aspirations at Old Trafford.

United have a good manager now, in Tommy Docherty. I shall miss playing. Everybody does, but I've never been a great advocate of player-managers and I certainly don't want to play for any other club when I do get fixed up in management. I'll always remember how lucky I have been at Old Trafford.

It has been my life.

Both Tommy Docherty and Sir Matt Busby wanted Charlton to extend his playing career by at least one other season, but he was steadfast in his decision.

I could go on playing, but I feel I have not much left to contribute.

If United had been relegated it might have been different. I would have owed it to them to continue.

As it is, I'm going to miss it like hell, but my decision is final.

There were countless plaudits from around the world, such was the esteem that he was held in. The remaining five games turned into something of a Bobby Charlton appreciation society national tour, amid presentations and applause.

A surprise 1-0 victory at Elland Road killed off any title aspirations that Leeds United possessed, while guaranteeing United's First Division safety. The two points, coupled with the recent fine run of results, pushing United up to a previously unimaginable twelfth place.

Although they couldn't be classed as local rivals, there had been enough spilt blood between the two sides in recent years to warrant this win as being one to cherish. The gates were locked well before kick-off, and the two Leeds supporters urged to return home by an announcement over the PA system (one as his house was on fire, the other because a car had crashed into his shop window) were spared witnessing their team's title dreams vaporise into the cold night air.

Survival had been a long and often rock-strewn road, but the relief felt within the club was unmeasurable, with no-one enjoying the more relaxed atmosphere than Sir Matt Busby. It had pained the man who had built the club from the ruined stadium, with an undistinguished squad in those immediate post-war years, to that of European Champions, only to see it all crumble around him.

'Things are going right again' he told David Meek in a rare interview.

There is a spirit about the club again and I feel the future looks reasonably good.

Tommy Docherty and Tommy Cavanagh have this knack of human contact and have created a good relationship with the players. They have given them spirit and the will to fight for results.

Tommy Doc has got this ability to communicate to players. He makes them feel part of it. He gives them something and in return they give something back. They have all responded to him, playing to win and running about to win.

Before Tommy arrived, it was like a nightmare. We were all under a cloud with embarrassment and headaches. I was beginning to lose hope. I thought an improvement would never come.

We were in a very perilous position and I just couldn't see us escaping without doing something. Now I feel we are over the hill. After the crystal Palace result I felt we had won the European Cup all over again. It is a tremendous feeling of relief.

What the club did has also been justified.

But the celebrations of Charlton's career were to be blemished on his home turf, with a dismal and ill-tempered 0-0 draw with neighbours City, followed two days later by an equally inglorious 2-1 home defeat by Sheffield United.

Bobby Charlton deserved a better send off from his Old Trafford home, a place where he had toiled in an attempt to restore the glory days of old, and where he had played a huge part in illustrating the history books with magical goals and memories. The crowd, as was now becoming the norm, invaded the pitch at full-time, some swinging on the cross-bar, the majority packing the area in front of the main stand beckoning Charlton to make one final encore. Not to disappoint, he appeared briefly in the directors' box and uttered a few discernable words towards the chanting crowd before leaving the stage for the final time.

Although leaving the Old Trafford stage, Charlton still had two United fixtures to fulfil. His final League appearance at Stamford Bridge, like his last hurrah at Old Trafford, ended in defeat. Chelsea, after paying homage to the player won by a solitary goal in 'a game so bad it was embarrassing' according to one account.

Many bemoaned the fact that no representatives from the Football Association had graced the occasion with their presence, making their own presentation to the man who had done so much for English football. Instead, they had merely insisted that Chelsea's 'farewell present' to Charlton should cost no more than £25.

Charlton's First Division send-off was somewhat overshadowed by the announcement on the morning of the game, that Tommy Docherty had given free transfers to both Tony Dunne and Dennis Law. The manager, already looking towards next season and believing that neither player fitted into his plans.

'Tommy Docherty has treated me well', said Dunne upon being given the news.

> He told me there was no hope of getting back in the first team, with three players fighting for the job. I didn't want to hang around until the end of my contract. I had the choice, but I want to get involved in the game.

The decision to give Denis Law a free transfer, however, was clouded in controversy.

Missing from the United line-up since early April, Law had been at the Cliff training ground for a light session. Before leaving he was called into Docherty's office, where he was told that he was being given a free transfer. Somewhat taken aback by this, as he still had a year of his contract remaining, Law told his manager that he would prefer it if he could simply announce at the time of his testimonial match the following season, that he was going to retire, before taking up the agreed coaching job with the club. 'No problem', said the Doc. Hands were shaken, and Law left to travel to Aberdeen for a short break to visit his mother. It was a bitter blow, more so because Law had been one of the players who had put in a good word for Docherty when moves were afoot to offer him the United job.

Back in his home city, unaware that the story of him being given a free transfer had already appeared in that day's *Manchester Evening News*, a lunchtime visit to a local pub left Law stunned when an announcement on television told him that he had been given a free transfer. The reign of the 'King' was over. Docherty had gone back on his word, and Law subsequently moved across town to rejoin Manchester City.

Upon returning home from Stamford Bridge, Charlton's boots had to be polished one more time as United travelled to Italy to fulfil their final fixture in the Anglo Italian Cup against Verona, his 752nd appearance for United. The curtain coming down as it had gone up, with the lad from Ashington scoring twice.

The 4-1 win against Verona was expected to bring to a close one of the most turbulent seasons in the club's history. However, the newspapers couldn't get enough of Manchester United who, despite their scrap for survival, still managed to be the top draw at grounds around the country, with six of their opponents enjoying their highest crowd of the season on United's visit, while more than 1 million people clicked through the Old Trafford turnstiles, producing an average of 46,000 per game (their highest gate was 61,500), almost 5,000 more than the next best.

Transfer speculation continued to take up the majority of written words, with reports of a definite move for Chelsea's Alan Hudson on the cards; the talented midfield player was seen as the perfect replacement for Bobby Charlton. Celtic defender David Hay, valued at £200,000 (£50,000 less than Hudson), was another player apparently attracting Docherty's attention, with recent signing Alex Forsyth being offered as part of the deal. Even George Best's name was to reappear. The Irishman, who now seemed to reside in Spain, had flown home for hospital tests, considered merely 'routine', while also hinting that he was 'keen' on a move to Aston Villa. Chelsea, Real Madrid, Barcelona and Valencia were also named as being 'interested' in the player as the sun at last shone over Old Trafford, with the players and supporters alike heading off on holiday to recharge their batteries for the forthcoming campaign.

6

A CHANGE OF POSITION

'I think we are just one player away from completing the side,' announced Tommy Docherty on the eve of the new season.

But even if we don't make that signing I'm confident the present squad can do well.

I didn't buy only to survive last season. I bought players for the future.

This is going to be a vital season for us. People want success quickly but I know it can take time. We need a good start and I want us to be in things right to the finish.

Manchester United didn't get that hoped-for 'good start', but they were certainly 'in things right to the finish'. However, not in the way that Docherty wanted, or indeed imagined. It was to be a turbulent season in the club's history. Not so much a rollercoaster ride, but a helter-skelter one. The ending, if suggested a handful of years previously, would have been laughed at, as it was to be, but not by anyone with an Old Trafford connection.

Pre-season was relatively uneventful, taking in fixtures from Hamburg and the Highlands of Scotland to a sun-kissed Spain, before kicking off the League campaign with a trip to Highbury to face Arsenal. It took all of 2 minutes for the travelling support, many of whom invaded the north London pitch prior to kick off, and everyone else connected with the club, to realise that little had changed from the previous campaign; United were once again going to have a fight on their hands if they were to keep their heads above the relegation zone.

United huffed and puffed against the Gunners, but could make little impression on the game in the warm, late summer, sunshine. Their tardiness, in midfield especially, was a major component in their 3-0 defeat.

There was little difference between this United side and that of last season, only Sidebottom and Charlton, who had played a few miles down the road in that final game at Stamford Bridge and did not feature at

Highbury – the latter of those had of course retired. Daly and James made up the dozen on show against Arsenal.

When two goals down, United did show some odd signs that they could compete and might have found further inspiration had Graham's header beaten Wilson rather than hit the bar. Over the course of the 90 minutes though, they did little to show that this season would be anything different than the last.

Back in Manchester, Denis Law, in the light blue of City scored twice, one a trade-mark bicycle kick. His presence would have been appreciated elsewhere.

Stoke City's visit to Old Trafford was United's 2,000th First Division fixture and they were to celebrate it with a 1-0 victory courtesy of a rare Steve James goal, allowing them to get the season up and running, determined not to be left clutching at the coattails of others. It was soon to be two wins out of three and seventh place in the League, with a 2-1 home victory over Queens Park Rangers. No runaway 8-1 success this time around, but it was still two points. That was all that mattered.

But despite the win, Docherty was far from happy. 'We were terrible, to put it mildly', said a dissatisfied United manager. 'I am being very kind if I say I was disappointed', he went on. 'I said to our lads at half-time, "Let's start working. We can only get better. We are a young team and we lack experience. Perhaps we need to talk more – help each other on the field."'

Tommy Docherty, however, was not the only one to voice his opinion about United over the course of the 90 minutes, as the visitor's sometime-match winner, often bad boy, Stan Bowles also had a few choice words to say. 'It was a scandal, they should lock them up for robbery like that' he protested, going on to say 'this United side are just not in the same street as the old lot. They're the worst team we have met. United are a really lethal lot. Crude you might say.'

So, only three games into the new season and already United, despite getting off to a favourable start, were displaying a rough edge – perhaps like last season, being determined to make up for any flaws in their make up with a touch of steel, attempting to knock their opponents off their game in order to grasp the advantage.

Even with only those two victories, the opinion was that it was still going to be a long hard winter for United, and Docherty still had much work to do as there were numerous problems surrounding his side and if progress was to be made, then it was going to cost them time and money.

Docherty was meanwhile still monitoring David Hay, Celtic's midfield-cum-defender, who had just been granted a transfer request by his club. Such was Hay's status, countless others were also keen to add the Scot to their ranks, not put off by the £200,000 plus fee. There was however, a player who was equally brilliant, but perhaps not quite as versatile, who could enrich United at no cost whatsoever – George Best.

Yes he could still be located around Manchester now and again, but could currently be found in Majorca, and he was being offered something of an olive branch by the club. 'We want him to come back and start training', said chairman Louis Edwards. 'The question of whether he plays for United again would have to be considered by the board.' Quite a turnaround from being told that he would never play for the club again, even more so due to the fact that Best had been informed when pre-season training was due to start, never acknowledging its receipt nor making an appearance at the Cliff on that particular date or any other.

Again, perhaps United considered cashing in on their still registered player, although his market value was now some way below that of even a few months ago, as a big question mark hung over his overall fitness – something that Tommy Docherty was quick to pick up on.

> This is a very critical period for George. I feel he must be at the point of no return. If he delays any longer he won't be able to make it physically.
>
> I hope he does come back, for his sake and the sake of football. If he does, we'll take it from there, but seeing is believing.

Best, perhaps wanting to prove to Docherty that he could return to grace his one-time stage, was quick to grasp the outstretched arm of Manchester United, or anyone else for that matter, by announcing that he was ready to return.

> I now feel the urge to have another game.
>
> A short time ago, I could not have thought like this. Now I want to get the feel of a football at my feet again. That will tell me what I want to know. People plead with me to play again. I had a Yugoslav musician with tears running down his cheeks imploring me the other night to play again. Things like that have an effect on you.
>
> I have always missed playing. It's the things outside football that create the pressures. This will have to be a comeback for keeps, otherwise everybody is just going to get sick of the situation.
>
> The longer I stayed away, the harder it was to come back. I have spoken to most of the other players recently and they all told me they wanted me back. I would like to think that the drinking problems I had, and the depressions they caused, are behind me.

The Irishman's name was on everyone's lips as they made their way to Old Trafford for the visit of Leicester City on Wednesday 5 September, and was still a major topic of conversation on the way home following United's 1-0 defeat, many eagerly hoping for his return in order to give a flagging United side a much needed boost. One season ticket holder declaring 'absolute rubbish. The worst side United have had in years.' He added 'I've called him (Best) all the names under the sun and he has been a fool, but I would give a lot to see even half an hour of George Best.'

Others felt that Docherty's team looked a different outfit from the one that had come under criticism against Queens Park Rangers four days previously, but there was still something lacking. But whether that 'something' could be George Best remained to be seen. It also remained to be seen whether Best would make a reappearance at the Cliff, as scheduled on Monday 10 September.

Before an additional training kit could be laid out in expectation, United had to travel to Portman Road to face Ipswich Town, where they once again staggered and tumbled through a disjointed 90 minutes, the 2-1 defeat pushing them further into the mire at the foot of the table, only three points adrift of bottom club Birmingham City.

Although only five games into the new season, it was now little different to the last, with every match report adjective strewn in criticism of United's performance. Few mentioned the name 'Best', as there was enough to fill those column inches without throwing him into the mix.

One report that did find space for his name hinted that it was just as well he was not present, as he might have changed his mind about his scheduled reappearance, the writer adding that he had been reliably informed that little had changed with the player, as he was seen leaving a Manchester club in the early hours of the morning.

'A limp and sorry challenge' was all United could offer against Ipswich, as they were 'feeble in defence, frail in mid-field and nothing but faint hope up front'. Not much going for them at all by all accounts, with Alan Smith of the *People* adding, 'I've got a half dozen sticks holding up my dahlias in the back garden than would have been more effective than any United defender in stopping Ipswich goals.' Holton, the one rock at the heart of the ailing club, was injured.

The result certainly mattered, as no-one wanted to see United involved in yet another relegation dog fight, most definitely not one that started in September and lasted until May. Few however, cared what the back pages said as for once, they could not wait for Monday to come around. Bestie was coming back, or was he? It was now like a séance, gathered round the Old Trafford Ouija board, hoping that a spectre from the past would make a reappearance. Many taking it all with a pinch of salt, others keeping their fingers crossed in the hope that he would materialise out of the misted past.

'Manchester United must be more merciful than Florence Nightingale or dafter than a brush', wrote Frank Clough in the Sun.

> The club that was once the most respected in the land are now ready to humble themselves once more at the feet of that mercurial genius George Best.
>
> They have tilted their chin like a novice heavyweight – an invitation to Best to either whack it or pat it. The great man has finally been talked in returning. Whether he'll make it after being out of the game so long is beside the point.
>
> What is important is what he might do in a few months' time if United are still struggling, if it's snowing and Best suddenly reads that there's a heatwave in Marbella. Another walk out at that stage would make United the laughing stock of the world.
>
> I admire their bravery, reckless though it is, in taking this gamble.

The odd truant schoolboy who would hang around the red gates, firmly shut, at United's Cliff training ground hoping to see his idols and obtain the odd autograph was elbowed out of the way by TV cameras, reporters and the distinctly curious who had made their way to Lower Broughton, as if it were Lourdes, hoping for a sighting, at the very least, but of a far from angelic, healing figure. Instead, a rounded, bearded Irishman, arguably a fallen idol, was the object they sought with an idealistic belief that a miracle could perhaps be about to be performed.

Many doubted Best's sincerity, but to his credit, he did turn up and equally surprising, on time, although he had been collected by Pat Crerand and driven there. Not trusted to find his own way. Then about an hour later, the waiting hoards were rewarded when the gates of the training ground were swung open, allowing them access and the opportunity to see the prodigal son put through his paces.

It was however, only to be a brief viewing, as a disgruntled Tommy Cavanagh complained about the intrusion of so many and dragged the players to a faraway corner of the training ground, before Tommy Docherty appeared and ejected the press corps who were soon afterwards accosted by an irate United manager and his assistant – two Glaswegians that you would certainly not want a confrontation with, and told to leave Best alone.

Due to Best's lack of fitness, there was obviously no immediate return to first team duty, but performances certainly required something to happen on the playing front, more so when your goalkeeper is relied upon to take a penalty kick.

Best's reappearance at the Cliff training ground was a shock to many. The sight of Alex Stepney leaving his goal and trotting up field to place the ball on the penalty spot, before firing it past Peter Shilton in the 66th minute of their game against Leicester City at Old Trafford, was an even greater one.

Stepney had scored from the spot in the pre-season match against Penarol in Murcia and had taken the odd one during training. Fair enough, but this was a First Division fixture and a crucial one at that, not some half-hearted kick about, or a funfair, with United desperate for the points and already trailing Leicester by two goals.

Fortunately, Stepney beat his opposite number, but United failed to claw themselves back into the game, a defeat that kept them in that precarious position near the foot of the table. A 3-1 victory over West Ham United and consecutive 0-0 draws against First Division leaders Leeds United and eighth placed, current champions, Liverpool earned them some credibility with the clean sheets, as well as the much needed points in that fight to get away from the foot of the table. The point against Liverpool, hauling them up to a more favourable fourteenth.

Although something of a change of fortune against long term rivals Leeds and Liverpool, both performances were not free of criticism and controversy. At Elland Road, Leeds were far from happy with United's approach, their tactics being brought into question and perhaps even more so as it robbed them of their 100 per cent record to date.

Docherty was certainly not going to apologise about United's match spoiling, time-wasting, negative approach to the game.

Here we were, facing a world class team with a young and inexperienced team ourselves. Anyone who says they are going to Elland Road to attack must be kidding.

They throw everything at you and before you know it, you are standing under your own cross bar. The onus to attack is always on the home team. I am not bothered about spectacle, we are trying to get a pattern, we want experience.

This was a great result for us. What's the point in coming to Leeds and opening out, losing 6-2. We go into the Second Division and I get the sack. I've got a family to feed.

People seem to forget that I am in the middle of rebuilding at Old Trafford. Success, and all the trimmings that go with it, doesn't come overnight and the first priority is to make Manchester. United a hard team to beat.

We have done three year's work in the months I have been here.

While defending his team's tactics, Docherty was also quick to point a finger at the referee's running of the game.

> I thought the referee was the most one-sided official I have ever seen. I saw late tackles allowed and some honest-to-goodness tackles were punished. He booked Jim Holton after only 4 minutes, yet other incidents which warranted the same treatment were allowed to go unpunished.

This was the same Leeds United who quite happily kicked their way through countless fixtures in the not too distant past, and who were involved in what was described as one of the dirtiest games ever – the Old Trafford 1970 FA Cup Final replay; a game when reviewed in more modern times by a top official, brought the verdict that it would have now produced six red cards and twenty yellow. A player had not been booked that season prior, the visit of United and *Sun* columnist John Sadler wrote of United 'snapping off Leeds's angels wings and used them for beating the First Division leaders over the head!'

Sadler also gave Docherty the name of 'Doctor Doolittle', as he talked to the animals due to the fact that 'United and those demented, foul-mouthed fans who follow them around, brought jungle law back to British soccer', adding that United didn't just halt the home sides record but 'bludgeoned it with a prolonged display of negative skulduggery.'

Arguments abounded over the current Manchester United, even in the offices of the *Sun*, as Sadler's stable mate, Mike Ellis, supported Docherty's tactics.

> From my observations, it is amazing that people expect United to be the glamorous team of old and forsake defence for goals and entertainment.
>
> At present, United are just not good enough to do that and the Doc realises this. Too many great players are missing. You can't replace Denis Law, Bobby Charlton and George Best and injured Ian Moore at the drop of a hat.
>
> United have been forced to substitute strength for skill in certain positions and until Docherty can get the players he wants, he has little alternative.

Against Liverpool at Old Trafford, amid thunder storms and gale force winds, the press, or at least some of those who took their seat in the press box, went from pointing the finger one week, to praise the next, as United grabbed yet another vital and most welcome point.

Tom Jack of the *Sunday Telegraph* wrote the following.

> First let us eat a few unkind words – those among us who had maligned United last week for taking the field at Elland Road with only a few dour defensive notions in their mostly Scottish heads. And especially those

who thought the Reds might have trouble finding an attacking idea there if they tried. For this was a tightly fought game in which United matched Bill Shankly's champions in both creatively and defence.

Time and time again, eight or nine United shirts could be seen bobbing in Liverpool's half. United have still not the magical legendary quality of their predecessors, but yesterday's attendance of over 53,000 shows they have hordes of followers who have still to be disenchanted.

But rather strangely, Mike Ellis of the *Sun,* who only a few lines ago we found supporting Docherty's defensive approach at Leeds, was now lambasting United over their approach of being 'set on a course which will take the goals out of the game but will bring in points, one at a time.'

It was a challenging time for United both results wise and performance wise, both of course interlinked, but as Docherty's team slid towards who knew what, many still clung to the belief that George Best's reappearance, although not on a white charger, would be enough to prevent slipping into an abyss, unable to claw their way back.

Best was apparently a reformed character. Not simply turning up for training every day, and on time, but staying behind for extra stints with youth coach Joe Lancaster, coupled with the fact that he had been put on a strict diet and hadn't touched a drop of alcohol since returning to the club.

How far he had progressed was still a matter of debate, but much would be revealed with his appearance in a testimonial match for the Portuguese legend Eusebio, when he would be guesting for a 'World All Stars X1', quickly followed by another testimonial outing, this time at Old Trafford, paying tribute to former teammate Denis Law.

In Lisbon, the city where he enjoyed arguably his finest hour, it was really only something of a token appearance, going through the motions for 45 minutes in a pair of borrowed boots, nursing a thigh strain and on doctor's orders to avoid any physical contact.

Against Ajax at Old Trafford, where 45,000 spectators gave Denis Law a rousing send off, despite him now being a Manchester City player, it was an emotional return for Best, running out at Old Trafford for the first time in ten months. His misdemeanours, tantrums and non-appearances presumably forgotten by the majority. Many however, could not forgive and forget, and never would.

On the night, Best was still showing signs of rustiness, but also looked comfortable with a ball at his feet and more so with the majority of the crowd behind him. Like United, he was on a long and winding road that might, or might not restore both to the pinnacle they once stood upon.

Scavenging points from the top sides was all very well but, as they would certainly not find themselves challenging those frontrunners come

May, it was also vital to gain the upper hand against the clubs with whom they shared the lower end of the table; losing 2-1 at Wolves was something of a minor disaster. The good work of the past fortnight was completely undone.

Goals were certainly one of the problems facing Docherty, only nine showing in the 'goals for' column with ten games played. The selling of MacDougall coming back to haunt him big style, as not one individual looked like leading the line and converting whatever opportunities came their way. There was nothing in the reserves to fall back on, or indeed promote. Too much lay in the hope that George Best would again be the messiah.

While his teammates, who were not exactly his friends, toiled in the Midlands, a crowd of over 7,000 made their way to Old Trafford for a Central League fixture, hoping to catch a glimmer of hope for the winter ahead with the reappearance of George Best in a red shirt, his first since 25 November last year. There was however, little in the way of encouragement for those cold Saturday afternoons ahead, as Best failed to inspire even United's second string to victory, Aston Villa winning 2-0. There was the odd drop of the shoulder in the attempt to get the better of a defender, the odd teasing dribble, the odd inch perfect pass. But they were all few and far between, and long before the end the crowd was dwindling away.

Still a little overweight, Best, although wearing the old number seven, played in midfield and according to reserve team coach Bill Foulkes, 'did everything that was asked of him'. The player himself, who was on the end of some harsh tackles, even retaliating against John Gidman, added, 'it was a great game. I enjoyed every minute of it, but I am not 100 per cent fit yet. It will take a few games like that.'

Confidence took a further knock with a home League Cup defeat against Second Division leaders Middlesbrough. Despite their lower status, the likes of Souness, Boam, Foggon and Armstrong would certainly not have looked out of place in the home dressing room, which was desperately crying out for reinforcements.

Disgruntled supporters leaving the ground spoke of the defeat as being a blessing in disguise, allowing the team to concentrate on avoiding relegation, something that was perhaps a little premature. Despite it being only October, this was something that was already preying on the minds of even the most staunched Red.

But all Manchester United's problems were not confined to performances on the pitch. The pressure surrounding the club continued to grow, and relations among personnel became strained. Docherty, never the easiest man to get along with and one who walked along a fine, often threadbare, line was certainly easy to fall out with – something that Lou Macari was to find to his cost.

Selected for a reserve tinted fixture at Mossley, a game that would have seen the Scot having played four times in seven days, left him far from happy, forcing an exchange of words with his manager. He did, however, still make the journey with the rest of those selected and was in fact prepared to play. Upon his arrival at the ground, the player was met by Docherty, who had travelled separately from the team and was told, 'Don't bother to strip, you won't be playing', and immediately headed for home. Soon afterwards came the announcement that Macari had been put on the transfer list and fined two weeks wages, for what was reported as a 'breach of club discipline.'

Docherty was later to say,

I gave Macari three chances to change his mind when I interviewed him at his home. Three times he rejected my friendly advice and turned his back on Manchester United. No player is bigger than the club.

Although I gave Macari every chance, personal feelings did not come into my decision. I simply decided that Macari should be transfer listed purely as a matter of discipline.

The manager added that things could possibly change once Macari recaptured his old form, 'but one way or another, I'm not particularly bothered.'

Macari, to his credit, admitted that he had reacted angrily to being told to go and train with the reserves, due to his pride being hurt more than anything else and the thought of having to play in such a minor fixture. He also spoke of the rumours that were circulating that he had not been trying during games in recent weeks.

He readily admitted,

I have been dispirited and down. I have found it hard to adapt to the change of attitude and style that has been demanded in leaving a successful club like Celtic, to join one battling to rediscover its former glory. Home and away, Celtic went for maximum points.

But at Old Trafford, out of necessity, we have to play a different game for the moment. This I accept, but for me the lack of goalscoring opportunities is like going hungry.

Now transfer listed at £200,000, Macari was a player more beneficial to Docherty in the first team than languishing in the reserves, or indeed playing elsewhere, certainly when there was no ready-made replacement. This was more apparent when there was now doubt over the future of Ian Moore, due to an ankle injury that had been troubling him since January and had seen the player make only two appearances since an operation to try and correct the damage.

Without Macari, Moore and also self-belief, United once again stuttered and stumbled through another 90 minutes of mediocre football against Derby County. Not that all of the 43,724 crowd witnessed every kick of the ball as, in what was now becoming a regular occurrence, many decided that enough was enough, well before full-time. For those who stuck it out until the end, the referee's whistle brought relief to the long-suffering diehard fans.

Tommy Docherty had hoped for a top six finish this time around, following the overall disappointment of the previous campaign, but such a dismal start to the current season had the cynics sniping that Manchester United would be rather fortunate to finish outside the bottom six going in their current form. Their predictions were strengthened by a solitary goal defeat against Derby County, achieved at their leisure and with considerable ease.

The United manager bemoaned that his team were not getting the breaks they deserved. Though with a quarter of the season gone, his team were only two points better off than the previous campaign and were languishing four points off the bottom. Many dismissed the 'bad luck' excuse for being nothing more than that, and pointed a finger at the lack of self-belief running through the side, along with the negative and unproductive tactics being played. Long balls launched more in hope than in accuracy, a lack of cohesion and composure in midfield and a virtually non-existent front line all adding to United's woes.

With a struggling side and a somewhat limited playing staff, the decision for United to risk players' fitness by playing a string of friendly fixtures throughout the season – a total of eight would be played, not counting the four pre-season fixtures, with six of those prior to Christmas, was something that could be debated long and hard. Some argued that such outings helped gel the team together, and allowed the management to try something different without the fear of losing points and dropping further down the table. Victories in those fixtures could also help in adding much needed confidence to the beleaguered side.

Those friendlies would also of course aid George Best in his long road to regaining something of his former physique and fitness, and it was with this in mind that Docherty took his team to Dalymount Park to face Shamrock Rovers, where around 20,000 turned up in the hope that the man pencilled onto the team sheet at outside left, would produce a minor memorable moment or two from his repertoire.

He didn't disappoint during United's 2-1 win, a game that only lasted 81 minutes due to spectators encroaching on the pitch, his cameo being enough to convince Docherty that it was worth the gamble to include him in the side to face Birmingham City five days later. 'I think he is fit enough' declared the United manager, with the player himself admitting that,

> I'm not worried about letting Manchester United down and if I find I am struggling against Birmingham, I shall ask to come off. I am not going to stand there like a spectator. It does not bother me if the Birmingham defenders are lining up to take a poke at me, they will be neglecting the rest of the team – and that will suit me fine.

It was not only George Best who returned to the fold against Birmingham City, as the inclusion of Lou Macari, who was still on the transfer list, showed the anxiety and desperation that surrounded Docherty.

The reappearance of the prodigal son added over 5,000 to the attendance and on a rain-soaked pitch. Though his contribution to the overall victory was minimal, there were odd glimmers of light under the dull Manchester sky offering some hope for the future to both club and player. It was, however, to take yet another Alex Stepney penalty, the only goal of the game, in order to secure victory.

With 13 minutes remaining, the returning one-time saviour and ultimate hero was substituted and somewhat embarrassed by the standing ovation given to him, with his own opinion of his first game back being summed up as, 'If I played every week like I played today, I would be worried about staying in the first team.'

He later made the confession:

> I found myself afraid to make mistakes early in the game. But later, I felt we were going to win and the longer it went on the more relaxed I became. I'm always reluctant to come off the pitch. I was really enjoying it, but I was tired. I might have took the penalty, but I was so tired my kick might not have reached the goalkeeper.
>
> The skill is still there. I'll never lose that. I just have to produce it.

Four days after the victory over Birmingham City, George Best once again tugged the heartstrings of the Old Trafford diehards, an apt description for the 17,859 who turned up for Tony Dunne's testimonial match against Manchester City. Dunne, like Law before him, had departed for pastures new since his testimonial was arranged. Perhaps the now Bolton Wanderers full-back did not expect a full house, but neither would he have expected his former club to be in such a state of disarray and playing so poorly, a huge factor behind many deciding that they could find better things to do.

Dunne would have been more than grateful for the £12,000 cheque, while George Best would have been equally delighted to get his name on the score sheet, notching United's goal in the 2-1 defeat, yet another step along the long hard road in an effort to get back onto his pedestal, which had stood dormant for so long.

He had said himself that it would take at least six more games before he was back to anything like the player of old. Going by his showing at Turf Moor against Burnley in United's next fixture, many were left with the opinion that such a suggestion was going to be a bit off the mark, as his contribution was as equally enthralling as the 0-0 score line.

Tommy Docherty was certainly finding life at Old Trafford far from comfortable, with the form of his team and their recent results disappointing to say the least. There was a lack of goals, panache and practically everything else that went with Manchester United and although Docherty had reverted to a three man front line against Burnley, nothing changed.

Juggling the side around brought little reward, and certainly did little to help matters. Buchan was being played out of position at full-back, a move that allowed the United manager to accommodate twenty-year-old Brian Greenhoff, with Steve James wearing the number six shirt. Tony Young was keeping Alex Forsyth out of the side, while sometimes filling in as an inside forward, with Welshman Clive Griffiths finding himself projected into the first team set up with Jim Holton suspended. It was still a side devoid of flare, charisma and a match-winning killer instinct, the DNA of the Manchester United of old, with the shortcomings of the present side ensuring that Docherty kept a watchful eye on the transfer market.

Lou Macari, David Sadler – who was finding his first team outings under Docherty limited to say the least, and Jimmy Rimmer were names that were still prominent on the United transfer list, with Brian Kidd the one player to be showing some signs of consistency, despite his lack of goals, attracting interest from other clubs.

One of those interested clubs was Everton with their manager Billy Bingham, keen to pair the European Cup winner with Joe Royle, so much so that an approach was made to tempt Kidd away from Manchester. Docherty refused to accept the initial straight cash offer, and even baulked at cash plus half-back Colin Harvey. He did, however, suggest that if Bingham offered Joe Royle, then he would happily do a straight swap. Needless to say it was a non-starter.

Docherty, having lost out on Sheffield United's Tony Currie and West Bromwich Albion's Asa Hartford, two individuals who would certainly have added much to United's midfield, had reportedly also approached Derby County with regards to signing Scottish international Archie

Gemmill. A fee of around a £250,000 was quoted by Brian Clough and was enough to end any initial interest. The United manager was later to say that he couldn't sign a player without Busby's say so and nod of approval. The transfer fee and weekly wage was also often a stumbling block when talks between the two Scots took place.

Goals had been few and far between in the opening three months of the season, as had performances of note, and the now common sight of supporters surging away from Old Trafford long before the final whistle was once again evident against Chelsea. Many might even have been inclined to head for home not long after having settled into their usual spot, as the Londoners took a third minute lead, but those supporters remained out of curiosity as United attempted to claw themselves back into the game. It was, however, to little avail, as Chelsea added a second 5 minutes into the second half.

The game dragged on slowly, and the exodus had begun when Best crashed a shot against the underside of the Chelsea cross bar, the ball bouncing precariously on the goal line before being kicked clear as the bearded Irishman stood arms aloft, claiming that his effort had indeed crossed the line. The referee was unimpressed and waved play on, but those who had given up on the cause, deciding that even luck was against their team were soon to be mocked, as with only 2 minutes remaining Tony Young was sent clear by Greenhoff before blasting the ball past Bonetti. A consolation if nothing else.

Strangely, with the referee already looking at his watch, United regained possession and with nothing to lose, surged forward, catching Chelsea, who only moments before had the game sewn up, on the back foot and in a reversal of previous move, Young set up Greenhoff for the dramatic equaliser.

Such a last gasp fight back to secure a point should have invigorated Docherty's team, propelling them onto better things, installing a confidence that had been missing to date. Sadly, following a 3-0 victory in Glasgow against Partick Thistle and a spirited performance at White Hart Lane, where many felt that the 2-1 defeat was undeserved, the inadequacy, lack of quality and often mediocrity of the performances was once again only too obvious during a six game run in November and December that was to produce a meagre two points – both from 0-0 draws.

Had Manchester United shown the same resilience as their Newcastle counterparts on 17 November, then those half dozen fixtures might have been more productive, but having taken a 2-1 lead at St James Park, everything fell apart in a 6 minute spell with the home side scoring twice to secure victory. It was a defeat that left United five points better off than bottom club Birmingham City, but there was little in their make-up to give anyone the impression that a more secure position could or would be achieved.

Those who had a passion for leaving Old Trafford early didn't even bother to turn up at all for the visit of Norwich City. Had they taken the trouble to venture towards the Ship Canal, then they would have at least been entertained by a pitch invading dog and a young United supporter who ran the length of the pitch to catch the unannounced 'twelfth man'. As it was, one journalist likened the afternoon to something akin to a Frankenstein movie – 'howling winds, scudding clouds and the terror of relegation gripping the game like a shroud.' Although there was no monster, the writer hinted that Jim Holton was the next best thing.

If there was one glimmer of light among the doom and gloom, it was George Best, whose name was once again taking up the headlines and even managing to make no-score draws against Norwich City and Southampton at Old Trafford interesting. 'Best is Bright Spot', 'Best Alone Transcends Mediocrity', 'Great Stuff, George', 'Best Shines in United Gloom' and 'Best Saves the Show', were all to appear following the Norwich match, with 'The Best of a Bad Bunch', 'Brilliant Best' and 'You're on Your Own Now, Best!' coming seven days later against the Saints. Although, it was also suggested that Docherty would have to be digging out the survival kit if he did not want to find his team in the unfamiliar and murky waters of the Second Division next season.

And it was still only the first week in December.

Despite dicing with the fear of being caught up in a relegation fight, friendlies continued to expand the fixture list, with some going as far as to hint that Docherty, as well as the club, must be making money out of such games due to their regularity when there was not really any real need to be playing them in mid-season. Some, like the testimonial for England international goalkeeper Gordon Banks, where United defeated a Stoke City X1 2-1, were arguably fair enough, but having ventured to Portsmouth eight days previously, to play under generator-powered floodlights could surely have been avoided. So much for players playing too many games during a season.

The postponement of the first of the season's local 'derby' fixtures against City at Maine Road on 1 December came as not simply disappointment to the supporters, who had made the journey to the ground that Saturday morning, but could have also have been seen as a form of punishment to the already suffering United support, as it meant three successive home fixtures.

For some, however, it was too many to endure, as attendances dropped from 36,338 against Norwich City to 31,648 against Southampton, then down again to 28,589 against Coventry City. The latter, the lowest home attendance for eight years, while at least delivering goals following the previous two blank fixtures, failed to brighten up Manchester, as the visitors returned to the Midlands with a 3-2 victory. A defeat that plunged United down to fourth bottom, three points in front of bottom club West Ham United. It was certainly not the ideal way for Tommy Docherty to celebrate twelve months since he was offered the United job.

Twelve months and United were certainly no better off than they were when he took over, with many questioning his appointment, as they had done with those of McGuinness and O'Farrell. From the goal-leaking defence to the inability of the forwards to score, United certainly did not do anything by half measures.

Turning things around to draw level twice against Coventry certainly indicated that the players had the willingness to fight for their First Division safety, if not their top flight lives, but they lacked the ability to hold on to whatever crumbs they could gather amid the winter gloom, allowing Coventry to snatch both points with a third goal, 13 minutes from time. Missing the rock-like central defensive figure of Holton was an excuse, but the defeat rested on more than one missing individual.

Letters to Father Christmas were posted earlier than usual, as a trip to Anfield loomed, but the old bearded one had only certain limitations and unfortunately, despite the wearing of red and white, did not extend to helping Tommy Docherty's team three days before he was due to deliver his yearly goodies. Neither were Liverpool, or indeed the match official, in any mood to be generous to the visitors.

When a team finds itself scrapping at the bottom of the table, luck is something they certainly seem to encounter little of, and so it was for United at Anfield with half an hour gone.

A cross from Callaghan into a packed United goalmouth saw several players challenge for the ball, but out of their midst came a hand to punch it away. Following consultation with the linesman, referee Iorwerth Jones pointed to the penalty spot, much to the disbelief of the United players, who immediately surrounded him in protest, claiming the hand was that of goalkeeper Alex Stepney. The 'keeper was duly sent the wrong way by Keegan's spot-kick, and continued his protests while leaving the field at half-time.

In reality, United could have considered themselves fortunate just to leave the field at the interval only a goal behind, and it wasn't until after the hour mark that they recorded their first shot on target. They could also consider themselves fortunate to leave the field at the end of the 90 minutes having lost only 2-0, as Liverpool outplayed them throughout the course of the game.

'I'm disappointed with Manchester United's position', proclaimed Docherty. 'Another six points and we would be in a comfortable position.'

Another twenty-three and they would be top, but that is beside the point, as the manager laid his thoughts on the line.

> All our troubles have stemmed from the goal famine. We've failed to score in seven games and you can't expect to succeed with a record like that.
>
> I've chopped and changed searching for the successful formula – and because of injuries – but planning a more settled line-up which I expect to take us to a mid-table position by the end of the season.
>
> I can't promise anything more. We are going through a transitional period – twenty-seven players have left the club since I took over a year ago – and I'm only £200,000 in the red on all my deals. I've not finished spending, but it will be only on the right players when they become available, although I would rather not spend at all.
>
> I'll be delving into the Third and Fourth Divisions if the occasion demands, but I don't expect to restore the flair that players like Crerand, Charlton and Law provided under Sir Matt Busby. What a job trying to follow that.
>
> The pressures these days are against all-out attack unless you are a great team like Leeds.
>
> The reason – the introduction of three-up and three-down. It makes managers cautious. If we drop into the danger zone then I'll not hesitate to tell my players, 'we've got to tighten up.'
>
> One thing is certain – we'll always attack like hell at home.

His expectations were certainly high, but considering a position of fourth bottom, not being in the danger zone and the declaration that he would be delving into the lower divisions in the search for players, was far from encouraging for the immediate future. There was a distinct lack of quality within the side and, although there would undoubtedly be some extremely good players in the lower divisions, a club of United's stature should be looking to recruit top international class individuals.

'Attacking like hell at home' was also a statement that seemed somewhat shallow as the visit of Sheffield United to Old Trafford on 27 December, which made it nine games without a victory. That United dominated for long spells was without question, but the failure to produce, and convert goalscoring opportunities were, yet again, to prove costly, as the Yorkshire side returned home 2-1 victors.

There was little encouragement from Tommy Docherty's mid-term thoughts, although he was certainly true to his words regarding his 'basement bargains', as he was soon to sign Stewart Houston from Brentford for £55,000, another Scot and a player he had signed for Chelsea six years previously. But there was more doom and gloom to come from a player who, in recent weeks, had arguably been the one individual who stood out – George Best. He admitted the following.

> One of the worst aspects of playing soccer for a living is that, at times, the very nature of your job can put a dampener on what should be a happy occasion. Last Saturday evening for instance, when most people were just building up to the Christmas festivities, I felt down in the dumps after our defeat by Liverpool.
>
> It wasn't only that we had lost a game – after all I should be used to that by now. What upset me was the inference people were placing on my performance in that game.
>
> To say I played badly would be the understatement of the year. That is hard enough to swallow. But when people start saying that I am up to my old tricks again, or have no stomach for a fight, that is just about the last straw.
>
> All right, I played badly, but everybody is entitled to a bad game ... and that includes me. I know I have made a rod for my own back in the past, but I am trying to live that down – if people will let me. But if that wasn't enough to dampen the Christmas spirit, our game against Sheffield United certainly was.
>
> I can never remember Manchester United players looking so upset after one isolated game. I don't feel ashamed to admit that I was near to tears after the match, and I could see that most of the lads felt the same. The feeling of sheer frustration after a match like this is hard to describe. You can see the way the confidence is draining out of the players because of this run of bad luck.
>
> I don't like it and neither does anyone else at Old Trafford. The question we have to answer now, of course, is: have we got the character and ability to climb out of danger?
>
> I once said that I would not play Second Division soccer with Manchester United or anyone else. I still don't relish the prospect and I hope to god I never have to make that decision.

As a dismal year drew to a close, there was finally something to shout about, an unexpected late Christmas present in the form of a League victory, the first for ten games, offering a ray of hope, a chink of light at the end of the long dark tunnel.

The two goals that secured victory over Ipswich Town at Old Trafford were both late in coming, but the 77th and 79th minute strikes by McIlroy and Macari were enough to earn the often criticised United players a standing ovation from the 36,000 supporters. It was not the most inspiring of victories, and whether it would transpire to be a cure for relegation sickness remained to be seen, but for now it provided relief in that such a long and worrying run without a victory had been brought to an end.

Any relief or hopes of an instant revival and a new beginning to coincide with a new year were firmly shattered, as United's decline continued at Loftus Road, where Queens Park Rangers were in no hospitable mood to their first-footers, despatching them from whence they had come with a 3-0 defeat.

Relegation was no longer a whispered word where United were concerned, as each nondescript performance found that dreaded 'r' word threaded into the match summary – normally within the first paragraph. Desperation seeped through the team, with right-back Tony Young booked within 3 minutes of the kick-off against QPR, having committed the first foul of the game seconds after kick-off. Best put in the effort, but that familiar burst of speed was missing, Bowles taking on the mantle of the 'great entertainer', with the visitors more than a little grateful to Alex Stepney for keeping the score at a respectable level.

'Told you so' cried the cynics when the news seeped out that George Best had once again failed to turn up for training in the wake of the Loftus Road defeat, and only two days before the FA Cup tie against Plymouth Argyle at Old Trafford. The player himself, was somewhat unperturbed.

> What's all the fuss about? I took a day off work for reasons that are very personal to me, and suddenly the whole world wants to know why.
>
> It's the kind of problem I've always had to live with so I don't suppose I should have been surprised by the reaction when I missed training. I've explained why I wasn't at the Cliff to my manager Tommy Docherty, and that's as far as I want to go.
>
> All the speculation about my absence has been wide of the mark. But with respect to the fans who genuinely take so much interest in my career, I don't want to reveal the real reasons publicly.
>
> I don't see any necessity to reveal my private life to the world. The only people who need to know are my employers at Manchester United and they have been told.
>
> There are no problems as far as my playing career is concerned.
>
> I'm still interested as ever in helping United to get out of trouble, and I want to play my part in beating Plymouth.

The player reported for training the day before the cup tie, and Docherty surprisingly included him in his squad of thirteen for the visit of Plymouth, telling reporters,

> the matter is not all that urgent. The incident will be dealt with according to its seriousness. It could be a small fine or a large fine.

It will be passed to the directors at the first opportunity and then we will decide collectively what action to take.

The United manager, however, did not wait for any discussion with his chairman or the directors, as he left Best out of his team selection, a decision made shortly before kick-off. His reasoning behind the move was given as 'a recent loss of form'. As good a reason as any I suppose, but as time went on, the rumour mill went into overdrive – 'he had turned up drunk' and 'he didn't show face until just before kick-off and had a female with him' were just two of many. Excuses, truths, half-truths; they mattered little. George Best did not play, his omission debated by the meagre 31,810 crowd well into the game, with his teammates struggling to overcome their Third Division opponents.

Plymouth Argyle had journeyed north unperturbed by either their hosts or the occasion, confident that they could repeat the victories that ousted Queens Park Rangers, Burnley and Birmingham City from the League Cup earlier in the season.

For just over an hour, United toiled and the majority were of the opinion that a long mid-week trip was on the cards. Had the visitors showed even a glimpse of the form that had produced their successful League Cup run, then thoughts of a replay would never have even surfaced. But their performance was poor, dragged down to United's level of late, with Stepney seldom troubled.

At the end of the day, the tie hinged on one decisive moment. Morgan won a throw-in on the right, collected the ball from Greenhoff before crossing into the Argyle penalty area where the diminutive Macari out-jumped a defender to head firmly past Furnell for what was the only goal of the game. The Scot was now United's leading scorer with four!

United were in the next round, but George Best was in hiding, the pre-kick-off confrontation with Tommy Docherty once again pushing him over the edge and prompting yet another missed training session. There was however, no actual disappearance. No worldwide search by the tabloid press to ascertain his exact location. Best was no further than Manchester city centre and his 'Slack Alice' nightclub, and he was the one looking for the press, not the other way about, as he wanted to sell his 'latest' story to the highest bidder.

In the past, many had sympathy with the player, but now no-one really cared. They had simply had enough. There problems surrounding the club were plentiful without another one rearing its head. Best had only shown odd glimpses of what talent he still possessed and had done virtually nothing to aid the fight for First Division survival. For most, it was now nothing more than 'good riddance and don't come back'.

'One of George's friends phoned me this morning and said, "George told me to tell you that he won't be coming in today and he is sorry,"' said a disappointed Tommy Docherty.

> I don't want to say anything at the moment. This is a very serious matter and I have my own ideas of what will be best for Manchester United.
>
> I cannot say at the moment if Best is finished with this club or if his attempts at a comeback have been a failure.
>
> He has worked well and until the last three or four games I was very pleased with him. Even after he missed training last week, I had a long talk with him and he impressed me that that it was only a temporary lapse.

As George Best's future was debated by all and sundry, the player himself did not wait for Tommy Docherty or the Manchester United board of directors to decide his fate, as he stepped forward and put an end to not simply the talk surrounding his latest truancy, but to his career at Old Trafford, declaring that he was finished with football for good.

> I came back because I was missing the game. I thought if I didn't give it another try I might regret it in the future. I got fit enough, but that spark, that extra yard of pace was not there. I felt I was not satisfied with myself. I said when I returned that if I could not recapture my previous form I would call it a day – I am just sticking to that promise.

In an exclusive interview with Paul Hince of the *Manchester Evening News*, Best was quite open about his decision and the reasons behind his quitting the game. Hince himself did not pussyfoot around the situation. When asked if United's current League position had anything to do with the situation, Best replied,

> Perhaps it has helped to make the decision easier – but this is not the main reason. I think even if I had been playing with Leeds United I still would have quit. I still believe I am a good First Division player, but I have to be better than that to continue. In the past I enjoyed being that little bit special – who wouldn't? I cannot face being just an average First Division player.

Best also confirmed that the doubts surrounding his future had emerged around Christmas, following a 'couple of indifferent games against Liverpool and Queens Park Rangers, and when I was dropped against Plymouth', but denied that he had only resurrected his career in order to obtain a licence for his night club.

While the majority were of the opinion that United were better off without the one-time superstar, Bob Driscoll of the *Sun* was writing 'Good Riddance United – Division One is better off without this rough stuff' alongside his report of the 2-1 defeat at West Ham, a result that pushed Docherty's team into second bottom place, three points ahead of Norwich City.

> The Second Division can start strapping shin pads to the goalposts. Manchester United are on their way down and when they get there nothing will be safe! Judging by the bruising but, almost certainly, losing battle they are waging for First division survival, it is going to be bloodcurdling stuff when they are fighting to get back next season.
>
> The latest horrific chapter in United's bullying story of decline was played at West Ham on Saturday when the tackling became so crazed that only fouls of spectacular proportions were worthy of the whistle.
>
> If United do go down, they will probably look back to this game as the one that pushed them over the brink.
>
> And if the game provided a true example of the manner in which they intend to leave, they will be no sad farewells.

Driscoll wasn't alone with his thoughts, as most of his colleagues in the press box echoed similar sentiments, while the nation's bookmakers had United marked as second favourites to be relegated at 1-2, just behind favourites Norwich City, who were 1-5. You could even get 7-2 on United finishing second bottom.

It was perhaps surprising just how far United had fallen in such a brief period of time. It was, after all, only six years since they had been crowned European Champions, with many of those who were regulars on the terracing and in the stands having witnessed, or had been brought up on the epic tales of the 'Busby Babes' of the 1950s. Now, few neutrals had any admiration for the team despite its memorable past.

Even their First Division opponents cared little for their current plight, with Arsenal's Alan Ball, preparing to travel north to Old Trafford, quick to insist that,

> Visiting teams hardly dared think about the prospect of winning there. Not now. I see a definite chance for us picking up two points on Saturday and no unbiased person would disagree.
>
> People say it would be tragic for the game if a club of United's standing were relegated. That's just not true. It would be tragic for them. It would take them a long time to recover.

But it certainly would not be tragic for football in general or the Second Division, which would benefit immensely from United's crowd pulling in particular.

Although United are heading towards relegation, it's still too early to be dogmatic. They still have twenty-six or so points from their last eighteen games to go for.

Ball's words acted as a form of inspiration to the off-colour United, who managed to grasp a point from what was an often bad tempered and frustrating 90 minutes. It was a game that they should have won but, as per usual, indifferent finishing was their downfall. From time to time, there was an ever so brief hint that United might prove all their doubters wrong and escape relegation, but Arsenal were equally poor, with a dismal record at Old Trafford, having won only thrice in their twenty-eight post-war visits.

Finding some form of constancy was one of Docherty's biggest problems. Over the past two months he had selected seven different full-back partnerships, but it was up front that his main problems lay, with the £300,000 overdraft needing to be increased, and if relegation was to be avoided, it had to be soon.

Never had Manchester United found itself in such a position. There had been relegations, threats of bankruptcy and worse, but as the supporters awaited the cavalry coming galloping along Chester Road to the rescue, frustration abounded and the whole club seemed to be in complete disarray.

Best had rocked the unsteady ship. George Graham, signed only twelve months previously, now found himself out of favour, at a time when his experience would undoubtedly have been a massive help and Docherty even found fault in reserve team coach Bill Foulkes, sending the long serving United home following a row between the Munich survivor and two other members of the back room staff. 'A situation occurred' said the manager, 'which meant I had to send him home for a few days. That does not mean he is suspended. It is a private club matter. It has been reported to the directors who will discuss it at their next board meeting.' Given the amount of time Docherty spent going to his directors, the carpet down that Old Trafford corridor must have been well-worn, while agendas at the monthly board meetings would have filled a considerable amount of space in the minute books.

It had been a few weeks since any friendly fixtures took the pressure away from the First Division grind, but the FA Cup fourth round tie against Ipswich Town at Old Trafford offered 90 minutes away from such doom and gloom, more so since the East Anglican side had been recently beaten, offering some much needed and seldom available confidence.

Although the 2-0 victory over Bobby Robson's Portman Road side had only been a month previously, results in the meantime had not exactly gone United's way. The chances of an extended cup run, never mind a trip to Wembley itself, were considered slim. Seven minutes into the Old Trafford confrontation, they were non-existent.

The Stretford End, still staunch in its support, while holding on to any small crumb of hope for survival, were stunned into an early silence when David Johnson rose to head the ball into the United goalmouth, Kevin Beattie heading past a helpless Alex Stepney.

From then on, it was a mediocre affair, with neither side contributing anything notable to the remainder of the game. Ipswich, content with their advantage, never looked in any danger of relinquishing their lead, and were more than content to let the game fizzle out. United failed to rise to the occasion, most probably because every game was like a cup tie to them; when a real one materialised, it was little more than another game and one that they found a struggle to successfully manoeuvre.

Following the 1-0 defeat, Tommy Docherty readily admitted, for once, that his team had played badly. 'We didn't even play at all in the first half', said the downhearted manager. 'We badly wanted a cup win to give us all a big boost, but now all that lies ahead is the hard fight for First Division survival.' Even the press, who could have a sympathetic side at times, often twisting the truth to make a drama out of a minor event, pushed the knife further into the already semi-conscious corpse, with Frank Green of the *Daily Telegraph* being more than just a little tongue-in-cheek when he wrote that the United support was correct in its assertions that their team were not a potential Second Division side, and that they looked more like a Third Division one during the Ipswich encounter.

Harsh words indeed, with more to follow seven days later when United lost yet again, Coventry City on this occasion only requiring a solitary goal to glean both points at Highfield Road. But a week is a long time in football and, having talked about his club being in a fight for survival, Docherty was now maintaining that his team would 'stay up' and that there was no crisis at the club, going on to say, 'It's not over yet you know, the teams at the bottom now (still three points from the bottom to be exact) are not necessarily the ones who will be there at the end of the season.'

Despite the brave face and the somewhat hollow words, Docherty was realistic and more than aware that his team were facing a grim few months ahead. He was also critical of those who were more than happy to point a finger at the performances of his team, and fought back against the accusations that he had forsaken United's attacking and charismatic play for a brand of football not previously associated with the club.

'So where are the man-eaters in my team?' He snarled.

There are more midgets than giants here. Outside of Jim Holton, new signing Stewart Houston and goalkeeper Alex Stepney, there is not a six-footer in the side.

Why can't people be more realistic? How can you run pretty flags up the mast when there are holes to be plugged in the hull? We are fighting for survival not going for a stroll in a perfumed garden every Saturday.

If they can't see this, how can I explain it to them? I can only trot out the old clichés and plead for time.

United's troubles are not the fault of any one person. All empires decline sometime. Life goes in cycles.

No matter who was in charge, even if it was Rasputin the mad monk, he could not alter the facts of evolution.

United had diced with relegation a decade before, but then they had players of the calibre of Bobby Charlton, Denis Law, Pat Crerand, Albert Quixall, Nobby Stiles, Johnny Giles and Bill Foulkes. Individuals certainly more talented than the present ensemble, and who were thankfully capable of turning the tide, going on to FA Cup success weeks later. The players of the current side were light-years away from those of the past, and silverware was what they kept in the drawers of their kitchens.

Defeat against League leaders Leeds United was inevitable, even if it was at Old Trafford, but the spirited performance from the home side surprised many and offered some form of encouragement for the grim weeks ahead. Weeks that would determine the immediate future of Manchester United. But with each passing week, the spectre of relegation grew larger and it was perhaps the Lancashire/Yorkshire rivalry, the simmering hatred between the two clubs and the top versus bottom confrontation that inspired United to a more spirited performance than had been witnessed in recent fixtures.

Even against ten men, United couldn't achieve a result, as Leeds United goalkeeper David Harvey played for 80 minutes in severe pain, having twisted his already dodgy right ankle in the opening 10 minutes.

If I'd been an outfield player I would have been off. But fortunately the whole team knew I was in trouble and sorted things out for me. You just tell Norman and the lads you are in trouble – and leave them to it. I couldn't get off the deck. And it was worse in the second half with the blinding sun in my eyes.

United did pick up on the injury, but could not exploit it and amid late winter sunshine the dark clouds remained.

Despite the current League position, coupled with the dismal results of late, a worse sequence than had seen Frank O'Farrell sacked, Tommy

Docherty was given a vote of confidence by Chairman Louis Edwards. When asked if there danger to the manager's position, he replied, 'No – none at all', adding that the board retained faith in the manager and that he still believed that relegation could be avoided.

Bobby Charlton took a much different viewpoint, although it pained him to do so.

Manchester United have no chance of staying in the First Division. That must be a simple fact of life for anybody not involved in the club and it really hurts me to admit it.

But, at the same time, it is not a shock. I've seen it coming for the last five or six years. The club has been living on borrowed time.

Pinpointing blame is virtually impossible. Certainly the present plight cannot be laid at Tommy Docherty's door, or that of his predecessor, Frank O'Farrell.

Long before that I could see it happening. Men like Paddy Crerand, Denis Law, Tony Dunne, George best and all the other highly talented players were not being replaced.

I don't mean by buying … by breeding.

Naturally, Tommy Docherty has done his best to replace me and all the other players of the sixties. But even if he had £1 million to spend he couldn't have done it.

Clubs don't sell their top players. Tommy spent a lot of money last season as a short-term answer to United's problem and it kept them up.

On reflection, he spent too much – and now he is left with no alternative but to develop a long-term policy – a youth policy. He has the effort, he must now instil more skill, more understanding. That is the only way back from the Second Division.

Docherty himself was now not so self-assured. Inwardly, he knew his team were paddling against the current and every dropped point, or two, pushed his team deeper into a position from which they would struggle to negotiate a route to safety.

We are in a position where one point will not do.

We have no choice but to place everything on attack and hope that the players who haven't been scoring as they should start to produce.

We're facing a situation where we are running out of time and games, and this is the only positive way we can correct the situation.

I don't believe we will go down. The biggest danger to me is that some of the younger players may start listening to all the relegation talk and start believing it.

But there's the same spirit and more ability here now than at this stage last season when we pulled out of trouble.

Yet we aren't getting the goals we should so there has to be a different approach. We shall have to go at teams more and if we fail it won't be through lack of trying.

The players, however, had slightly different opinions, with one stating, 'If I were manager, with the same players, we wouldn't be where we are today.' While another hinted that Docherty's assistant, Pat Crerand, could not be entirely happy at the club, as the team was in total denial of everything he believed in.

United's position was certainly precarious, now 1-5 to go down according to the bookmakers, but they still managed to create records – their 60,025 against Leeds United was the biggest crowd anywhere in Britain this season. They were also the first club to prop up the rest, but still be able to pull England's top average attendance despite being two points and one position worse off than last season. Not only was their position slightly more delicate than that of the previous campaign, if the results from last season, against the opponents they were still to face were taken into consideration, then they were well and truly doomed as their points total would be a mere twenty-eight – a haul that was not enough to save West Bromwich Albion twelve months previously.

The 'let's go for it' attitude kicked in against Derby County. It initially proved to be too frantic, as United found themselves 2-0 behind following goals from the home side in the 17th and 31st minute. Much to the relief of the travelling support, the interval had something of a calming effect on the players and within 3 minutes of the restart, Brian Greenhoff had beaten Boulton with a rasping drive from 30 yards.

It was a goal that left Derby hanging on in desperation, when they had earlier been strolling to a comfortable victory and a goal that gave United some inner belief. Twenty minutes later, they clawed their way back into the game with an equaliser from Houston, who sliced his attempted cross and the ball swerved past a stranded Boulton in the Derby goal.

Seven days later, another point was claimed in the 0-0 home draw against Wolves, although it was more a point lost than one gained, due to a missed Alex Stepney penalty. The United 'keeper seeing his 73rd minute penalty saved by his opposite number Gary Pierce, while also being relieved that Wolves could not capitalise on him being at the wrong end of the pitch, as they somehow failed to keep the rebound in play.

The attempt to claw some inspiration from playing recorded highlights from the 1968 European Cup Final over the public address system before kick-off, coupled with the point from the Derby encounter, was little more than disillusionment, with the game bringing a return to the harsh realities that faced the club with an insipid and slipshod performance. It was one that left them only one point in front of bottom club Norwich City and two behind third bottom Birmingham City, both of whom they still had to play, with thirteen games remaining.

Thirteen certainly did not prove to be unlucky, as suddenly United turned in their most impressive performance for weeks, against Sheffield United at Bramall Lane. Their first away win of the season and their first on any ground this year. Strangely, it was Hope in the home goal who offered United just that, by failing to stop Macari's shot 10 minutes before the interval. A speculative effort he would normally have had no trouble in stopping.

Macari should have made it an even more comfortable victory by scoring a second, but after rounding the Sheffield 'keeper he was left with too tight an angle to push the ball home. Few cared as United managed to hold onto that solitary goal lead to claim both points.

Of slightly more concern to the supporters, and indeed the local Old Trafford residents, was yet another little needed friendly, taking up a blank Saturday on the fixture list when a relaxing weekend might have been more productive in the long run. Problems could be expected with some regularity at the majority of home fixtures, but the visitors due in Manchester on this particular Saturday afternoon were Glasgow Rangers. Not exactly the guests you would have welcomed with open arms. Their reputation certainly went before them, and many decided that this was one fixture that they would happily give a miss, with the official attendance later given as 22,215, with an estimated 7,000 of those coming from north of the border. Obviously, there was a large number of United followers who were certainly no angels, but even they were put in the shade by a disgraceful afternoon down by the Ship Canal.

Quite why Tommy Docherty or the Manchester United officials sent an invite to Ibrox inviting Rangers is unknown, but as the Glasgow club had been banned from European football for two years following the 'Battle of Barcelona' in 1972, it was a powder keg waiting to be lit.

There had been numerous problems with the Scottish contingent on their journey south and, prior to kick-off, around 500 charged across the Old Trafford pitch, with fighting breaking out all over the terraces. Countless arrests were made before, during and after the game, while many others required hospital treatment. It was reported that some seventy-seven Rangers supporters were arrested and appeared in court on charges ranging from police assault, assault and disorderly and threatening behaviour. One man was charged with being in possession of a fireman's axe.

In the cold light of day, United secretary Les Olive said, 'We expected hundreds (of Rangers supporters), but thousands arrived. Obviously these incidents, which we deplore, will make us think very carefully before arranging another friendly.'

As for the game itself, it was arguably one of the better 90 minutes of the season to date, with United twice going in front, before conceding a third – a goal that gave Rangers victory. There is, however, no record that this third Rangers goal was 'fixed' in order to prevent further trouble from the visiting support.

For the second consecutive fixture, unsavoury incidents blighted the 90 minutes, but on this occasion, although there was trouble on the Maine Road terraces with reports mentioning 'an orgy of wrecking and terror', the main protagonists were players from either side, not those who professed to be supporters.

Postponed from early December, it was perhaps not the best time for the two local rivals to meet, more so with the return fixture at Old Trafford only a matter of weeks away. United had enough problems without a couple of nail-biting 'derby' encounters thrown into the mix.

The game never really got going as an actual football match, and had simmered away before Holton and Summerbee clashed in the 28th minute, both players being booked for dissent. Three minutes later, Macari reacted angrily to a Doyle tackle, picking up the ball and bouncing it off the City players head. Doyle retaliated, with the situation soon developing into a free for all.

Morgan and Summerbee, the two captains, tried to calm the situation before referee Clive Thomas stepped in and sent both players off. Macari and Doyle were somewhat reluctant to leave the pitch. Much to everyone's surprise, the referee decided that if the two offenders were not going off, then everyone else was and as the crowd stood stunned, all the players left the pitch and headed for the dressing rooms.

On the terraces, it was total disbelief. It took a loudspeaker announcement to inform the supporters that play was only suspended on a temporary basis. While this was going on, the referee, who was later to come in for much criticism due to his handling of the game, visited both dressing rooms to inform Macari and Doyle that if they did not remain where they were then he would abandon the game.

Following the 5 minute 'cooling off' period, play resumed and there was little in the way of physical confrontation during the remainder of the 90 minutes. Neither were there any goals, simply havoc and destruction outside the ground at full-time as hundreds went on the rampage.

No goals, but another point in the fight to remain a First Division club, something that Docherty had set his heart on prior to the game judging by his team selection, a curious mix-match of individuals, an eleven with only one recognised goalscoring forward in Macari, who only lasted 30 minutes. Paul Bielby was surprisingly given his debut, while Brian Greenhoff took the number nine shirt. Even George Graham managed a rare outing, his first for six games, coming on as substitute.

The next fixture was crucial, against Birmingham City away, the club sitting third bottom, one place above United and holding a one point advantage. Victory here was imperative.

Despite the haunting spectre of relegation hanging over the club, the spirit within the camp was strong despite rumours to the contrary. 'It's as good as it was when we were doing well', confirmed Alex Stepney.

> We've got a good boss, good staff, the directors are behind us. All right, so we might go down and there will be a few who won't be sorry. But it's not the end of the world. It might take a couple of years to build again and get back into the first Division, but we can do it. Others have and they weren't Manchester United.

On the manager who had sold him to United, Stepney said, 'Tommy Docherty? He was always a character, a hard man, but he was always an honest.'

Forty-eight hours prior to the visit to St Andrews, Docherty paid out £60,000 for Sheffield Wednesday's Jim McCalliog, a talented individual, obviously Scottish, and one who had been a one-time target for Sir Matt Busby. The twenty-seven-year-old had been on the verge of joining Aston Villa, having agreed terms, but Docherty stepped in with a better offer and clinched a deal for the player he had once sold to Sheffield Wednesday whilst manager of Chelsea.

Sadly, McCalliog's inclusion in the relegation encounter at St Andrews made little difference to the eventual outcome, with the journey back to Manchester made in silence by players and supporters alike, as once again, luck deserted United in their time of need.

They were fortunate not to be a goal behind minutes before the interval, when Stepney tumbled backwards after saving a header from Hynd, taking the ball over the line in the eyes of many, but in those of the match official, he declared that the whole ball was not over and waved play on.

Giving the anxiety of both teams to secure maximum points, play was often scrappy and unimpressive, and at times there was more bite on the terracing than on the pitch, more so when Birmingham City scored the decisive goal in the 83rd minute.

The goal itself was as untidy as the general play, with Gallagher simply launching the ball towards goal, and it flew over the head of Stepney and into the net. A raised linesman's flag for offside against Hatton attracted the referee's attention, and a lengthy conversation between the two officials ensued, but the outcome changed little as the goal stood.

Worse was to follow. Four days later, Norwich City, who had been propping up the rest of the First Division for longer than they cared to remember defeated Birmingham City 2-1 at Carrow Road, a victory that saw them leapfrog over United, enjoying a one-point advantage despite having played two games more. The realisation now well and truly set in that any hope of survival had all but evaporated, something that was more emphatically drilled home with the 1-0 defeat at Old Trafford by Tottenham Hotspur on an afternoon when the vitalised Norwich City hammered Stoke City 4-0. United were now three points adrift.

With only one goal in the past five fixtures, United had the unwanted record of having the worst scoring record in the Football League, with only twenty-five goals in thirty-three First Division outings. Admitting the failing that his team just could not score goals, Docherty was now beginning to change his tune from his 'we will survive' to 'if we cannot string four or five wins together, that's it.' Had he kept faith with Ted MacDougall would the situation that he now found himself in been any different? The answer can only be 'yes', and the situation that United found themselves in was Docherty's own making.

Suddenly, however, something within Old Trafford began to stir.

A trip to Stamford Bridge to face Chelsea on 30 March was expected to yield little in the way of comfort, with Docherty looking to salvage a point by playing Brian Greenhoff once again in the number nine shirt in place of Brian Kidd. A baffling selection to some, but one which offered an additional defender should desperation set in. It was to be a decision which paid off, but not in the way it was expected, as centre half Steve James suffered a kick in the face around the half hour mark and Greenhoff's forward role was cut short, as he was forced to move back to partner Buchan in the heart of the United defence.

By that time, however, United were a goal in front, a rare occasion in itself, Greenhoff setting McIlroy scurrying down the left, whose pass to Morgan saw the United captain fire home from all of 30 yards. It was a goal that did little to stir the home side out of its indifference, but a goal that gave Morgan the confidence to go on and enjoy an inspired afternoon.

United managed to hold onto their solitary goal lead until half-time, but after the break found a new lease of life. On the hour they went two ahead, McIlroy chasing a loose ball to the goal line before crossing to Daly who beat Phillips. Seven minutes later, Morgan out-foxed Harris and Houseman before crossing to McIlroy to make it 3-0.

The home side did pull one back 9 minutes from time, but a dishevelled Chelsea were never going to mount any form of a comeback.

Was there still an outside chance of survival some wondered?

Much would depend on how the other results went, as United were still bottom with only eight games remaining, although one of those was against fellow strugglers Norwich City. Sitting on twenty-four points, they were one behind Norwich, who had played two games more. Third bottom Birmingham City had played one game more and were five points in front, while Southampton and West Ham United were both nine points better off. With three clubs going down, they were certainly in a precarious position, but with victories, luck and other results going their way, who knew what would materialise in the final month of the season.

Next up was Burnley at home, and buoyed by the excellent result at Stamford Bridge, United stormed into a thirty-two second lead through Sammy McIlroy, with the ball pinging from Daly to Martin, to McCalliog before the young Irishman coolly chipped the ball over the head of Parton in the Burnley goal.

Hopes that United were going to gain some advantage on the back of the Turf Moor club's recent FA Cup semi-final defeat were soon dispersed, as the visitors drew level 12 minutes later when Waldron's centre beat Stepney and Nulty headed against the United crossbar. Fletcher reacted quickest to nod home the rebound.

The goal seemed to inspire Burnley, with Collins, Fletcher and Hankin all causing United problems, while Stepney did well to keep out efforts from Thomson, Hankin and James. But having failed to turn their advantage into goals, they were caught on the rebound 23 minutes into the second half, when Forsyth fired home a free-kick after Parton handled the ball outside his area.

It was a lead that United held for little more than a minute. Burnley attacked from the re-start and, as Collins closed in on goal, was brought down by Stepney and James scored from the spot. Six minutes later, James once again strode up to the spot after Holton had fouled Fletcher and again had the beating of Stepney.

Burnley were now in command, but character and determination had now been embodied into United's DNA. With only 3 minutes remaining, with many having decided that the Lancashire neighbours were about to claim both points and nudge United even closer to the drop, Holton redeemed himself, sneaking in to head the ball home from a McCalliog cross.

Despite conceding three, United were off the bottom of the table on goal average, .04 better off than Norwich. Three days later, they intended to have points separating them, never mind a fraction of a goal, as the relegation battle swung onto a head-on clash at Carrow Road.

It was a game that would more than likely decide the destiny of one club, which one was the major question as the pendulum could swing either way.

Norwich were unbeaten in five, while United had suddenly discovered that they could score goals, with six in the past couple of games. However, it was worrying that this was 15 per cent of their overall total.

In football, however, as in life, there was always more than a possibility of something, or someone coming back to haunt you. Lining up for Norwich was a certain Ted MacDougall, neglected, or perhaps we should say shunned, by Tommy Docherty; if ever there was an opportunity to gain revenge for his lack of opportunities and everything else under the United boss, then this was it.

Had it not been for Alex Stepney, United would have been dead and buried at the hands of their former striker after only 20 minutes. The 'keeper pulling off two superb saves to capture many of the following day's headlines and offer his teammates confidence and inspiration.

The opening 45 minutes saw an evenly matched, but goalless encounter and it remained so until the 65th minute when Lou Macari, recalled to the battlefront after suspension, latched on to an attempted lob back to his own 'keeper by MacDougall, brushed off one attempted challenge before lifting the ball over the head of the advancing Keelan.

MacDougall almost made amends 5 minutes later, but was once again denied by Stepney as Norwich pursued the equaliser, forcing United into some desperate measures as they fought to hold onto their advantage.

No matter how hard the home side pressed, they could find no way past a resilient Holton and the equally defiant Buchan, with the seemingly unbeatable Stepney behind. Then, with 4 minutes remaining their efforts were all to prove worthless as United cleared their lines, the ball orbiting through the air towards Greenhoff. Looking for a linesman's raised flag for offside, which failed to materialise, Greenhoff continued his run before beating Keelan with a low shot.

One down, two to go. United were still hanging on.

'This team is fighting for United', said Docherty.

We can still do it. We have picked up five points from our last three matches and it is the teams above us who must be worried. Easter will decide the whole business.

I can't ask more of my side at the moment and this is the kind of team I have been trying to get together all season. But I admit that time is running out.

At least we are trying to play some football. Before we were just hitting long, hopeful balls upfield hoping someone would get a shot in.

Jim McCalliog has made a big difference.

McCalliog, once he had settled in, certainly had made a difference in the short period of time that he had been at the club, but something else had stirred Docherty's team from its slumbers. From its early season, they couldn't put a foot right nor string two victories together, to showing something akin to championship challenging form: things had changed. From trudging home dejectedly, often well before the final whistle, to dancing around the terracing, tartan scarves held aloft, the supporters were riding the crest of the wave, while being well aware that a huge wave could engulf them at any moment.

'Sometimes I thought some of the younger players were more interested in their own personal problems – like playing for Scotland – than playing for the club', Docherty admitted.

> Some were very quiet. It was as if they were overawed about coming to United, which is, and always will be a hell of a big club.
>
> But suddenly the lads are starting to play for each other. There is a chance. They are talking to each other on the field, shouting to each other. Helping each other.
>
> The Irish lads for instance, wouldn't say boo to a goose. Look at Gerry Daly. It has taken him twelve months to settle down.
>
> Alex Forsyth had played for Scotland, yet he would be the first to admit he had a terrible time when he first came to us. But he got back into the team recently and has been magnificent.
>
> So why are we struggling at the wrong end of the table? My answer is simple – we are not scoring enough goals.
>
> If we were not creating chances then I would be almost insurmountable. But at times we have played some great stuff and lost simply because we haven't turned those chances into goals.
>
> We do everything right … until we reach the penalty area. Then tension takes over and the chance is lost. But at least we have shown the skill to make the opportunity in the first place.

Norwich were down and the pencils and paper were now out, United supporters scribbling away to see if they could work out the mathematical chances of survival. How many points would save their club from the drop? The answer, among the ifs and buts appeared to be thirty-six. If that was the case, United required nine points from their final six games.

That total was reduced by two the following Saturday when Jim McCalliog made an even bigger difference, scoring the only goal of the game against Newcastle United at Old Trafford, his first for the club and one that could prove crucial in the days ahead.

Newcastle, to be honest, were without five regulars through injury or whatever, with the others, and more than likely those who were missing as well, suffering from a common end of season disease which went by the name of 'Wemblyitis'. An FA Cup Final date with Liverpool was waiting on the horizon. They were, however, two points off that line in the sand, the magical thirty-six point mark.

'We played four kids that day, a fortnight after we had beaten Burnley in the FA Cup semi-final', recalled Malcom McDonald.

> Dave Crosson (a right-back), Dennis Laughton (a centre half played in midfield and looked totally out of position), Alan Kennedy (left-back) who went on to do great things at Liverpool, but was a poor defender who was terrific going forward. Finally Keith Robson played up front with me but was never a front man as such who preferred a withdrawn role that the team was wholly unused to. Our priority on the day was don't get injured and miss the FA Cup Final.
>
> As for United, they had become a flair-less and unimaginative side that was little more than workman like, a massive change from what had been just a year or two before. Players were filling numerous positions that would have struggled to get in the reserve side three seasons earlier. It was sad to see a great club go down the pan so quickly.

Playing with something of a different game plan, United placing more emphasis on keeping possession and building cautiously from the back, took the lead in the 12th minute. Crosson, on his First Division debut, fouled McIlroy when there was little need and from Houston's free-kick to the far post, Holton rose to head back across goal towards the lurking McCalliog who stooped forward to head the ball past McFaul at the far post.

Missed opportunities at either end, littered the remainder of the game. Laughton and MacDonald could have nudged United closer to the Second Division, while Sammy McIlroy wasted a golden opportunity to relieve the tension on the Old Trafford terraces. The score line however, did not alter. Players were filling numerous positions that would have struggled to get in the reserve side three seasons earlier. It was sad to see a great club go down the pan so quickly.

It was now seven points from five games.

Two days later, Everton made the short journey along the East Lancs Road, heading to an Old Trafford cauldron bubbling with enthusiasm, belief and hope, creating something of a party atmosphere in the warm spring sunshine. Doom and gloom had been replaced with a sparkling enthusiasm, an un-burstable bubble, with the impossible dream edging towards reality.

A lackadaisical Everton, some fourteen places above United in the First Division, were never allowed to get a grip of the game, as United picked up where they left off against Newcastle and their superiority, along with a different match official, should have produced a score line of 6-0. Greenhoff and McIlroy were guilty of astonishing misses, while the referee decided that he had spotted an infringement, one that no-one else had, when Daracott nudged McCalliog's shot into his own goal with 3 minutes remaining.

Jim McCalliog was once again the hero of the hour, notching two in the 3-0 win, leading the Everton defenders a merry dance, while leaving the United support debating what might have been had he made the move to Old Trafford much earlier.

The first of his double came in the 21st minute when he curled a free-kick into the top corner of Lawson's net, after Macari had been fouled by Seargeant. His second in the 56th minute, something of a simple effort, tapping the ball home with the 'keeper beaten after McIlroy's shot had rebounded off the post. His celebration captured the mood of the afternoon and indeed that of recent weeks, when he rushed towards the touchline at the Scoreborad End, lifted up a ball-boy and waltzed with him into the penalty area. In between times, Houston had scored United's second, rising above two Everton defenders to head home a Morgan free-kick seconds before half-time.

Victory saw United leapfrog Birmingham City, if only on goal average, while Southampton dropped a point at home to West Ham and Coventry City found themselves sucked back into the relegation battle, having lost at Derby. Over the next two days, both Birmingham City and Norwich City picked up points. The former in a 2-2 draw at home to Burnley and the latter, also at home, in a 1-1 draw with Newcastle United. The bottom of the table read as follows –

16 Arsenal	Played 38	Goal average 0.89	Points 36
17 Manchester City	Played 40	Goal average 0.80	Points 36
18 Coventry City	Played 40	Goal average 0.78	Points 36
19 Southampton	Played 39	Goal average 0.67	Points 33
20 Birmingham City	Played 39	Goal average 0.73	Points 32
21 Manchester United	Played 38	Goal average 0.84	Points 31
22 Norwich City	Played 39	Goal average 0.61	Points 27

It was now five points from four games. Four games that would decide United's immediate future.

On 20th April took United to the Dell, where the gates were closed an hour before kick-off, with a reported 2,000 locked out. The Southampton police and dog handlers provided the pre-match 'entertainment', clearing the pitch of marauding youngsters spoiling for a fight.

There was an obvious nervousness within both teams. To their credit, they did attempt to play football, sensing that a draw was not the end of the world, but a victory would do wonders for their respective League positions. Neither was there a distinct physical aspect to the game, the supporters showing more fight than any of the twenty-two players.

Almost midway through the first half, United gained the initiative, Martin, the Southampton 'keeper, brought down McIlroy as he chased after the ball, more in hope than anything else. What prompted the 'keeper to make such a rash challenge was anyone's guess, as the United forward looked to be going nowhere. From the spot kick, McCalliog made no mistake, for what was his fourth goal in three games.

It was a decision and a goal that knocked the stuffing out of the home side, as they struggled for the remainder of the first half, allowing United to dominate the remainder of the first half. But it was a domination that failed to produce any further goals, a factor that was to prove vitally important as the second half got under way.

That second half was barely 60 seconds old, when Young failed to control the ball, allowing Peach to send a cross into the United penalty area. Gilchrist and Osgood both had shots blocked. Amid the chaos, Greenhoff took a wild swing at the ball and missed, allowing Channon the opportunity to blast home the equaliser past a helpless Stepney.

Desperation set in momentarily, but United rallied, although it was soon to become obvious that they would be more than happy to settle for a share of the spoils, rather than risk all-out attack and lose both points. 'This means that one of us will go down,' admitted Southampton manager Laurie McMenemy after the 1-1 draw.

It was a point, but one that did little to ease United's plight. Their only advantage was that they had a game in hand, with victories in those three remaining fixtures producing that magical thirty-eight points total. Only fifth bottom West Ham could achieve that.

Southampton lost 3-0 at Burnley two days later, then Birmingham City hammered Queens Park Rangers 4-0 on the same night that United travelled to Goodison Park to face Everton, a couple of hours on which so much hinged.

Up against the double threat of Latchford and Royle the United defence coped well in the game's early stages, but their approach to the game in general was best described as negative. Gone was the hint of aggressive confidence and instead of a 'let's go for it' style of play, they were more than content to over-work Stepney with countless back passes, even from near the halfway line. It was more or less we have a point at the start, so let's keep it scenario.

In rare ventures into the Everton penalty area, Greenhoff forced Lawson into making a fine save, then on the half hour, Morgan rose to a Houston cross, but once again the 'keeper was alert to the danger, saving at the foot of his post.

All the football came from Everton, and although United somehow managed to keep them at bay during the opening 45 minutes, it was of little surprise when the home side took the lead 4 minutes after the interval. Royle was fouled in midfield and from the free-kick, the ball bobbled about the united penalty area before Lyons managed to prod the ball past Stepney.

It was not the ideal start to the second half, neither was the news of Birmingham City's half-time lead against Queens Park Rangers. Time was now against United, with their thirty-six-year stay in the top flight of the English game now in real danger of coming to an end. Knowing that they had little to lose, they adapted a more attacking approach, but other than two efforts from the slightly subdued McCalliog, Lawson was seldom tested.

Everton did have further opportunities to increase their lead, but failed to take advantage of the visitors who, as the game went on, looked resigned to their fate. Their performance in the Liverpool Post considered as being 'pathetic'.

After the recent performances, which created something of a false dawn, United offered little on Merseyside and the defeat, coupled with Birmingham City's victory over Queens Park Rangers left United seeking a miracle rather than two points, against cross town rivals City at Old Trafford. In theory, their destiny was out of their hands. A victory over City would only aid their quest for maintaining First Division status if Birmingham City, managed by former United defender Freddie Goodwin, lost to Norwich. Victory for the St Andrews side would nudge United over the edge, no matter what.

So the sun rose over Manchester on the morning of 27 April, a far from normal day, certainly in the eyes of those who followed the fortunes of either of the city's two football clubs. The blue half were buoyant, feasting on the fact that a victory over their arch rivals would send them into the Second Division. They cared little if it could be interpreted differently if Birmingham City won, it would be seen in their eyes that it was City's victory that sent United down. Across town, there was no excitement around the breakfast table, if indeed such a meal could be eaten, as an unusual nervousness preceded the Old Trafford fixture. The usual spring in the step for a home fixture and one against City at that, was missing. The journey towards the Ship Canal made slowly, in silence. It could after all be a funeral they were attending.

Approaching the ground, the Union Jack flag had twisted around the flagpole on the roof of the stand in the afternoon breeze, making it look as though it was hanging at half-mast. Not the most welcoming of sights, neither was the odd scrimmage between rival supporters, making early entry into the awaiting arena the safest option.

Once inside, the tension hung over the pitch like a shroud, but it was large numbers of supporters, mainly from the Stretford End, who were to envelope the playing surface prior to kick-off, the last of numerous 'invasions' coming as the United team took to the field. Mobbed as if they achieved a major success.

United began briskly, Morgan out foxing Donachie and Oakes before crossing the ball into the City penalty area where Corrigan plucked it off the head of McCalliog. Thirteen minutes into the game, United almost snatched the lead. A Morgan corner reached McIlroy at the far post, the Irishman lobbing the ball back into the goalmouth where Corrigan fumbled in his attempt to catch. McCalliog headed the loose ball towards goal, but it was cleared by Donachie standing on the line.

Most of the tension was restricted to the terraces, although it spread to the pitch when a loudspeaker announcement informed everyone that Norwich were ahead against Birmingham City. The inevitable booking, however, coming in the 32nd minute, when Doyle obstructed Macari, at a time when City were slowly beginning to creep into the game.

The lack of scoring power that had haunted United throughout the season continued to do so as the second half got underway, with no one up front to finish off the good work done by the likes of Greenhoff and Daly in midfield. One rare attempt at goal again saw McIlroy denied by a City defender on the line with Corrigan beaten.

Morgan was pushed forward, but still a breakthrough would not materialise and, as the minutes ticked away, City began to press forward, caring little for the discomfort it caused their opponents. Tueart hit the bar and then saw Stepney turn another effort round the post as the game looked to be heading to stalemate.

Then with 8 minutes remaining, and City continuing to press forward, their supporters having been quick to inform their hosts that Birmingham City were now winning, as were fourth bottom West Ham, Lee snaked his way across the United penalty area before slipping the ball forward to Law. With his back to goal, the former United favourite somewhat nonchalantly back-heeled the ball and was stunned to see it slip past a wrong-footed Stepney.

Law, with head bowed, walked away from the scene and continued his walk towards the sanctuary of the dressing room as hundreds of youngsters swarmed onto the pitch from the Stretford End, and smoke began to appear behind a rather concerned Joe Corrigan at the Stretford End of the ground. The City 'keeper having already been hit by a dart. 'It hit me in the back of the leg', said the 'keeper, 'and a knife, the kind you would use to cut linoleum, went flying past me. I gave them both to the referee and got on with the game.'

Many were on the pitch out of pure devilment, following others like sheep, while some were hoping that their actions would bring about the abandonment of the game, forcing a replay, as had occurred in the Newcastle United v. Nottingham Forest FA Cup tie at St James's Park few weeks previously, which saw the home side win the rearranged fixture.

City players, along with numerous police officers, were caught up in the tidal wave of bodies and amid the mayhem were punched and kicked. 'I was struck several times on the side of the head', said full-back Donachie, while arch-United enemy Mike Doyle added, 'I wasn't worried when the fans came on because I expected a few whacks.' Not so brave was Dennis Tueart, who admitted to being 'terrified'.

Somehow, the police managed to clear the pitch in just 3 minutes, but a second invasion, as the smoke poured out from the Stretford End, saw Sir Matt Busby make a fruitless appeal to the invaders to keep off the pitch. With both sets of players in the safety of the dressing room, the referee made the decision to abandon the match. The announcement that followed only inspired even more individuals to clamber over the fencing to further blacken the name of the club.

'It was abominable, bloody abominable', uttered chairman Louis Edwards, while Frank McGhee of the *Daily Mirror* wrote,

> The Football Association should not close Manchester United's ground for a couple of matches at the start of next season. The FA should close the Stretford End of that ground for the whole of next season. And they should also make it clear that if there is any further trouble from loutish. Mindless moronic scum at Old Trafford then ALL the terraces there will be kept empty of customers and only seated fans allowed in the ground.

As for the outcome of the game, the result mattered little, as Birmingham City defeated Norwich City 2-1, sending United into the doldrums of the Second Division. Few out with Old Trafford shed tears. Even less were surprised.

In the *Sun*, Frank Clough had predicted relegation as far back as September, but had hoped that such a fate could be avoided, stating that he liked style, class, character and charisma, and that was why he liked United. He admitted to have been privileged to have watched the likes of Charlton, Best, Crerand and Law. Learned about humility and listened to the other man's point of view through chats with Matt Busby and to having sang and danced when United won the European Cup in 1968. He now declared that he had,

> Watched with increasing despondency their decline. The directors had never seemed to get to grips with the problems of the Old Trafford once Busby decided to leave the arena.
>
> When they should have plonked a £50,000 cheque in front of the noses of men like Don Revie or Jock Stein to tempt them to take over, they didn't.
>
> They settled for second best and now they are paying the penalty.
>
> I don't blame Tommy Docherty, though I don't doubt that he has made mistakes too. He was asked to save a sinking ship but, the gaps were too wide for him to repair. Only recently has the Doc given the team its head. But it was too late.
>
> If the Doc wants to make the point that it was too late long before that, I wouldn't argue too strenuously with him.
>
> The writing was on the wall.

So, a thirty-six-year stay in the top flight of the English game had come to an end with a resounding crash, but before those ties with the First Division could be finally torn asunder, there was still with final fixture to fulfil, a visit to Stoke City.

There were periods during the game when United showed some of the form that had almost rescued them from the drop, with McIlroy and Morgan both coming close to scoring, but an 18th minute goal from Ritchie was enough to secure victory for the home side. Smith hit the bar, while Pejic, and Jimmy Greenhoff both came close to increasing the home side's advantage.

Off the field, the United support, welcomed by the majority of the Staffordshire Police force and enough dogs to keep Crufts happy, were well searched before entering the ground with a hatchet and a foot-long knife seized. Once inside, they at least kept their improper behaviour to the terracing rather than the playing surface. Bonfires were lit and police cleared parts of the standing areas, but on the whole the game passed without incident and only eighteen arrests, taking the season's total to 343 and ensuring United of the unwanted accolade of having the country's worst following by more than 100. No fanfare of trumpets would greet Manchester United's arrival in the Second Division.

Everyone had their opinion as to why United went down. Leicester City's Graham Cross, who wasn't surprised by the events that unfolded, pointing his finger at the fact that 'they should have started planning for the future two or three years ago by introducing youngsters into the side on a gradual basis, especially as the likes of Law and Charlton were nearing the twilight of their careers.' He added that he also considered that they were not scoring enough goals to survive.

Former captain Noel Cantwell was another not shocked by the recent events surrounding the club he captained to Wembley glory in 1963 and was slightly more critical in his assertions.

> To be frank, this situation has been developing during the past two or three seasons, so I am not shocked.
>
> As an outsider, I would say they were relegated because the players aren't good enough. Plenty of enthusiasm and hard work was expended, but how on earth could the club hope to survive in the big time when their leading goal scorer finished the campaign with a mere six goals.
>
> If George Best had knuckled down, the club would have stayed up. United enticed him out of retirement and although George made a gallant effort to recapture his old form the whole situation misfired.

The empire had not simply crumbled over the past couple of years or so, the foundations had been unsteady for much longer. Looking back, one individual said,

> The only thing that united us was glory and success. Denis and Bobby didn't get on. Shay Brennan, Bill Foulkes and Bobby, survivors of the pre-Munich club, resented the newcomers. It was their club, and the newcomers were carpetbaggers.
>
> They were all little groups of two and three, mutually antagonistic. Never a family. It couldn't be with all these players coming from the outside. But it could have been rebuilt with the youth policy. A new family could have been built, but never was.
>
> And the players had too many outside interests. They were at the club from 10 to 12 and that was it. They were professional players. I think they enjoyed it on a Saturday, but a lot were just doing it for the money. And no-one wanted to talk about football. Horses, dogs, birds, but not football.

There was talk of a junior player who voiced his opinion about things being thumped in the stands, while it was suggested that Busby had the wrong people around him, while exerting his influence if ever a vacancy came up at boardroom level. The board were also criticised for their lack of forward planning. David Herd, the goalscoring hero from the sixties, was not alone when he summed up the situation, saying 'the club was not United any more. Just an ordinary club.'

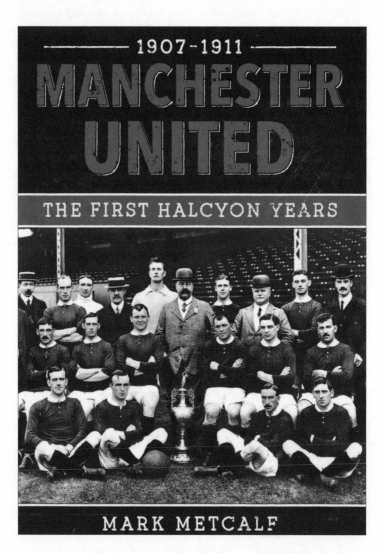

Manchester United: The First Halcyon Years

Mark Metcalf

Manchester United may be world famous today, but back in 1907 the club had yet to win either the League championship or the FA Cup. Things were to change dramatically over the following four seasons.

978 1 4456 2238 5

192 pages

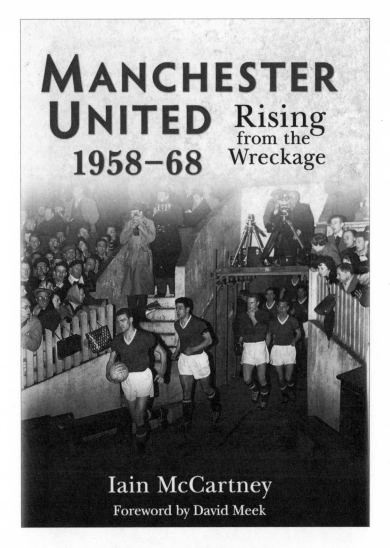

MANCHESTER
UNITED Rising
1958–68 from the
Wreckage

Iain McCartney

Foreword by David Meek

Manchester United 1956–68:
Rising from the Wreckage
Iain McCartney

The definitive story of Manchester United's resurgence from the ashes
of a German runway to a balmy May evening at Wembley and the
pinnacle of European football.

978 1 4456 1798 5
352 pages

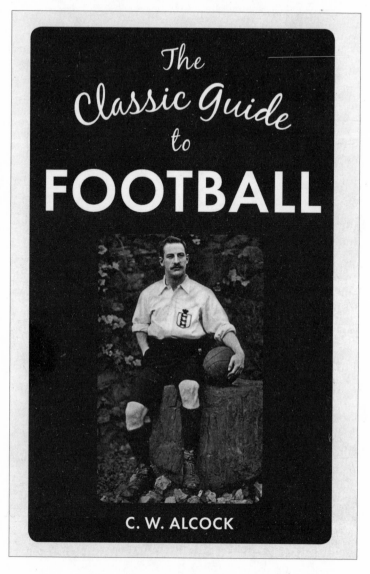

The Classic Guide to Football

C. W. Alcock

The history of the beautiful game from one of its founding fathers.

978 1 4456 4016 7

160 pages